Backyard Birding and Butterfly Gardening

T0346468

A pileated woodpecker excavates a hole in a tree stump

Backyard Birding and Butterfly Gardening

Randi Minetor
Photographs by Nic Minetor

LYONS
PRESS

Essex, Connecticut

An imprint of Globe Pequot, the Trade Division of The Rowman & Littlefield Publishing Group, Inc.
4501 Forbes Blvd., Ste. 200
Lanham, MD 20706
www.rowman.com

Distributed by NATIONAL BOOK NETWORK

British Library Cataloguing in Publication Information available

Library of Congress Cataloging-in-Publication Data

Names: Minetor, Randi, author, photographer.
Title: Backyard birding and butterfly gardening / Randi Minetor ;
    photographs by Nic Minetor.
Identifiers: LCCN 2021058510 (print) | LCCN 2021058511 (ebook) | ISBN
    9781493066094 (paperback) | ISBN 9781493068395 (ebook)
Subjects: LCSH: Bird watching—United States. | Butterfly gardening. | Bird
    attracting | Backyard gardens. | Gardening to attract birds. |
    Birds—Food—United States.
Classification: LCC QL682 .M57 2022 (print) | LCC QL682 (ebook) | DDC
    598.072/34—dc23/eng/20211209
LC record available at https://lccn.loc.gov/2021058510
LC ebook record available at https://lccn.loc.gov/2021058511

Contents

ACKNOWLEDGMENTS

Birders across the country continue to be delighted to share their sightings, skills, and backyards with fellow enthusiasts. We can't say enough about all the people who opened their yards and nurseries to us, and who pointed us in the direction of our targeted birds, butterflies, plants, shrubs, trees, and landscapes.

Many thanks to the members of the Rochester Birding Association in western New York State, as well as friends and neighbors in western New York and far beyond. For their help in filling the first edition of this book, we thank Randy Anderson, Pam Bartlemus, Bob Beal, Doug Beattie, Linda Bender, Nancy Casper, John Colagrosso, Amy and Jim Coté, Laurie Dirkx, Karl Goldsmith, Kevin Griffith, Lucretia Grosshans, Bonnie Hawk and Robin Hamm, Bob and Muriel Haggerty, Diane Henderson, Karen Huey, Vicki Kadow, Jim Kimball, Paula and Rich Landis, Ann McCracken, Jane Miller, Gay Mills, Jim Moser, John and Suzanne Olson, Andy Rueby, Martha and Peter Schermerhorn, Gretchen Voss, and Bethany Zinni Brooks, all of whom allowed us into their backyards to photograph birds, feeders, and gardens.

Our quest to find native plant species across the country led us to Rockingtree Floral & Garden Center in Sturgis, South Dakota, where owner Carol Hallock and her staff provided tremendous assistance.

We are always grateful to the Bird House in Rochester for their ongoing support, allowing us to photograph some of the items in their store's extensive inventory, and inviting us in for book signings and other special events.

Southeastern Arizona is a magical place with many more than its fair share of hummingbird and oriole species. Luckily for its human visitors, several homeowners open their property to bird enthusiasts so that we can see these extraordinary birds. We can't say enough about the late Mary Jo Ballator and what is now the Ash Canyon Bird Sanctuary in Hereford, Arizona; the Paton Center for Hummingbirds, formerly the Paton residence in Patagonia, Arizona, and now managed by the Tucson Audubon Society; and the Madera Kubo Bed & Breakfast in Madera Canyon, Arizona.

For this second edition, we add our thanks to the Baldpate Inn outside of Rocky Mountain National Park for allowing us to photograph broad-tailed hummingbirds at their feeders; and Dominic Sherony for his loan of excellent photos, his insights, and his assistance with tricky identifications. Lucretia Grosshans and Shirley Shaw provided their knowledge of butterflies as well, for which we are most grateful.

In addition to so many individual backyards, we spent a great deal of time in America's backyard—at last count, we shot photos for this book at no less than thirty-eight national parks, monuments, and historic sites, from Cape Cod in Massachusetts to Fort Bowie in Arizona and Mount Rainier in Washington. We extend a special thanks to all of the national park rangers and volunteers who directed us to birding locations, blooming wildflowers, and shrubs full of berries across the nation.

We thank all of our relatives and friends who support us with their hospitality during our travels and their good wishes at home: my brother and sister-in-law, Mike Bassow and Merry Guild, and our friends and hosts Dawn and Kevin Wiley, Ken Horowitz and Rose-Anne Moore, Lisa Jacomma and Kevin Hyde, Richard and Jane Patterson, and Diane and Chris Hardy.

Many, many thanks to Rick Rinehart and the team at Lyons Press for their work in bringing this book to fruition. Regina Ryan, agent extraordinaire, continues to shepherd us through one project after another with such grace and goodwill.

A male Rivoli's hummingbird rests in the sunlight

Spotting an indigo bunting turns nonbirders into birders

Preface to the Second Edition
A TINY MIRACLE

March 2020 will forever be remembered as the month when everything stopped. Millions of us gathered in our living rooms as our places of business shut their doors, bewildered by the sudden, complete absence of activity. We huddled around screens and watched news channels from early morning to late at night, waiting for a glimmer of good news that would end the pandemic and allow us to get on with our lives. Some of us worked from home in spare bedrooms, in basements, on kitchen or dining-room tables, or propped up with pillows on beds. The pastimes that occupied so much of our lives became out of reach, redirecting us to jigsaw puzzles, home improvement projects, and baking bread. In a sense, we nested.

As time dragged on, the season reached its equinox. Dreary March skies gave way to sparkling, bright blue days, and temperatures warmed. People desperate for a change of scenery began working in their gardens, walking around their own neighborhoods, and venturing farther than ever before into parks, refuges, and other open spaces, where they could maintain their social distance. Others, locked in front of their computer screens by endless Zoom meetings, turned their heads and looked out the nearest window.

That's when a tiny miracle happened: they discovered birds. Right there in their own backyards, in their neighborhoods, and in what became their favorite outdoor spaces, people who had never had time to spend outside saw a slice of the natural world open up before them. And they wanted more.

It didn't take long before stores that sold feeders and bird food saw a major influx of new bird enthusiasts. Backyard birding stores across the country have logged significant sales increases, and the birdseed industry faced unprecedented shortages in supply, even with reports of record production from sunflower farmers. Audubon.org reported in August 2020 that a birding store in Maine saw its biggest single month—May 2020—in sixteen years of business; a store in Ohio enjoyed a 50 percent business increase. Neither store expected the demand to ebb anytime soon.

Why so many sales of feeders and food? Just like those of us who have birded for decades, these new birders wanted to see lots of different birds. They became fascinated with these little flying jewels, each with their own personality and habits, performing backyard ballets and mini-dramas full of confrontations with other species, battles for dominance, raising unruly children, and survival of the nimblest, cleverest, boldest, and most persevering.

If you are one of the untold thousands of people who have just discovered the wonders of birds and birding, it's my pleasure to welcome you to the flock. Birders love to share what they know, so this book is packed with information to help you invite more birds to your yard. It details the birds you are most likely to see in your region, what those birds eat, what they require for nesting habitat, and which seasons bring them to your area—in short, everything you need to know to make your yard a place where birds want to be.

One of the great bonuses of creating a backyard bird habitat is that birds are not the only creatures that will enjoy it. Trees bring caterpillars and places for them to cocoon and metamorphose—and that process produces butterflies, impossibly delicate and varied insects that manage to triumph in spite of the enormous odds against them. You can give these airborne gems a boost toward continued survival by planting specific flower species with which some butterflies have a symbiotic relationship—the flowers provide food for the butterflies, and the butterflies carry the flowers' pollen from one blossom to the next, ensuring the plant's good health and reproduction. If you took a closer look at butterflies during your pandemic walks in the wilderness, you may be especially pleased to discover that you can invite them into your own backyard as well, by selecting the right plants and trees to sustain them.

If you find diversion and socially distanced solace in watching birds and butterflies in your backyard, this second edition of our book is certain to delight you. It continues to be Nic's and my pleasure to share the fun and the variety of birding with kindred spirits across the United States. May you bring many birds to your yard, may you defeat your plundering squirrels, and may your feeders always be productive.

Introduction
NATURE AT YOUR DOOR

They're out there every day, flashing through your yard on the wing or perching, inquisitive, in a tree above you while you putter in your garden or enjoy a cool drink on your patio. They collect on the utility wires above your apartment or suddenly congregate around puddles on your front walk.

Winter locks your yard in an icy stasis, but still the birds arrive—gathering to huddle in a shrub, taking refuge just inside a hole in your shed, or poking through tree litter scattered on the snow's frosty surface. One morning, as the days grow longer before the cold relents, you're awakened by the clear glissando of a northern cardinal, the first herald of approaching spring.

Birds telegraph the change of seasons, they clear last year's berries off your bushes and reduce the number of grubs in your lawn, and they brighten your mornings with their song. They already share your backyard and your neighborhood with you, but you haven't formally invited them over for dinner.

Luckily, it's never too late to do so.

Why do nearly 20 percent of all Americans watch birds? Perhaps it's the birds' seemingly infinite diversity in limitless combinations—the remarkable variety of sizes, colors, songs, and behavior patterns we can observe. Once we look beyond the sooty pigeons at the bus station or the starlings soaring in synchronized flocks over congested highways, the diversity of this family of the animal kingdom is staggering. In North America alone, the American Birding Association's July 2021 checklist counts 1,127 bird species that either breed in the United States and Canada or put in regular appearances around the continent's fringes as they drift over from faraway shores.

Dedicated backyard birders in nearly every state and province can tell you that over the course of a year, you might see more than seventy different species in your own yard—from hawks, geese, and gulls passing overhead to many varieties of sparrows, finches, blackbirds, and other small birds at your feeders and in your shrubs and trees. If you're fortunate enough to live on the edge of a pond or lake, in a farming community, or near a desert—or if you have a large property with many trees—your backyard visitors may expand to number more than one hundred different species.

A northern mockingbird rests in a yaupon holly bush

Tiny flashes of glitter in the sunlight, hummingbirds dart from flower to flower so quickly that you never quite get a close look. Goldfinches, their yellow feathers some of the brightest you've ever seen, zip through your yard on the way to more interesting pickings next door. Orioles, almost too flamboyantly orange to be real, scold you for the lack of fruit and berries in the shrubs around your home. All of these birds would be perfectly amenable to getting to know you better, if only you knew how to get them to linger.

And while you watch, another class of visitor flits silently through your garden, looking for its favorite flowers to sip their nectar. Butterflies, some even brighter and more delicately decorated than the birds, are very selective in their sustenance, with some species' larvae—the caterpillars that fascinate children and adults alike—choosing only one flower on which to feed. Planting a butterfly garden in your yard can attract the caterpillars, provide places for them to pupate, and encourage the emerging butterflies to remain throughout their short lives. In this second edition of *Backyard Birding and Butterfly Gardening*, you will find the information you need to bring more butterflies into your own yard, giving you excellent opportunities to observe them at close range.

Whether your backyard is a compact square in a tract of regimented squares, an expansive suburban lawn, or a mowed oasis surrounded by open land or forest, you can bring your region's birds into your yard to enjoy their life cycle of courtship, nesting, raising young, and departing for warmer climates. You needn't be a master gardener or a top-notch birder to engage with the feathered creatures in your area, or to attract fluttering insects with gorgeously painted wings—in fact, all you need to do is follow a twentieth-century song lyric: "Find out what they like and how they like it, and give it to them just that way."

OUR ORIGIN STORY

My first backyard bird was a ring-necked pheasant I flushed while trying to identify wildflowers in an open field behind the apartment building in which we lived. I was twelve years old and eager to explore my environment, such as it was—picking my way through what my mother called a "vacant lot" to put names to morning glories, goldenrod, and chicory. In an instant, I stepped too far too fast and nearly fell backward as a rush of wings and tail feathers erupted directly in front of me. The sun caught the pheasant's shockingly red and green head as he took flight, and I stood, mouth agape, thinking I would never again see something so beautiful.

By then I had a young student's understanding of butterflies, watching one make its way out of its pupa in a glass jar nurtured by my fourth-grade teacher. Five years in the Girl Scouts introduced me to many more butterflies on trails throughout Upstate New York, trudging through parks and surprising the fragile creatures as the members of my patrol and I emerged from forests on the edges of open grasslands. While most of the places we trekked are now suburban housing tracts, I maintain a healthy patch of Joe-Pye weed and common milkweed in my own yard and enjoy lengthy visits from monarchs, tiger swallowtails, cabbage whites, and red admirals as summer edges into fall.

My husband, photographer Nic Minetor, learned about birds at his mother's elbow, reaping the benefits of her keen ear for birdsong and her delight at every new individual in her yard. Growing up with an amateur naturalist in the house gave Nic an innate understanding of the synergy between food, water, and shelter as birds' basic hierarchy of needs. Now he captures the wonders of backyards across America in digital images, with a photo library that holds more than 450 bird species and dozens of butterflies.

Our mutual backyard birding adventure began innocuously enough, with a simple plastic feeder suction-cupped to our urban apartment window. A few hours after we installed our humble offering, I glanced at the window and discovered two little birds, their faces a deep purplish pink, greedily attacking the pile of yellow, red, and black seeds. Pink birds! I'd never seen anything like them. I grabbed the field guide we'd bought the day before and flipped through it. In minutes I determined that we were playing host to two male house finches, both of which brought their streaky brown mates to our feeder shortly thereafter.

The heady rush of bringing a bird I'd never seen before right to my window became a deliciously addictive experience. When we bought our home a year later, creating habitat and feeding stations for birds became one of our highest priorities—and, as it turned out, a never-ending process of trial and error. Our eventual successes came at the price of exotic plant species that withered in our garden, and hundreds of pounds of bird food devoured, not by birds, but by squirrels and the industrious eastern chipmunk, a critter that can squirm its way into hopper feeders that slam shut on the heavier squirrels.

Yes, we'll tell you how to keep the squirrels at bay—a process of watching, waiting, and removing every possible raceway to your food supply. Your squirrels will remain in your yard, but we can help you keep them confined to the ground, where they will clear the scattered seeds the birds dash from the feeder.

Many a beginning backyard birder can point to experiments that failed and plants that perished—but you don't have to suffer through such wallet-draining mistakes. This book will help you make the right choices the first time, whether it's the purchase of shrubs that will fill your yard with berry-eating birds all winter, or the selection of the most effective house sparrow baffle, with tips to maximize its usefulness.

What are the secrets? In a nutshell, bringing birds and butterflies to your backyard involves a combination of feeders and natural food, enough variety to tempt a wide range of palates, a source of water, and the native trees, shrubs, and flowers that create a familiar, safe, and practical environment for the birds and butterflies that live in your area.

We offer many recommendations for plants that actively attract birds and butterflies—some for the seeds they produce when the flowers fade, and others for their wealth of fruit, nectar, dense foliage that provides cover, and strong limbs that serve as stable nesting or pupating locations. As you plan your own garden or transform your existing landscape with native species, we urge you to consult your local nursery to find the hardiest species for your climate and region.

To photograph all the birds, butterflies, plants, and trees we needed to represent the entire continent in this book, Nic and I traveled from our home in Rochester, New York, to southeastern Arizona, through the grasslands of the Great Plains, out to the Grand Tetons and other Rocky Mountain destinations, and into the Pacific Northwest. The result is a compendium from America's backyards to your fingertips, with information that will be useful in whatever climate or habitat your own backyard may provide.

Today, as Baltimore orioles devour grape jelly from feeders in our front and back yards and American goldfinches munch a combination of nyjer seeds and sunflower chips inches from my back door, I'm so pleased to join with Nic and Lyons to bring some of our not-so-secret methods to you. By following the principles in this book, you can share in this visual bounty and turn your backyard into the habitat of choice for all manner of marvelous birds and butterflies.

Western bluebird on a post

1: Backyard Birding and Butterfly-Watching Essentials

Before you begin choosing feeders, buying bags of bird food, and planting flowers that will produce seeds and nectar, make sure you're ready to enjoy the birds and butterflies that will most certainly arrive in your yard.

Just as the birds need food, water, and shelter, you need a few essentials to make your backyard birding and butterfly-watching experience as rich and colorful as it can be. Let's start with the nature-watching basics and come back to the birds and their needs in the next chapter.

A CLEAR VIEW

Where in your house can you sit comfortably and look out a window? Whether you have a wide bay window in your dining room, a sliding glass door off of your kitchen, or a portal near your desk in your home office, you'll want to place your bird feeders where they can be seen from that window. This is particularly true if you live in an area above the frost line, where wintry weather can keep you from spending a lot of time on a deck, porch, or patio. Looking out the window over your morning coffee and watching a variety of birds feasting at your feeders can make a frigid, overcast winter day seem a great deal brighter.

You don't need a panoramic, ceiling-to-floor window to enjoy the view of birds and butterflies visiting your yard. Choose the window that reveals the greatest number of natural features—trees, shrubs, water (puddles count!), and lower plants. Be sure to select comfortable furniture for your viewing window. You may find yourself sitting for extended periods, so have a well-padded chair, a table on which to take notes, and quick access to food and drink. It's no wonder that most people choose their kitchen table to serve as Nature Watching Central.

Test out each of the windows in your house that might serve as your primary viewing station. We often look out windows without really seeing what is there: overgrown shrubs that block the view, vines that crisscross the glass, or old, dirt-clogged screens that obscure what lies beyond.

If your house was built before the 1920s, your windows may have a weird, wavy appearance. This is a result of the manufacturing process used to create windows in the late nineteenth and early twentieth centuries. The waves are part of the original structure of the glass; they have not "sagged," as some myths about glass would have you believe. If you don't like the distortions these waves may cause when you watch birds and butterflies, it may be time to replace these old windows.

Next, look past the glass to the scene beyond. What features of your yard can you see? Are there trees and shrubs that could provide places to hang viewable feeders? Where might you add a birdbath or brush pile that will attract birds within your line of sight? Can you see a place to plant a tall garden of flowers to provide nectar for butterflies and hummingbirds?

This first examination will help you begin a plan to turn your yard into habitat for many varieties of birds and butterflies.

Remember, nothing brightens a room or improves a view more than a clean window. Wash your windows with warm water and mild soap at least twice a year, using a soft cloth or old T-shirt. Use a squeegee to help minimize the potential for streaking. If you've got stubborn stains or embedded soils, many professionals swear by a solution of two parts distilled white vinegar and one part water. This will remove hard-water spots, dirt, and other gunk without generating harmful ammonia fumes.

However, beware of the dangers that clean windows will pose to the birds outside. Birds may see only the reflections of trees, sky, and clouds and fly headlong into the glass. The startling report known as "Three Billion Birds," published in the journal *Science* in September 2019, revealed that window strikes are one of the primary reasons that the world's bird population has diminished by 25 percent since 1970—in fact, up to one billion birds die annually in the United States and Canada from flying into windows.

You can help protect birds by installing one of several low-cost products that deter birds from approaching windows. Acopian BirdSavers, for example, are lengths of nylon parachute cord (also known as paracord) that hang on the outside of large windows. The thin cords barely interrupt a person's view looking through the window, but when birds see them, they steer clear to avoid colliding with the cords. The American Bird Conservancy and the Cornell Laboratory of Ornithology recommend these "Zen curtains" as a tested and effective way of reducing bird strikes. You can purchase them at most birding supply stores, or even make your own by following the directions Acopian provides at its website: www.birdsavers.com.

A FIELD GUIDE

You may think at first that a field guide is only for serious birders or butterfly watchers who get up at dawn to catch glimpses of unusual species. The first time a bird or butterfly you don't recognize lands at one of your feeders or flits through your garden, however, you will wish for a quick-reference guide to tell you what has arrived in your yard. This may be a book, a laminated folding guide, or an app on your smartphone—and you may want different guides for various activities.

How do you choose the right guide for you? First, look for a book or app that has "Field Guide" in its title. Many books and apps offer photos or illustrations of birds or butterflies, but only the field guides are fully comprehensive. Many field guides cover the entire bird or butterfly population of the eastern or western half of the United States, with the Mississippi River as the rough dividing line. Others focus on one bird family, such as warblers, sparrows, hummingbirds, or shorebirds. Even if you believe that you will never see anything very unusual in your backyard, you will likely be pleasantly surprised by the wide variety of species that stop at your feeders or gather in your berry-laden shrubs, and the changes in your backyard visitors throughout the different seasons. You'll want to be able to identify them all, so choose a guide that covers your region or half of the country at the very least.

Many birders turn to smartphone apps to consolidate their field guides—and some of these apps can even identify a bird in a photo for you, reducing the amount of uncertainty new birders experience as they learn about male versus female plumage, seasonal variations, and all the other elements that can make bird identification tricky.

The most popular of these is Merlin Bird ID, a free app created by the Cornell Laboratory of Ornithology and Bird In Hand, with the assistance of legions of birders and scientists. Merlin uses computer vision technology developed at Caltech and Cornell Tech to identify birds in photos, drawing on hundreds of millions of sightings birders have recorded in the online eBird database (more on this shortly). In 2021, Merlin added birdsong identification to the app, giving birders the ability to record a nearby birdsong and identify it in seconds. It uses the lab's Macaulay Library of bird sounds—the world's most comprehensive source for audio recordings, photos, and videos of birds—to access the songs of more than 450 birds and match them to the ones in your recordings.

If it feels like cheating to use an app to tell you what birds you are seeing and hearing, you can still carry a field guide (or more than one) on your phone for fast reference in the field. Among the ones that are popular with new and experienced birders are iBird Pro, Audubon Birds and Butterflies, the Sibley eGuide to Birds, National Geographic Birds, Peterson Birds, and BirdsEye; all of these can be used offline once you have downloaded them. Some of these apps provide both photos and illustrations of birds, as well as multiple birdsongs for each species, so you can listen to various songs to help you identify the bird you may be hearing.

If you are new to birding, some apps provide tools to help you narrow down which bird has paid a visit to your yard. Audubon allows you to browse birds by shape, while Merlin and iBird take you through a menu that filters possible birds by shape, color, size, location, and habitat, among other prompts. As you learn what different bird families look like, your needs will change, making it faster and easier to use the larger and more complex apps.

A number of apps also make butterfly identification easier, with online tools like ButterflyIdentification.org, GardensWithWings.com, and Butterflies and Moths of North America (butterfliesandmoths.org) providing quick-reference guides and simple questionnaires to aid in identification. The free app Picture Insect identifies all manner of bugs from your photos, including butterflies and caterpillars, but it does not contain a field guide that you can browse to make your own identification. Audubon's smartphone app mentioned earlier provides a field guide to both birds and butterflies in one, making it a handy addition to your nature app collection.

BIRDING LIBRARY

A good home birding library should include a comprehensive, region-wide or nationwide field guide, and specialty guides for birds that interest you most.

Choosing a Field Guide

Photos or illustrations? Try both kinds of guides to determine which you prefer. Photo guides provide single, vivid examples of each bird, usually in breeding plumage. Illustrated guides provide many drawings of the same species. These guides give you an idea of all the possible plumage variations, revealing fine shades of identification. Many bird lovers have one of each kind to improve their ability to identify an unexpected species—or to recognize a bird that looks like a familiar species, but may be in juvenile or winter plumage.

Go to your local bookstore or birders' specialty store and browse through the titles. Look at the size and weight of the guides, and think about where you will keep this guide in your house. Do you want a guide that will fit in a coat pocket, or one that offers larger type and illustrations on a bigger page?

The best field guides provide many different views of the same bird species, so you can see the differences between the male and female birds of the same species. Other views show you how the bird might change in winter, or how an immature bird might look. There's a map on each page as well. Map colors tell you where the bird lives in each season: summer, winter, or year-round, and its migratory path.

Don't feel that you must restrict yourself to one choice. Many experienced birders keep a copy of every field guide on the market along with their binoculars. The ability to compare different photos and illustrations can help you sharpen your identification skills, while giving you enough information about a bird's size, markings, and behavior to make a well-informed decision about the bird's species.

BINOCULARS

Whether your passion is birds or butterflies, you need binoculars.

Even if you only watch the creatures in your own backyard, the day will come when a bird or butterfly will land in a distant tree, and you'll want a closer look at an unfamiliar wing pattern or unusual breast color. Binoculars open up the world of nature to the casual viewer in a way that no other tool can.

But which pair is right for you? Here are the most important things to understand about the way binoculars work:

You'll see what looks like a size or formula, usually stamped on the focus knob. It may say 7 × 35, 8 × 50, or 10 × 40, or another combination of numbers.

The first number is the number of times the binoculars magnify the image for you. If the first number is seven, for example, the binoculars show you the bird or butterfly at seven times its normal size.

So you may think that a magnification of ten would be the best, right? The fact is that 10× binoculars can be very hard to hold still enough to see a clear image at ten times its normal size. Unless you're using the binoculars exclusively on a tripod, the 10× pair will probably frustrate you more than thrill you. Most people prefer a pair with 7× or 8× magnification.

The second number (35, 40, 42, or 50) is a measurement of the amount of light that comes through the large end of the binoculars. It's actually the diameter of the objective (larger) lens in millimeters. Here, larger is better, as it allows you to see more clearly in low light situations—near dusk or on overcast days.

Ask your retailer about the binoculars' field of view. A wider field of view is better for spotting your target, as you have more area that you can see—giving you a greater opportunity to find the bird or butterfly in your lens.

For observing butterflies, the ability to focus at very close range can be critical to your enjoyment. Binoculars made for general use may only focus well on subjects that are 20 feet away or more, while most birding binoculars achieve a close focus of about 10 feet. You may have the ability to get much closer

Binoculars are the right size for you when you can hold them in one hand

to butterflies without scaring them off, however, so binoculars that can focus on a subject as close as 6 feet away are ideal. This information should be in the manufacturer's description of the product.

Finally, look for optics that are fully multicoated. This is critically important, as binoculars with full, multiple coatings will reduce color fringing, producing a clear, crisp view. A sharp, well-defined image is the result of many different coatings on each lens. Just about all of today's binoculars have some coatings. Some very reasonably priced optics are fully multicoated, which means that every piece of glass inside the binoculars—as many as eighteen surfaces—has multiple coatings. Each layer reduces the reflective scattering of light between these glass surfaces, eliminating glare and distortion. Coated optics look dark and often greenish or bluish when you look at the objective lens.

NO FRINGING

When you're trying out binoculars, watch out for the blue or yellow halo around images you see through the lens. This is color fringing, an effect that's caused by poor color correction. Cheap optics with single-coated or noncoated lenses can't correct these annoying patterns. These optics don't have the lens coatings required to increase the color contrast as the light passes through the lens. You will become dissatisfied quickly with binoculars that produce this effect.

The Right Fit

Binoculars should fit comfortably in one hand. Ideally, you should be able to hold them in one hand as you look through them and record notes with the other hand. You may still use two hands, but be sure that your optics are not too large to hold steadily. If you're buying your first pair, go to your favorite outdoor sports store and try several pairs in person. Take them outside and test them before making a choice.

The Right Price

The top binoculars may run as much as $1,500 per pair—which is extreme for backyard nature observation. Don't feel that you must purchase the absolute best. Instead, buy the best you can afford. If you are new to birding and butterfly watching, you may want to begin with a modest pair. You might choose a smaller-diameter objective lens or a lower magnification, but don't skimp on the coatings! Spending $250 instead of $100 will make an enormous difference in your enjoyment.

If you're just getting started with backyard birding and butterfly watching and you have a fairly standard city or suburban yard, a spotting scope may not be a high priority. Using a scope also may be self-defeating for butterfly watching, as the scope's narrow field of vision may be too restrictive to follow an insect in flight. But if your property backs up to a pond or lake, a big open field, or a wetland, or if your neighbors have large trees or shrubs that attract birds, a scope will bring many out-of-reach birds into sharp focus.

Birds have a frustrating tendency to hide just beyond your ability to see them. A scope can help extend your viewing range, sometimes by hundreds of feet, so you can see the scarlet tanager in your neighbor's oak or the Scott's oriole at the feeder across the street.

Just as binoculars come in many shapes and sizes, scopes run the gamut of varieties as well. A visit to your favorite birders' specialty store or outdoor outfitter will reveal the wide range of spotting scopes available. As you will see, a good scope is a fairly major investment.

You may choose either an angled or straight scope—an angled scope has an eyepiece offset 45 or 90 degrees from the barrel, while straight scopes have aligned eyepieces. The difference is a matter of personal preference, but straight scopes are better for digiscoping (see next page).

Scopes generally begin at 20×, magnifying the bird twenty times for your enjoyment. On some models, you can choose an eyepiece that zooms in to an astonishing 50× or 60×, making birds look so close they could be sitting on your hand. Look for fully multicoated optics, which will decrease distortion, increase the contrast of the image, and give you a sharp, clear, vibrant view of the bird. Get the largest objective (front) lens you can afford. A 60 or 65 mm lens is excellent; an 80 mm lens will let in much more light and deliver a brighter image.

There's more to a scope purchase than the scope itself. Your scope is only as good as the tripod that holds it upright. You need a tripod that will hold steady while you look through the lens, even if you're outside on a windy day. A tripod that vibrates or sways will make it very difficult to get a clear view of the subject.

Digiscoping

Scopes have become very popular in recent years because of digiscoping—taking digital photos of birds and butterflies using a digital camera or smartphone attached to the scope's eyepiece. This method provides excellent opportunities to take an image to analyze and identify later. If you plan to digiscope, you will have the best luck using an adapter to attach your digital camera or smartphone to the scope. The adapter holds your camera steady, leaving your hands free to move the scope while you focus on the bird or butterfly.

Digiscoping is easy with a smartphone-compatible mount

FIVE TIPS FOR DIGISCOPING

- Find the bird or butterfly and focus the scope on it before you attach the camera.

- Set the camera's shutter priority at 1/500 second or faster.

- Shoot at your eyepiece's widest (lowest) magnification—you can crop the photograph later with your computer software.

- Shade your LCD screen when you're outside so you can see if you got the shot.

- Take lots of shots—just keep shooting as long as you see the bird.

KEEP A YARD LIST

Keep a list of every bird and butterfly you see in and around your yard. Whether you start writing down the species you see to track them from day to day, month to month, or as a year-to-year comparison record, keeping a yard list will become your passion in no time.

Start by jotting down the species you see. Keep a pad and pen by the window from which you watch your feeders and your garden. Write down what you see that day, or during that week or month. Make additional notes

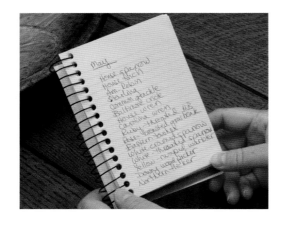

if you see behavior that strikes you as interesting. If a bird arrives in unusual plumage, note this as well. Soon you will have a sense of which birds and butterflies arrive in various seasons, and which birds are with you year-round.

Why keep a list? You might begin by simply writing down each new species that visits your yard to get a running total of the number of different birds and butterflies that show up. This list becomes your "life list," the total number of species you've seen in your lifetime. Birders and butterfly enthusiasts find tremendous satisfaction in seeing their life list grow.

Once you have a list established, watching nature in your backyard provides a wonderful opportunity to enjoy the natural change of seasons. You might begin writing down all the birds and butterflies you see each month, starting a new page on the first of the month and recording the dates on which you add species to the month list. As you see bird species for the first time during the year, you will know that the bird migration has begun—often before any significant change in the weather occurs. By comparing one year's list to the next, you can know when it's time to put out your hummingbird and oriole feeders, when the woodpeckers and nuthatches will need the extra protein in raw suet, or when you might begin to see the first caterpillars of the year in your trees and shrubs.

What counts as your backyard? Most birders and butterfly watchers agree that a backyard list includes anything you can see from your yard—birds that fly over your yard, birds and butterflies in your neighbors' yards, or, if you're lucky enough to have more than an average suburban yard, anything you see throughout your acreage. If your yard backs up to a "forever wild" patch of open space, a wildlife refuge, the Mojave Desert, or the Pacific Ocean, the birds and butterflies you see beyond your lot line certainly count.

Digitize Your Records

If you are interested in going paperless, there are several excellent bird and butterfly listing apps available. These digital lists allow you to record the date, time, place, and conditions under which you saw each species, and how many of each came to your yard. Some even have spaces for your photos, so you can keep your notes and pictures together in one place. Listing software is available for both Windows-based and Macintosh computers, and for both iOS and Android smartphone platforms. Some are built right into the field guide apps, allowing you to check off a bird or butterfly when you identify it. Keeping your lists on your mobile phone can help you increase the number of birds and butterflies on your life list while providing an instant field guide when something new flies into view.

You can also keep track of your sightings using apps that contribute to the global community of birders and butterfly watchers. The Cornell Laboratory of Ornithology's eBird gives you the opportunity to enter your observations into a database that spans the globe, joining millions of birders in tracking the whereabouts of birds everywhere. Your daily yard lists become part of citizen science, providing current information on bird migration, arrivals in your area, breeding success, feeding habits, and

Bird Pro is one of several field guide apps that covers all the birds in North America

overall movement of birds from one place to another. The free app is available in Apple's App Store and Google Play.

There's a similar effort in progress for butterflies as well. The Butterflies and Moths of North America (BAMONA) project collects photos shared by butterfly watchers throughout the continent, who enter their sightings at the project's website. The information provided helps track butterflies' shifting ranges and numbers as the climate changes. You can register for an account and start submitting your photos at https://www.butterfliesandmoths.org/user/register.

Hairy woodpecker on suet feeder

2: Food for the Birds

Believe it or not, birds can be even pickier about what they eat than humans—many choose only a couple of foods from the multitude of options available at your feeders and in the wild.

WHAT BIRDS EAT

While survival instincts extend some birds' diets during the months when their first-choice foods may be scarce, most birds are specialists when it comes to seed, suet, nectar, and the delicacies we provide at our feeding station smorgasbord.

Many of the most colorful and tuneful birds will not approach feeders at all. Warblers, vireos, flycatchers, kingbirds, gnatcatchers, swallows, swifts, and a wide range of other birds are insectivores, beginning their migration south as soon as the bugs begin to wane at summer's end. These birds may come to your yard if you have a healthy population of yummy insects, but they are more likely to remain in the wilds of your area's forests, wetlands, chaparral, desert, or mountainsides where their appetites are more easily satisfied.

A handful of bird species are generalists in their diet, feeding on hard-shelled seeds when these treats are available, but turning to berries and insects during nesting, feeding, and fledging their young. Cardinals and grosbeaks top this list, catching their food as they need it and frequenting feeders when their reproductive schedule allows it.

Sparrows, finches, chickadees, and chickadee "allies"—bushtit, verdin, and various titmouse varieties—are voracious seedeaters. Pine siskins are often found at seed feeders, as are grackles and blackbirds. Cardinals and jays choose various kinds of seed before many other foods found in the wild. Finches of all colors prefer nyjer seed—also known as thistle seed. This light, slender seed holds little interest for other birds or for squirrels.

Some birds prefer to feed on the ground but will come to a well-stocked platform feeder that allows them to eat in their accustomed position. Good platform feeders simulate ground-feeding behavior. You may see juncos, jays, grackles, titmice, and blackbirds come to a platform feeder. Doves are fond of platforms as well, especially the ubiquitous mourning doves. If the feeder contains a mix of peanuts and sunflower seeds, nuthatches, flickers, and some

Tufted Titmouse on platform feeder

woodpeckers may make occasional stops as well.

Hummingbirds, those most desirable of all feeder birds, love nectar, the basic sugar water mix with which we fill their feeders. Orioles are also nectar lovers and are more likely to come to nectar feeders with perches that allow these larger birds to linger. Even more than nectar, orioles are very fond of fruit—especially oranges. Slice an orange in half and place it on an oriole feeder or in the crook of a tree branch.

Woodpeckers and nuthatches go nuts for suet, whether it's the pure stuff you buy from your butcher or the packaged cakes that slip easily into suet cages. Jays, grosbeaks, house sparrows, and chickadees will come for suet blends that include seeds and nuts, while titmice and house finches may put in appearances to nibble as well.

Starlings are also big fans of suet. Your winter woodpeckers may suddenly be crowded off your suet feeder by starlings as the first signs of spring arrive, and when juvenile starlings leave the nest and start looking for their own food.

CHOOSING SEED BLENDS

There's a basic rule of thumb for buying seed and seed blends for your feeders: cheaper is not better. Those inexpensive seed blends contain lots of seed that birds throw out of your feeder and onto the ground. These add pounds to

Birding Tip: Keep Feeding Year-Round

There's a common misconception that suggests we should stop feeding birds in summer or fall, when natural food sources are plentiful. The truth is that birds will supplement their diets at your feeders while taking advantage of the food around them. Go ahead and continue to feed year-round; the birds will take what they need and go elsewhere for the rest.

Undesirable blend   Better blend   Pure sunflower seeds   Nyjer seed

the seed bag but do nothing to attract interesting birds to your yard. Even the squirrels turn up their noses at fillers like golden millet, red millet, and flax.

Better blends that contain a variety of seeds, including sunflower, safflower, and white millet, will attract birds' attention. White millet is popular with many birds, including chickadees, doves, jays, finches, towhees, buntings, juncos, and some sparrows. Some premium blends contain bits of calcium carbonate, which female birds need for the formation of sturdy eggshells. The birds you attract will make you glad that you chose the pricier blend or the sack of pure sunflower seeds.

Sunflower seeds are the most favored seed by the widest variety of birds. Choose from the softer-shelled black oil sunflower seeds, or black striped sunflower seeds, which are harder for some birds to open. Filling your feeders with black striped sunflower seeds can be a quick deterrent to house sparrows and blackbirds, which prefer the softer seeds.

Nyjer seed (also known as thistle seed, although it does not come from thistle plants) generally comes from countries in Africa. It's been treated so that it will never sprout, making it a risk-free backyard offering. This seed is a little more expensive than most blends, but it's a magnet for American and lesser goldfinches, house and purple finches, pine siskins, and other small birds that thrive in areas of tall grasses. Nyjer seed requires a feeder with smaller holes than the feeders you fill with sunflower and other seeds.

You will see many varieties of seed mixes at your local do-it-yourself, hardware, farm supply, and birding specialty stores, with names for their mixes that are meant to tempt your wallet. Be wary of fancy naming strategies; instead, read the bags and see exactly what's in the mix before buying. In particular, don't buy seed blends that include chemicals advertised as vitamin supplements. Generally, these are meant for caged birds that cannot hunt for their own food. Wild birds get their nutrition from the foods they eat, so these chemicals are unnecessary.

SUET

Extraordinarily popular with a wide variety of bird species, including woodpeckers, sapsuckers, nuthatches, and even warblers, suet has become the favorite offering of backyard birders. With its rise in desirability has come a startling selection of varieties, all pressed into cakes, rendered for year-round use, and readily available in discount stores and supermarkets, as well as birding specialty stores.

Pre-packaged suet cakes

Unprocessed butcher suet

Suet provides birds with a concentrated source of protein, one of the most important elements in helping them maintain energy throughout the nesting and breeding season. Overwintering birds require energy for warmth—in fact, some birds must eat constantly all day to take in the protein and fat they need to survive a frigid winter's night. They replenish their stores of fat by frequenting your suet feeders, making winter backyard birding a treat for nuthatch and woodpecker lovers. The same birds will return during the spring and summer, taking mouthfuls of suet to their nestlings. Suet blends that contain fruit and nuts provide important nutrients to baby birds.

You can buy cakes of pure suet or suet blended with seed, nuts, fruit, or even insects. Blends with fruit and insects can attract wrens and spring warblers, especially if migrating birds arrive before insects become plentiful. Orioles may take an interest in berries or orange essence mixed into the suet. Blends with nuts attract chickadees, nuthatches, grosbeaks, sparrows, and jays. Just about any kind of suet cake will bring woodpeckers to your yard, while house sparrows, starlings, and grackles will establish residency to feast at your suet feeder.

Many birders in colder climates prefer to use suet purchased from the local butcher, supplying birds with animal fat in its purest form. The greatest advantage to this is that squirrels are generally disinterested in this stuff, while they will hang upside down for long intervals to chow down on manufactured suet and seed cakes.

Suet cakes from reputable manufacturers are processed to remove impurities that make raw suet melt or spoil. These rendered cakes are stable up to about 100 degrees Fahrenheit, making them appropriate for all climates expect the hottest desert areas. Some manufacturers refine suet even further to make it usable in temperatures above 100 degrees. Look for varieties with "no melt" on the label.

NECTAR

Everyone wants tiny, beelike hummingbirds in their yard, and the primes of nectar-seeking orioles can have backyard birders getting up at dawn just to watch their nectar feeders.

It's easier than you might think to make your own nectar—and infinitely preferable to the powdered or bottled varieties you find in stores. It takes about ten minutes, and homemade nectar provides the nutritional balance birds need to keep their energy up throughout the nesting, breeding, and migration seasons. Commercial nectars contain additional ingredients beyond sugar, none of which improve the taste or benefits of the nectar itself.

Anna's hummingbird at nectar feeder

As your local weather warms and the sun heats your nectar feeders, you will need to change the nectar every couple of days to keep it fresh. Sugar water ferments in heat—this is the basic principle involved in making beer and wine—and the soured brew is bad for the birds. To keep up with the demand, you can make gallons of nectar to have on hand, especially if you feed hummingbirds at many feeders and your tiny friends frequently empty your reservoirs. The nectar will keep in your refrigerator for several days or longer in many cases.

Nectar feeders come in many shapes and sizes, from the simplest plastic bottles to decorative stained glass with wrought-iron trim. The birds don't care about the decor, however—as long as there's something red on the feeder to catch their eyes as they seek nourishment. If your feeder does not have red elements, tie a red ribbon around the top or hang red streamers from the bottom. The birds will spot it easily—and once they've found it, they will keep coming.

Female hummingbirds congregate at feeders with plenty of perches

Oriole nectar feeders are often very similar to those that attract hummingbirds, except they may be larger and usually have orange trim. Orioles prefer to perch rather than hover, so feeders that provide a foothold will attract these stunning birds. You may find orioles coming to your hummingbird feeder to drink the nectar you offer—it's not critical that you have a separate nectar feeder. Orioles also feed on insects, fruit, jelly, and nectar produced by flowers.

Hummingbirds will congregate on a feeder with multiple perches, providing you with great opportunities to identify different species or male and female birds. Choose a feeder with several openings and perches to allow more than one bird to feed at a time. Be sure to wash the feeder thoroughly and change the nectar every few days.

FRUIT AND NUTS

From the first strawberries of early summer to the nuts that drop from trees in the fall, your backyard can supply birds with a steady, nutritious diet. By sharing the bounty of your shrubs and trees with the birds, you provide them with the kinds of foods for which they would forage on their own—and you get to watch them in action.

Many birds that devour insects from spring through fall find themselves without this basic sustenance in winter. Not all of these birds migrate to the balmy climate of Central and South America, however—in fact, some of these birds move southward from northern Canada to the northern United States, where they find alternative food sources among the nuts and berries that linger in the trees throughout the winter.

Others do not migrate at all, shifting their dietary focus from bugs and grubs to fruit, seed cones, and acorns to generate the energy they need to survive the winter. The American robin is just one of many species that will switch from invertebrates to berries, seed cones, or nuts over the winter. Northern backyard birders associate robins with the onset of spring, so they are often startled by the sudden appearance of dozens or even hundreds of robins in the middle of January. These birds have not started the migration early; they've probably been in the area all winter, feeding on juniper berries, baneberry, and the orange berries of the mountain ash.

American robin eating juniper berries

In spring and summer, some birds—orioles and jays in particular—are readily attracted to fruits and jellies set out for them in your backyard. Baltimore and orchard orioles in the East are quick to come to feeders with half an orange added to the fare. Blue jays, tufted titmice, and robins will

Mexican jay heading for an orange

Birding Tip: How to Make Nectar

- Determine how much nectar your hummingbird feeder will hold.
- Add that much water to a saucepan.
- Stir in 1 part sugar to every 4 parts water—so if the feeder holds 2 cups of water, add ½ cup sugar.
- Bring the water to a boil.
- Boil for 10 minutes, stirring until the sugar dissolves.
- Let the water cool, and fill your feeder.

White-breasted nuthatch at peanut feeder

vie for mouthfuls of citrus fruit as well. In the western states, Bullock's and Scott's orioles line up for fruit, as do jays like Woodhouse's scrub-jay, California scrub-jay, and Mexican jay.

Nuthatches and woodpeckers love to pick peanuts out of feeders. As the peanuts are fairly challenging to remove, the birds linger at these feeders for several minutes at a time, giving you plenty of opportunity to enjoy their long-billed exploration. Trees in your yard that produce black walnuts, pinyon nuts, acorns, or cones will attract a fascinating variety of jays, grosbeaks, and—in colder climates—crossbills, which dig seeds out from between cone scales with their uniquely shaped bills.

You can enjoy a host of colorful birds throughout the year by combining feeder treats with cultivated nuts and berries the birds can find on their own. Having fruit at your feeders and in your garden can boost the number of species that feed in your yard. Many woodpeckers, warblers, grosbeaks, titmice, and sparrows choose berries and other fruits. You may even attract more unusual species, especially in winter: redpolls, dickcissel, quail, buntings, and tanagers all supplement their insect diets with berries.

GRIT IS GOOD!

Birds need grit and gravel to aid in the digestion of the foods they eat. Their digestive system includes a gizzard filled with grit, which breaks up seed hulls and grinds hard foods into bits that can pass into the small intestine. Wild birds know instinctively to add grit to their diets. You can help by leaving some part of your backyard or driveway unfinished so birds can find natural sources of gravel at the ready.

MEALWORMS

Most beginning backyard birders would not think to provide insects at their feeders. When birds are busy raising their young in late spring and early summer, an easily accessible supply of dried bugs may ease the strain on busy mother birds. You can do a great service to your resident bluebirds, robins, wrens, and others by adding a dedicated platform feeder stocked with dried or live mealworms. These creatures provide nutrients including protein and vitamins A and B, which are important to a bird's health and longevity.

Mealworms are the larvae of the darkling beetle, cultivated by commercial growers and packaged for home bird feeding. It's easy to pour a supply of these into a platform feeder without handling the worms at all. You can purchase them at birding specialty stores, at grain and feed stores like CountryMax or Fleet Farm, and at some DIY hardware chains. Fishing specialty stores also carry live and dried mealworms, as the larvae make excellent bait.

Live mealworms are the most effective in attracting birds, as their movement catches the eye quickly. To keep live mealworms in place, use a feeder with a slippery bottom and sides—a glass or hard plastic dish with sides at least 3 inches high. The mealworms will not be able to negotiate the slick sides, but they will keep attempting to do so—and birds will see them moving and come in to eat. If the idea of storing live larvae in your refrigerator is not particularly appealing, roasted or dried mealworms will still attract bluebirds, thrashers, robins, and wrens, although it may take more time for the birds to find them.

Dried mealworms often come in plastic containers or bags and also come mixed with additional fruit flavors, or even with dried fruits like cranberries or raisins. They can be found in cans or in special vacuum packaging, both of which retain the worms' moisture and make the larvae more palatable and attractive to birds. As dried mealworms do not move, mixing them with fruits will help attract birds more quickly. Mix dried mealworms with a little vegetable or olive oil to make them look juicy and shiny. If you're feeding with dried or roasted mealworms, place the feeder near a birdbath, recirculating pond, or fountain with moving water to help the birds find it. Once the birds discover the mealworms, they will come back again and again to this ready supply of tasty nutrition.

Use dried mealworms in the heat of summer or over the winter, when the extreme temperatures can kill the live ones. Dried mealworms can be stored on a shelf in your garage or utility room, while live mealworms must be kept in a container in the refrigerator, where they will go dormant until you move them to the feeder. Leave mealworms out throughout the fledging season to see adult birds bring their young to your feeder.

Dried or live mealworms are only two of the choices available to backyard birders who want to attract colorful insect-eating birds to their gardens. Some suppliers also sell waxworms, the larvae of bee moths, or fly larvae, which are smaller than either mealworms or waxworms. Any of these will attract insect-eating birds.

Eastern bluebird (female) eating from mealworm feeder

House finch on feeder near branch clamped to porch

3: Bird Feeders and Optimal Placements

If you love watching birds, turning your garden into a feeding paradise is a great way to bring birds to your yard. Birds are very adept at finding their own food in the wild, but like any other creature, they will take the path of least resistance to a good meal—especially if that meal is offered consistently and in quantity.

The birds may take some time to find your new feeders, especially if you live in a recently built neighborhood or if no one in your area has offered food for birds recently. Keep the feeders full of fresh food, and in a matter of days or a few weeks, the most adaptable species—usually house sparrows, chickadees, or house finches—will arrive to check out your offerings. In spring and summer, other birds will spot the activity at your feeders from the air and will come down to join them. In winter, many different species come together in flocks to forage for food, so the variety of birds at your feeders can be fascinating.

The key to attracting a wide variety of bird species is to offer several different kinds of food using different kinds of feeders in various locations throughout your backyard.

TUBE FEEDERS

The most popular feeders with birds and backyard birders alike, tube feeders provide twofold benefits: they are easy to use, and they attract plenty of active, colorful birds to your yard.

Place your tube feeders where birds can benefit from the three things they need most: food, water, and shelter. A tube feeder on a post in the middle of a wide-open, mowed yard will attract fewer birds than a feeder positioned near the cover of shrubs or trees. Birds are constantly on the watch for predators like hawks and cats, so they will choose feeders that offer them instant hiding places behind leaves or among thorns.

Tube feeders should be spaced so that birds have room to maneuver between them. Some feeders provide many openings through which birds can access the seed; these may attract small flocks of finches or chickadees. Place the feeders at least 10 feet apart to make sure there's plenty of room for all of the birds to rest and eat.

This cloth feeder is filled with nyjer seed, a special favorite of American and lesser goldfinches. Placing a nyjer feeder in a tree or shrub gives these colorful birds ready access to leafy cover, where they can hide when a hawk or owl passes overhead. Lesser goldfinches, seen here, are very social birds that move in small flocks, often accompanied by house finches. If you have one goldfinch, your feeder soon will attract others.

Space between feeders offers the added benefit of keeping squirrels at bay. Squirrels are comfortable leaping through the air from one feeder to the next, so if your feeders are too close together, your furry backyard buddies have ready access to every seed you supply.

You may want to place feeders close to windows to give you a clear view of the birds (but see "Birds and Windows" later in this chapter), or even to hang them from your eaves on hooks or plant hangers. Just be sure to position the feeders over or near bushes that provide sheltering leaves and branches. You can also purchase a feeder hanger (also called a shepherd's crook) from a DIY or birding specialty store and hang your feeders in the middle of a bed of native flowers. Birds will be attracted first by the color of the blooms and the potential for natural seeds. They will stay to feed on the seeds or nuts you provide, and they will keep coming back as your flowers produce their own seeds.

Tube feeder with perches on a pole in garden

Placing a feeder in a tree solves all kinds of bird-feeding issues. Birds, such as the pine siskins seen here, have ready access to food in an area that they frequent, making it easier for the birds to find the feeder for the first time. They can feed under the cover of leaves over their heads, masking their location from hawks. If ground predators see them, they can hop or fly to a hiding place in no time.

Finally, take careful note of what's under your feeder. Keep in mind that active feeders produce a litter of shells, and that inevitably birds will leave their droppings as well. If you're planning to hang a feeder on a porch or deck or very close to your house, be sure that the leavings will not mar your floor, house siding, children's play area, or any other surface that you'd prefer to keep clean.

HOPPER FEEDERS

Birds have voracious appetites, and once they begin to arrive at your feeder in flocks, you may find that your feeder runs out of seed at an alarmingly rapid rate.

Hopper feeders offer a set-and-forget alternative to smaller tube feeders. These larger feeders often hold up to five pounds of seed or more, dispensing the seed through multiple holes at the bottom of the feeder.

Larger birds like woodpeckers, doves, and jays cannot perch comfortably on a tube feeder, as their size and weight make it difficult for them to get to the seed once they've settled on a perch. Hopper feeders offer larger perches, more space between the bird and the seed-dispensing hole, and a stable perch that does not sway so easily under a bird's weight.

Use any kind of seed that you wish in a hopper feeder. The holes are large enough to accommodate whole sunflower seeds or even shelled peanuts, and the tray construction at the bottom of the feeder can keep fine seeds like nyjer from spilling out.

A common grackle lands above a female house finch on a hopper feeder mounted to a deck railing

Hopper feeders are most stable when they are mounted on top of a wooden or metal stand-alone post. This keeps the feeder from shaking or rocking when larger birds land, providing a secure station at which they can feed comfortably. Some hopper feeders come with a threaded mounting sleeve, so you can screw them onto a metal post made to fit the feeder. This makes installation easy. If you have a fence, gate, or deck railing that will accommodate a hopper feeder, the post can provide a strong, stable stand.

Fences and railings can become highways for squirrels, however. Choose a hopper feeder with built-in squirrel deterrents to keep these voracious animals out of your seed. Some hopper feeders have guards that will close under the squirrel's weight, cutting them off from the seed within.

Hopper feeders can also hang from a sturdy branch in a tree. This places the food right where birds live, providing all the benefits of shelter and convenient access. If you have a fairly new yard with young trees, choose a smaller hopper feeder—perhaps with a one- or two-pound capacity—so the weight of the seed doesn't overtax the branch.

Northern cardinal feeding on house-shaped hopper feeder hanging in a tree

WOOD, PLASTIC, OR METAL?

- Wooden feeders are particularly susceptible to squirrel or chipmunk invasion. These little animals will gnaw through wood in no time to gain access to the food inside.

- Plastic feeders are more resistant to unwanted intrusion. Choose a feeder that won't yellow in the sun so you'll have a clear view of the contents for years to come.

- Metal feeders stand up best to weather and to attacks from hungry animals. All-metal feeders can be pricey, but they will return your investment with their longevity and their ability to protect your seed from squirrels.

Choose a hopper feeder that you can take apart easily for cleaning. Some hopper feeders allow ridges of seed to harden below the holes, making it necessary to get inside the feeder and clean out compacted seed regularly before it begins to decay. The more readily the feeder comes apart, the easier it will be for you to protect your backyard birds from molds that can cause illness.

Also consider a hopper feeder with panels made of glass or Plexiglas, so you can see how much seed remains. Clean the feeder regularly—at least once a season—to keep the panels clear. Clean feeders filled with fresh, visible seed attract more birds.

WINDOW FEEDERS

If your yard has no trees, or if you don't have a yard at all, you can still feed birds with great success by installing a window feeder.

You'll find a wide variety of window feeders available. These range from simple plastic structures that adhere to your window with suction cups, to sill-sized feeders that install inside an open window to bring birds right into your room.

If you can see the birds through your window, the birds can see you as well. Don't run right up to the window to view the birds in the feeder—they will be startled by the sudden movement and fly off. Move cautiously, a few steps at a time, toward the window—or enjoy the birds at a distance from the comfort of your favorite chair.

Many birding specialty stores carry one-way film with which you can cover your window, so the birds see a mirror image of themselves while you maintain your clear view of the birds at your feeder. This film usually clings to a clean window, so there's no adhesive involved.

House finches in a window feeder

BIRDS AND WINDOWS

Birds have a tendency to fly into windows, colliding with the glass and knocking themselves senseless. In fact, the Birds and Buildings Forum estimates that one billion birds are killed every year by flying into windows. Birds don't see or understand glass—they see trees and bushes reflected in the glass, so they fly right into it as if these reflections are really trees. Window feeders actually help birds survive, because the birds slow down and land when they see the food. You can also hang paracord on the outside of the glass, following instructions available at Acopian BirdSavers (birdsavers.com), as the birds will avoid the strings and stay back from the window.

As with all feeder placements, choose a window that has shrubs or other vegetation below it or nearby to give birds the shelter they need from predatory hawks. Look under the window to be sure that falling shells or bird droppings will not adversely affect the surface beneath it.

NECTAR FEEDERS

One of the best things about hummingbirds is that they don't mind being close to human beings.

This means that you can place your nectar feeders right under the eaves of your house, or on your porch, deck, or patio, and enjoy hummingbirds up close throughout the spring and summer months. If you want to see your hummingbirds' reflective feathers light up like neon, put your feeders where they will catch the sun.

Nectar feeder hanging near weigela

Hummingbirds will find your feeders quickly if they hang over or near tubular flowers like trumpet vine, weigela, cardinal flower, or penstemon. The hummingbirds will feed on the flowers and spot the red decorations on your feeder. As hummers spend their lives seeking new food sources, they will visit your feeder as part of their regular rounds.

Orioles are a little more skeptical of human presence—but the lure of sugar water is strong, so they will perch on nectar feeders even when they hang close to household windows and doors.

Space nectar feeders along the side of your house, hanging them where you can see them from inside. If you have many feeders, label them with numbers to help you, your family members, and guests bring one another's attention to new arrivals. "Broad-billed hummingbird on feeder 4" becomes a mantra for families lucky enough to live where many hummingbirds frequent their feeders.

Where you live has a great deal of impact on how many hummingbirds you will attract to multiple feeders. Residents of the eastern United States may see only one species—the ruby-throated hummingbird—as this is the only species that breeds dependably east of the Mississippi River. Western residents may see anywhere from three to fourteen different hummingbird species depending on their proximity to the Mexican border. More feeders may not increase the number of species you see, but they are likely to draw more birds to your yard.

A young Anna's hummingbird hovers between nectar feeders #2 and #3

Nectar feeders come in many shapes and sizes, including diminutive feeders that can be inserted in hanging plants. You may find yourself filling these little feeders more than once a day during peak hummer seasons.

Bees come when the nectar spills or leaks from the feeder. Once the sticky residue is on the outside of the feeder, there's no getting rid of the bees except to take down the feeder, clean it, and move it about 30 feet away from its original spot. In addition, bees are attracted to the color yellow. Choose a nectar feeder that does not feature yellow bee guards. The bees don't keep the hummingbirds from feeding—they bother humans much more than they do birds.

SUET FEEDERS

Many birds love suet, but you're probably feeding with this natural fat product because you want woodpeckers, nuthatches, creepers, and other tree-clinging birds to come to your yard. These colorful birds can make fascinating guests with their industrious, purposeful movements—these are birds that behave as though they have important jobs to do.

If you hang a suet feeder in the middle of your mowed yard or from a plant hanger off of your house's eaves, the birds you want are very unlikely to put in an appearance. Woodpeckers and nuthatches search for their food within the bark of trees, so they may never notice a feeder in a clearing. They dig for insects, finding them behind the bark or burrowed into tree trunks or branches.

Downy woodpecker feeding at cage feeder containing raw suet

Birds that frequent suet feeders are accustomed to clinging vertically to tree bark, or even to hanging upside down as they scavenge along a tree branch for insects. They prefer the cage-style suet feeders that offer them wide, solid bars onto which they can cling, with plenty of room between the mesh for their large bills to probe the suet.

For the best results, hang your suet feeders in trees close to the trunk, or tie the feeder directly to the trunk. Mounting a feeder in a tree or right on a tree trunk will attract more woodpeckers and nuthatches more quickly. To fasten a

Hairy woodpecker feeding from suet spread on tree bark

suet cage to a trunk, don't drive nails into your tree—instead, secure the feeder using strong plastic-coated wire. Thread the wire through the back of the cage at the top and bottom, and twist the ends together on the other side of the tree. Once the feeder is secured, bring the suet out to the feeder to fill it. Remove the feeder and clean it once each season.

Many backyard birders get excellent results by skipping the feeder altogether and smearing suet on the bark of a tree. This is especially good for attracting brown creepers, which do not frequent feeders and search for food by creeping up a single tree over and over, always returning to the bottom to begin again.

While some commercial blends are available in spreadable form, you can make your own suet spread. Grind the raw suet or chop it into small bits. Melt it into a liquid in a saucepan over low heat. Strain the liquid through cheesecloth and let it cool. When the suet has cooled to a solid, repeat the melting and straining steps to fully render the suet. Let the suet cool a second time until it's the consistency of soft paste, then spread it on the tree bark with a spatula.

Feeders shaped like small logs are uniquely attractive to woodpeckers and other tree-clinging

Red-bellied woodpecker feeding from a log feeder with holes stuffed with raw suet

birds. Manufacturers make sticks of suet blended with nuts and seeds to insert into the holes of these feeders. You can use any kind of suet in these, however, as long as it's stuffed securely into the hole. (Suet on the ground attracts squirrels, not birds.) Birds gravitate to the familiar shape and find treats in each of the holes. Hang one or more of these feeders in your trees to attract repeat visitors.

If you want to be sure that only tree-clinging birds feed on your suet, choose feeders that only offer access to the suet from the bottom. The only birds that can enjoy these feeders are those that can hang upside down.

PLATFORM FEEDERS

A wide variety of birds, both small and mid-sized, prefer to feed with both feet on the ground instead of perching or clinging to a feeder.

Doves, white-throated and white-crowned sparrows, blackbirds, and juncos may be just as interested in seed as are the chickadees, house sparrows, and finches that perch on your feeders. They will land below your feeders to clean up what other birds drop, but this may not be enough to satisfy their appetites. Also, they're not likely to find high-quality food discarded by the insatiable eaters above them.

Common grackle on a platform feeder mounted to a post

Platform feeders provide a ground-like experience for juncos, doves, pigeons, migrating sparrows, and jays. These flat feeders allow birds to land on a stable structure and search for food on the surface, a more comfortable method than reaching into awkward holes on a tube feeder to pull out seeds.

Birds that feed on the ground will come to a seed-laden platform even if it's several feet off the ground. With this in mind, position your platform feeder where it's easy for you to see. This will give you great views of birds you may be missing when you watch from inside your home. Install the platform on top of a post or pole, but close enough to trees or bushes to provide quick cover when hawks circle over your yard.

The best platform feeders hold seed, nuts, and even mealworms between two layers of mesh or screen. The first layer keeps the seed from blowing away or being brushed off the feeder by messy eaters. The lower screen has a finer mesh, which allows rain to fall through to the ground while keeping the seed in place and relatively dry.

- Use dried corn to attract large ground birds like ring-necked pheasant, quail, bobwhite, and wild turkey.
- Add nuts—especially shelled peanuts—to bring jays, chickadees, woodpeckers, and flickers to your platform and ground feeders.
- Mealworms in a platform feeder can bring you bluebirds, wrens, and thrushes.

Some platform feeders have feet that allow you to place the feeder right on the ground, making it easy for ground-feeding birds to find it quickly. This kind of feeder may expand the variety of birds you attract, adding quail or even wild turkey to your list of backyard birds.

Placing a platform or tray feeder on the ground can help you attract these birds to a specific place in your yard, where you can observe them easily from a window. Choose a feeder with legs that lift the tray a few inches off the ground to allow rainwater to drain away from the seed. Migrating birds looking for food sources will see the commotion on the ground at your tray feeder, increasing the number of species in your yard during spring and fall.

Many homeowners simply place a wide, low dish of seed on the ground for juncos, doves, flickers, and sparrows. If you choose this inexpensive method, drill small holes in the dish to allow water to drain out, to keep the seed from getting moldy.

In all cases, limit the amount of seed and nuts you place in a platform or tray feeder. Too much seed can clog the drainage holes or mesh, turning the food into a soggy mess that will not appeal to any bird.

Hang a tray or flat basket-style feeder under a tube feeder to catch discarded seed as it falls. This reduces the amount of seed waste you need to rake up later, while providing a steady diet for birds that feed on flat surfaces. Leave enough room between the tube and the tray to accommodate larger birds like jays, grackles, and doves.

FEEDER MAINTENANCE

One of the most positive and effective things you can do for your backyard birds is also one of the simplest and least costly: clean your feeders regularly.

Seed feeders should be disinfected at least once a season, or any time the seed has had a chance to decay or become moldy inside the feeder. If birds eat the spoiled food, they can get sick.

Beyond the seed itself, birds often leave droppings on top of feeders and on perches. Studies have shown that bird droppings—especially house sparrow, pigeon, and starling droppings—may cause as many as sixty diseases in humans.

If you feed your birds with raw suet in the colder months, remember to discard this suet and switch to commercial no-melt suet products as the weather warms. Raw suet becomes rancid in warm weather, so don't wait until the birds reject the smelly stuff—toss it and clean the feeder in which it spent the winter.

Nectar and jelly feeders should be washed thoroughly every time you refill them. As nectar hangs in a clear glass or plastic feeder in the sun, it begins the process of fermentation—essentially the same process by which breweries make beer. Hummingbirds don't care for fermented nectar, and they will avoid your feeder once they've tasted the sour swill. Washing the feeder thoroughly will remove any residue, keeping your nectar fresh tasting. It may take a while for the birds to trust your feeder again, but keep it full of fresh nectar regardless of whether you see hummingbirds.

Black-capped chickadees on a platform feeder secured under a tube feeder

Jelly and fruit feeders inevitably attract bugs, so washing these will remove any dead insects (usually ants) that have accumulated. If you're feeding with orange halves, cleaning the feeder will remove any mold the fruit may have fostered on the feeder itself or on the pegs that hold the fruit in place.

The latest tube and cage feeders disassemble easily to allow you to clean them thoroughly. These cleverly designed feeders open at the bottom as well as at the top, so you can wash away all the seed residue that works its way into every tight space. Ask for easy-clean feeders at your birding specialty store or wherever you purchase your feeders.

Keep your feeder-cleaning tools separate from other tools in your basement, shed, or garage. Create a kit that includes a long-handled feeder-cleaning brush, a sponge or other scrubber, a measuring cup for bleach, and a long pointed stick to reach into the bottom of a tube feeder. Rubber gloves are also handy, especially if birds have left their droppings on the perches or on top of the feeder.

DIY: KEEPING FEEDERS CLEAN

Step 1: Remove Waste

Start by removing all the wet, sticky, or moldy seed from the bottom of the feeder. Use a stiff brush or long stick to reach into the bottom of the feeder. Tapping the bottom or sides will help loosen the residue. Deposit the waste into a trash basket lined with a plastic bag.

Step 1

Step 2: Total Immersion

Fill your washtub or utility sink with enough hot water to immerse the feeder completely. Add one part bleach for every ten parts water: if you use two gallons of water (256 ounces), add about 26 ounces of bleach. Disassemble your feeder as much as possible. Some feeders have removable perches or unscrew at the bottom; others may only have a removable top. Immerse the feeder and all of its parts completely in the hot water with bleach.

Step 2

Step 3: Wash Thoroughly

Use a clean brush with a long handle to scrub the inside of the feeder. Make sure all of the seed residue, dust, and clinging mold gets cleaned out completely. Wash around each of the seed-dispensing holes, where birds perch and eat. Use a sponge or brush to clean any droppings off the outside of the feeder.

Step 3

Step 4: Dry Completely

Allow the feeder and all of its parts to dry thoroughly before reassembling and refilling. Filling a wet feeder with seed will only restart the spoilage process as the seeds come in contact with the moisture. If you need to get your feeders out quickly, use a blow-dryer to hasten the drying process.

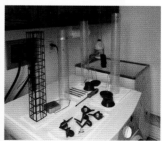
Step 4

Pine siskins in a garden birdbath

4: Neighborhood Watering Hole

There's no better way to attract birds to your yard than with moving water. Sources of water can be scarce for birds in areas with large human populations, especially in suburban areas or cities. Birds need water just as much as we do, so a clean water feature can bring mixed flocks to your yard on a regular basis.

In addition to hydration, birds need to clean themselves, and they will use your birdbath to do so. You'll see birds stand in shallow water, fluff their feathers to allow the water to reach their skin, and splash themselves with their wings. Some birds actually jump into the water and out again very quickly, seeming to bounce back and forth compulsively as they wet themselves thoroughly. Your water feature does a great service to the birds, and it's sure to provide you with some entertaining observations of bird behavior.

How do birds find the water? Moving water—a simple drip into an otherwise still pool, or a babbling recirculating fountain—will catch birds' eyes as they fly over your property.

Water has the added benefit of attracting birds that will not visit your feeders. Warblers and vireos will drop from their high perches in the treetops to visit your birdbath, as will flycatchers, kingbirds, and all manner of sparrows.

CHOOSING A BIRDBATH

When you think of a birdbath, a single image may come to mind: a carved stone basin on a Grecian-looking pedestal, filled with standing water.

If this vision doesn't appeal to you, you're not alone. An entire industry has developed to provide us with a wide range of options that not only bring much-needed moisture to our birds but also complement the style and layout of our gardens.

The carved stone birdbath is still available, but in new materials that stand up to the elements and in colors and models that add panache to your yard. If you've dreamed of having a small pond, it's easier than ever to create one, even in a yard with no natural water features. The sound of gently trickling water can be part of your backyard experience for a small investment and a minimum of technical effort.

Drip water feature with bathing American robin

The best outcome of the new birdbaths is this: the days of stagnant, standing water are gone—and not a moment too soon. The greenish, odiferous water that so often filled those ancient stone birdbaths took on that ghastly shade because there was no circulation pump, automatic dripper, or other mechanism to keep the water moving.

Most important, birds are attracted to the flash and clarity of moving water, just as we are. You'll see more birds in your yard if you bring that glimmer home and extend your feathered friends some sparkling hospitality.

PEDESTAL BIRDBATHS

Pedestals now come in a range of styles that can match any home, whether your house is a painted Victorian lady, a midcentury modern colonial, a turn-of-the-century Craftsman, or an adobe abode.

The majority of pedestal birdbaths are made from plastic or resin, which makes them virtually impervious to heat, cold, snow, and rain. For sheer durability, these are baths you can use as a centerpiece or accent for a garden of any size, whether you're tucking a birdbath into a corner of a small city yard or creating an expansive habitat filled with native flowers and shrubs.

A birdbath of cast stone or ceramic construction may be more to your taste. These offer no additional advantage to the birds, but they may match your home's style or be the perfect natural accent to your garden. The potential for chipping, cracking, and storm wear are higher with natural materials. Keep this in mind for climates in which severe cold or violent storms are part of the annual picture.

While most manufacturers have taken water level into consideration in the design of their birdbaths, be sure to look closely at the

Terra cotta pedestal birdbath with lesser goldfinch

depth of the bowl. The water should be shallow around the edges so that birds can perch on the edge of the bowl and drink comfortably.

At the same time, the center of the bowl should be just deep enough to allow a sparrow to stand and bathe, fluffing out his feathers to splash water through to his skin. If the bowl is too deep, the birds will reject it as a water source.

If you've already got a pedestal birdbath and the water is too deep for comfort, place a rock in the center of the bowl. The rock should be large enough to rise above the water, giving birds a place to perch and drink, or to retain their footing while they splash themselves.

Some birdbath setups create a small fountain in the bowl, addressing the issue of water depth while giving birds more than one place to drink or bathe. The best of these are solar-powered, requiring no electrical lines or batteries. As the water circulates automatically, you can fill the reservoir once and refill when birds and evaporation lower the water level.

Pedestal birdbath made of modern materials

Resist the temptation to place the birdbath alone in the middle of your well-mowed yard. Like feeders and birdhouses, birdbaths need to be near trees or shrubs to allow the birds to escape to shelter. Leaves and other detritus may drop into the water, but the birds will actually stop to drink here, so the occasional clean-out of fallen twigs and other bits will be well worth your effort.

Birds will find your birdbath because there is water in it, but beyond this basic requirement, the design of your birdbath should reflect your personal preferences. Many artisans fashion remarkable, unique birdbaths, like this one

Birding Tip: Cat Deterrent

Pedestal birdbaths have an important benefit: they're harder for cats to reach. If you've got a cat, or if your neighbors allow their cats to wander, sooner or later a cat will find its way to your backyard and your feeders. The leap to the edge of the pedestal birdbath, however, may be more than a well-fed suburban cat can handle, especially if thorny bushes edge the bath.

Metal artist Paul Knoblauch made this ornate pedestal birdbath

by metal artist Paul Knoblauch. If you're considering a truly one-of-a-kind birdbath, check to be sure it can accommodate a circulating pump or a dripper to create the moving water effect that will attract birds.

DISH BIRDBATHS

Shaped like lily pads or painted with elaborate designs, dish birdbaths can sit on the ground, hang from planter hooks or shepherd's crooks, fasten to the side of a deck railing, or stand at the edge of a patio.

- Birds will go wherever they have a safe path of escape, so place your dish birdbath close to cover.
- Group potted plants around a birdbath on the ground or in a corner of your patio.
- Hang the birdbath next to a shrub or tree at the edge of your deck.
- Place it on the ground beneath a rosebush or hawthorn, where the thorns will protect the birds.
- Hang it in a pine tree with sheltering needles.

For the most part, dish birdbaths are less expensive than their pedestal or circulating counterparts, making them good choices for a beginning backyard birder. The least expensive dish birdbaths are often the most durable: a simple, natural-colored dish on a round metal frame will last for many years with regular cleaning. It's easy to fill this birdbath from the garden hose, even if it needs filling more than once a day. A watering can will do the trick as well. To clean it, just pop it out of the metal ring and wash it in a utility sink. Scrub it with a brush to remove droppings and sediments.

Hanging birdbath

It's this versatility that makes dish birdbaths so popular with backyard birders in homes of every size. Equally important, dish birdbaths are easy to clean on a regular basis. Most can simply be lifted from a frame or hanger and emptied, or even brought into the house to wash in the basement laundry sink.

Female house finch in a plastic bowl birdbath

DIY: CLEANING YOUR BIRDBATH

1. Pour out all the water in the birdbath.

2. Wear rubber gloves.

3. Using a stiff-bristle brush, scrub out all the soils and sludge accumulated in the bottom of the bath. Rinse with a garden hose.

4. Wet down any bird droppings to make them soft, and scrub them off with the brush.

5. Empty the droppings into a plastic garbage bag and discard.

6. Finally, fill the birdbath with a solution of ¾ cup of household bleach to 1 gallon of warm water. Let it sit for ten to fifteen minutes to kill algae and bacteria. Rinse thoroughly.

Dish birdbaths are generally shallower than many pedestal baths, topping out at the ideal bird bathing depth of 1½ inches. If you've got your heart set on a dish that's deeper, remember the trick of placing a rock in the center to give birds an extra place to perch. Partially filling the birdbath also works well; check the water at least daily in hot weather and refill it if the sun evaporates the shallow pool.

Finally, look for dish birdbaths with ridges or other decorative elements around the edges that provide additional footholds for the smallest birds.

YOUR OWN POND

Even very small spaces can accommodate a manmade pond, and the addition of this water feature to your yard can bring you many hours of pleasure—and many birds with which to share your small oasis.

Ponds do not need to be large, but they do need a well-constructed sand base and a strong rubber liner to keep the pond filled and contained. A pond is more than a hole in the ground filled with water. It's a self-contained mini-ecosystem that you create to attract species that thrive in an aquatic habitat.

To keep your pond healthy and useful to birds, amphibians, and small animals, plan to include a pump that will keep the water moving. Without the pump, you risk creating a stagnant pool filled with algae and bacteria instead of a lovely addition to your landscape. Worse, mosquitoes love standing water. A pump will circulate the water and could even create a small waterfall, generating the visual effect and soundscape you desire. The best pumps are noiseless so that no motor sounds will mar the sound of trickling water.

Pond with manmade recirculating falling water feature

You may choose simply to keep your water slightly agitated with a small pump, an effective safeguard against a major buildup of surface scum and noxious organisms. If you dream of having your own waterfall, several manufacturers offer kits that make it fairly easy to create the cascading effect. How big a pump do you need for your pond? Experts say that your pump should be able to move half of your pond's capacity in an hour—so if your pond holds two hundred gallons of water, you need a pump that flows at the rate of one hundred gallons per hour.

Fountains actually lift the water above the pond's surface, so there are more elements to consider. Pond filters, pipes, and fittings all create resistance as the water moves through the fountain system. You will need a pump that can overcome this resistance. Your garden store can help you calculate the pressure

Pond with fountain effect

you need. Be sure to ask lots of questions before you begin the installation so that you can eliminate costly issues up front.

Your pond will become a focal point around which you can create a delightful garden, so choose its location carefully. Avoid placing your pond directly under a tree. Flower petals, leaves, seeds, and fruit dropping from the tree will cover your pond regularly, giving you an unnecessary cleaning chore to do. If your pond is in a sunny spot, be sure to check the water level on hot days when evaporation could reduce the contents. Use your garden hose to add water.

Algae grow in water, but they also need light and nutrients to survive. You can control algae growth by cutting off nutrients and altering the light.

- Create a lip around your pond to keep rainwater from carrying fertilizer into the pond water.
- Keep your filter clean.
- Use an outdoor-rated ultraviolet (UV) sterilizer to kill the algae.
- Place barley straw in the pond, where flowing water will make it decompose and turn into hydrogen peroxide, which kills the algae.
- Use an algae inhibitor that is not toxic to other plants, birds, or animals.

Surround your pond with a rock border to cover the edge of the plastic liner, and also to define the edge and give small creatures a place to perch while they drink.

Think carefully about the plants that surround your pond—you'll need plants that grow best in very moist soil, or even right in the water. Create a stepped effect with low, mid-sized, and taller plants, giving your pond a natural appearance while providing suitable cover for birds of all kinds, whether they prefer to feed on the ground or to perch at the top of ornamental grasses or cattails. Your favorite nursery will have many suggestions for pond-loving plants that thrive in your climate zone. (See the map in appendix B to determine your zone.)

Plants make a pond more inviting to birds

This tufted titmouse chose a
fence-mounted box for its nest

5: Nest Boxes, Nests, and Nesting Behaviors

One of the most popular ways to bring birds into your yard is to invite them to nest. Providing birdhouses—typically called "nest boxes"—can encourage many bird species to make your yard a seasonal haven.

BIRDHOUSES

It's a common misconception that birdhouses become a bird family's home, to which the birds will return year after year. With a few exceptions, this is rarely the case; birds use a nest box for laying eggs and raising young, usually vacating the premises once the young birds have left the nest. If a mated pair raises a second or third brood in a season, they usually move on to a new nesting location.

A shopping excursion for a birdhouse will reveal dozens of different varieties, from the very ornate to the simplest pine box with a hole in it. Choose whatever style of house you like to complement your yard or garden, but rest assured that birds are attracted to the size and position of the hole, not to the pretty paint or the detailed gingerbread trim on some very attractive nest boxes.

Why are there so many shapes and sizes? Different boxes attract different bird species. The choices are nearly as varied as the eighty bird species that will use nest boxes.

Which Birds Use Boxes

Birds' process of laying eggs, sitting on them until they hatch, and caring for their nestlings is so fascinating to us that we go to great lengths to invite birds to do all of this in our own backyards.

Not every bird requires the assistance of a manmade nest box, however. In fact, the vast majority of birds do quite well in building their own nesting place and raising their young without any human intervention at all.

To make your yard as interesting as possible to the widest variety of nesting birds, choose nest boxes that are appropriate for birds that already nest and breed in your neighborhood.

Nest boxes are most attractive to cavity nesters: birds that look for holes that lead to snug, sheltered spaces in natural or manufactured places. A great many backyard birds are cavity nesters, including house sparrows, wrens,

Mountain bluebird establishes residency in a post-mounted birdhouse

nuthatches, woodpeckers, chickadees, titmice, tree swallows, some flycatchers, bluebirds, and purple martins. American kestrels also use cavities for nesting, so you may find a pair of the nation's smallest falcon occupying a nest box of the appropriate size (15 inches deep, with a 3-inch hole about 12 inches from the bottom) if your property includes open fields.

Chickadees, nuthatches, and titmice all prefer cavities at about 5 to 6 feet off the ground. Choose a wooden box with a small hole, no larger than 1⅛ inches across, to allow these small birds to enter the nest box while keeping larger birds out. The nest should be in a tree, either tied to the trunk or suspended from a solid tree branch.

> **Birding Tip: Location Is Everything**
>
> Placement of your nest boxes is a critical part of attracting the right birds to the right boxes.
>
> - Red-bellied woodpeckers prefer boxes high up in trees.
> - Great-crested flycatchers generally prefer boxes up to 20 feet off the ground.
> - Tree swallows like boxes made for bluebirds, especially when they're secured on dead trees. Violet-green swallows look for nest boxes in trees in sparse or open woodland.
> - Red-breasted nuthatches will come to boxes in cone-bearing trees like pine and spruce. White-breasted nuthatches like boxes in leafy trees, but they won't turn down coniferous woods.
> - Wrens will come to just about any nest box, even one hanging below the eaves of your house. They will defend other nest boxes in the area, however, even if they've already rejected them.

Bluebirds of all varieties prefer nest boxes on posts or poles in open land, where they have a wide view of the meadows or grasslands that surround them. If you live in a thickly developed suburban or city neighborhood, bluebirds are highly unlikely to find your nest box.

If your country yard does attract bluebirds, watch your nest box carefully for marauding house sparrows. These aggressive birds are known to drag young bluebirds out of the box and co-opt it for themselves. House sparrows are not protected by wildlife laws, so you are welcome—even encouraged—to pull a house sparrow nest out of your bluebird box and discard it.

An eastern phoebe builds a shelf nest on barn rafters

Cavity-nesting birds use the nest box for the sole purpose of raising young. Some birds may return to a nest box in winter to roost overnight or to wait out storms in relative comfort.

Some birds prefer the open architecture of a shelf, a roof beam, or even a retail store sign as the ideal nesting location. Robins are shelf nesters, choosing to nest at the tops of bushes, on open tree limbs, or on nesting platforms you can make or buy. Barn swallows and phoebes are also fond of this nesting style, often nesting exactly where you wish they would not.

When you know what birds you're likely to attract, visit your birding specialty store to get the best information on what boxes will interest your birds.

NEST BOXES THAT WORK

What makes a good nest box? While each bird species has its own preference for hole size and placement, some basic rules of thumb apply across most species.

Birds are attracted to what they know, so the best material for birdhouse construction is natural, untreated wood. Your nest box does not need a coat of paint or a chemical finish—in fact, the most practical nest boxes have no outer coating at all. Look for nest boxes made of wood from cone-bearing (coniferous) trees like fir, pine, or cedar. If you're building your own box, there's no need to spend the extra money on pricey hardwoods—the birds are happy with the bargain-basement materials.

You can skip the sanding as well: birds prefer an unfinished interior with rough walls. A slanted, overhanging roof helps deflect rain from the hole and shades the interior from the sun.

Hole size is the most effective way to control the birds that have a chance to nest in your box. To keep house sparrows out of your nest boxes, make the hole no larger than 1⅛ inches. House wrens, chickadees, titmice, and nuthatches will still be able to enter. Bluebirds require a larger hole, up to 1½ inches. Songbirds like Carolina wrens can also use a hole this size.

Birdhouse with a 1½ –inch–size hole

Beyond the entrance hole, the nest box needs additional small ventilation holes to allow fresh air to enter once the nestlings have hatched. Small holes in the floor will allow moisture to escape when heavy rains hit, as they often do in humid climates during the summer months.

Don't add any perches outside the entrance hole—these are just an invitation to predator birds and invasive species like house sparrows to gain access. It's your job to keep predators from reaching into the box to steal eggs or grab nestlings. You have several choices for this. Buy or make a wooden hole extender that turns your birdhouse opening into a longer tube, making it too far for raccoons to reach inside. A cage-style hole extender also narrows the approach to the nest box opening, discouraging long-armed mammals, grackles, and jays. These methods will deter house sparrows as well.

Finally, choose or make a box with a hinged roof and walls to allow you to open the box once the birds have moved out and clean out the abandoned nest. The birds will not return to the nest, and the remains can attract parasites and other vermin that are not good for birds.

When you choose a strong, durable nest box, you have the opportunity to see birds select this box, build a nest inside, incubate a clutch of eggs, and raise the young—all right in your own backyard.

House wren	1 to 1¼ inches
Chickadee	1⅛ inches
Bewick's wren	1¼ inches
Titmouse	1¼ inches
Downy woodpecker	1¼ inches
Nuthatch	1⅜ inches
Carolina wren	1½ inches
Bluebird	1½ inches
Tree swallow	1½ inches
Violet-green swallow	1½ inches
Hairy woodpecker	1¾ inches
Great-crested flycatcher	1¾ inches
Purple martin	2¼ inches
Flicker	2½ inches
American kestrel	3 inches

SPECIES-SPECIFIC BOX REQUIREMENTS

We've talked about construction materials and the size of the opening, but these are just the initial steps in attracting birds to your nest box. Some of the eighty species that will use a nest box require very specific features before they'll turn your birdhouse into the seasonal family manse.

If you know exactly which species you'd like to have nesting in your box, you can create the perfect nesting environment for that bird. For example, purple martins are well known for their preference for social nesting. These birds need wide-open spaces like farmland or the "forever wild" of a wildlife refuge, where they can swoop and dart to catch insects—and a lake or pond with plenty of mosquitoes will help attract these birds. Martins will return to the same nesting site year after year, as long as there are no structures or trees within 40 feet of the nest box pole on all sides.

First, be sure that the birds you want actually nest and breed in your area, and in the kind of habitat you can provide. If you live in the middle of a

Purple martin house

northeastern city, for example, you will have no luck attracting varied thrush, a bird that is native to the states of Washington and Oregon. By the same rule, a California home can attract Steller's jays and California scrub-jays, but not the blue jays, which rarely venture that far west.

Next, your nest box needs to be in a habitat in which your target bird is comfortable. If you have a large lot with some dense stands of trees, you'll have better luck attracting black-capped chickadees—and your odds improve if you stuff the nest box with wood shavings and sawdust so the bird can excavate its own cavity. If evergreen woods including aspen, ponderosa pine, and spruce trees surround your home—and you live west of the Great Plains states—violet-green swallows may adopt your nest box fairly readily.

Box height is a large factor for certain species. Northern flickers, eastern screech owls, and American kestrels all prefer higher nests, as much as 30 feet off the ground. Many small birds, including the Carolina, mountain, and chestnut-backed chickadees, Carolina wren, prothonotary warbler, red-breasted nuthatch, and tufted or juniper titmouse, are comfortable in nest boxes from 5 to 15 feet off the ground. Bluebirds and house wrens look for lower nest boxes, with wrens topping out at 10 feet and bluebirds choosing to be 3 to 6 feet up.

Many birds establish an area in which only one mated pair can nest. This is the birds' territory, and birds will defend that area from all other birds of its species that might approach. Kestrels, for example, will not nest within half a mile of one another. Even little chickadees establish significant territory, permitting one nest in an area of several acres. Once birds choose your nest box, your yard becomes their territory, and they will defend the area—sometimes aggressively—against avian intruders.

Nest boxes are usually very utilitarian in design and construction, but birdhouses can become ornamental additions to your yard or garden. Artisan-style birdhouses may or may not attract birds, depending on their placement in your yard, the size of the entrance hole, and the interior space (cavity) the birds find once they enter. Remember that if birds do nest in a decorative birdhouse, you will need access to the inside of the box to clean it out at the end of the breeding season.

INVADERS

It's lovely to consider the possibility of nuthatches, titmice, or bluebirds nesting in your yard, but the fact is that aggressive invasive species may be the first to find the boxes you've placed for more desirable birds.

House sparrows and European starlings are exotic, invasive species, introduced to our skies and woods by well-meaning Americans in the mid- to late 1800s.

As invaders, they had no natural predators, so their numbers multiplied with exponential speed. Today these two species are among the most populous in the world—in part because they can nest and breed just about anywhere, including in nest boxes meant for other birds.

House sparrows are particularly partial to bluebird boxes. Many birders (including us) have observed house sparrows actively pushing bluebirds out of nest boxes and killing their nestlings. Starlings also kill bluebirds; if

This house sparrow usurped a box meant for bluebirds

that's not reason enough to discourage them, they also are noisy, they roost in huge flocks, they devour your seed and suet and chase away smaller birds, and they leave their droppings all over your property.

As house sparrows and starlings are not native to the United States, the Federal Migratory Bird Treaty Act of 1918 does not protect them, so we are within our rights to discourage their nesting behavior. That being said, whether or not you want to take house sparrow matters into your own hands is entirely your decision.

Nest with Carolina wren and cowbird nestlings

It may feel squeamish to remove starling or house sparrow nesting material and even their eggs from your nest boxes. The fact is that one removal may not be enough. House sparrows raise up to four broods per season, so you may find yourself with another nest to deal with just weeks after you've dispensed with the first.

In the end, the only way to defeat the birds may be to take down your nest boxes. Even this is a small step, however, as house sparrows will nest just about anywhere: in your rain gutters, in signs at retail stores, or through a hole in your garage or eaves.

Beyond sparrows and starlings, there are more insidious dangers to nesting songbirds. Brown-headed cowbirds are "brood parasites," laying their eggs in other birds' nests and leaving the other birds to incubate and raise their young. Often the cowbird nestling is born first and is many times the size of a bird's other offspring—as you can see here, in comparison to a Carolina wren nestling. The baby cowbird's aggressive feeding behavior may starve the other nestlings. What you do with a cowbird egg is your business, but remember that it is illegal for humans to remove a cowbird egg from another bird's nest.

NEST BOX MAINTENANCE

Most birds build a new nest every year—or several, as they raise more than one brood each season, and each clutch gets a fresh nest.

DIY: HOW TO CLEAN A NESTING BOX EFFECTIVELY

Step 1: What's in There?

First, put on your gloves. Open the nest box and see what's inside. Usually you'll find a nest made from any number of materials: twigs, string, grass, leaves, bits of paper or cloth, yarn, or even spider webs or cocoons. You may see eggshells as well. It's also possible you'll find a dead nestling.

Step 1

Step 2: Clear the Nest

Remove the nest with your gloved hand and drop the nest into your bag. You may have some scraping to do to get the guano (droppings) off the cavity walls and floor. If the guano is hardened, use a spray bottle to wet it down. This will help make it soft. Scrape all the material out and directly into your bag. Be very careful not to breathe in any of the dust from this material.

Step 2

Step 3: Disinfecting

Once the nest box is cleaned out, disinfect it with a mix of one part bleach to nine parts water. Use a spray bottle to apply the water/bleach mix to the inside walls of the box. Don't use any commercial disinfectants, flea powders, or insecticides! These are very bad for birds. The bleach/water solution is enough to kill any remaining blowflies or parasites. Let the box dry completely.

Step 3

Step 4: Good Things to Know

If you find an unhatched egg inside the box, you may be tempted to keep it. The egg may be rotten, however, as the fetus inside either did not develop at all or died before it could hatch. Even if the egg seems harmless, it's a breeding ground for viruses like E. coli and streptococcus. If the infertile egg breaks, it can spread these viruses. The best thing to do is discard the egg.

Step 4

The nests from the previous season or brood may seem like keepsakes or teaching tools for your children, but the fact is that they can become havens for parasites, lice, and mites. Equally important, the droppings and other leavings in the nest can be harmful to humans if we inhale the dust from these materials.

Some birds will build a new nest right on top of an old one, but this creates new hazards for the birds inside. The new nest is closer to the entrance hole, so it's easier for predators to reach in and get to the eggs and nestlings. In addition, parasites may inhabit the lower nest and may come through the new nest to affect the birds.

Once the nestlings have fledged, the birds abandon the nest. It's time for you to clean out the nest box, making it ready for the next breeding birds to consider it as a nesting site.

Start by assembling the tools you'll need to clear the nesting material and other detritus from the box. You'll need a pair of nonporous gloves, an ice scraper or other tool with a sharp blade for scraping, and a thick plastic trash bag.

Once you've cleaned the box thoroughly, winterize it for roosting birds by placing a piece of cardboard in the bottom. This will block the drainage holes, which will help keep the wind from blowing in. Place dried grasses inside to help roosting birds keep warm through the winter.

NESTING MATERIALS

Imagine sitting for weeks on a pile of eggs. What kind of material would you want under you while you waited for the eggs to hatch? If you answered "something soft," you're thinking like a bird.

Bird nest on shelf in a barn

Birds do indeed feather their nests, often picking their own down off their breasts and underparts to create a softer, warmer bed for their eggs. This method can only go so far before it compromises the mother, however, so birds look to their environment to provide more lining material.

Parent birds look for nesting material that will form the structure of a nest—usually small twigs, grasses, and leaves—and then focus on the nest lining, the part that comes into contact with the eggs.

The nest lining helps keep the clutch of eggs close together, maximizing warmth and protection. In some cases, the lining materials help keep the nest waterproof, shedding rainwater easily.

Birds have a broad choice of materials. They may choose moss, tufts of fur shed by other animals, leaves, grasses, pine needles, and fluff from cottonwoods, cattails, or dandelions. Many use mud to hold the nest together. Hummingbirds weave spider webs into their nests, tightly securing the structure that will hold their eggs.

Many birds—especially ground nesters—also look for materials that will help disguise the nest, keeping the eggs and the brooding mother safe throughout the gestation period. Bits of wood, twigs, larger leaves, and last year's grasses can serve to hide the nest from view until the nestlings are close to fledgling size.

You can help by placing a variety of materials in your yard within reach of the birds in places they frequent—hanging on the branches of shrubs near your feeders, on the ground under your platform feeder, or near favorite perching or roosting haunts.

Natural Nest Material

You don't need to hang up a variety of nest boxes to invite birds to nest in and around your yard.

Birds have been nesting without our help for millions of years, and most species prefer trees, bushes, natural cavities, and crevices in manmade structures to the boxes we craft so carefully.

What nearly every nesting bird needs is suitable material with which to build a sturdy nest. The shape, size, and construction of the nest varies with each bird species: some appear to be a haphazard pile of loose sticks, while others are intricately woven baskets lined with petal-soft feathers, leaves, or even pussy willows. Your yard can be a treasure trove of supplies for busy builders.

It takes weeks for a bird to complete the nest construction process for each brood, so you'll see birds gathering nesting material throughout the spring and summer, first building the firm foundation that will hold the nest in place, and then creating the armature

House sparrow carrying nesting material

to cradle the eggs. The last step is the nest lining, ingeniously designed to be moisture resistant, to help keep the eggs warm, and to create a soft seat for the incubating mother.

How can your yard and garden assist in the nest-building process? Your trees, shrubs, and flowers can produce many of the essentials for strong, sturdy nests.

Brush Pile

Resist the urge to rake and bag up every fallen leaf and errant twig from your yard, as these are integral elements of a good nest. Instead, make a brush pile by raking together fallen or pruned branches and twigs. Choose a corner of your yard in which you can leave these limbs permanently. When you prune your trees or shrubs, add more to the pile. Birds will use bits of the pile for nesting material, and perhaps even nest within it.

Last Year's Leaves

Leaves often collect under shrubs and trees. It's customary to rake and bag them, but if we let them be, birds will use some of them as nest lining. When you clear last year's leaves from your yard in spring, leave some piles under your shrubs. Even beyond nesting, ground-feeding birds forage under leaves for grubs and insects, so you may draw more thrushes and wrens to your yard. The added bonus: the leaves will decompose and serve as natural mulch.

Grasses

How do birds make their nests so strong? Some use long, supple grasses to weave the twigs together in a basket shape. Add native grasses to your landscape, allowing them to grow naturally high in summer and die back in the fall and winter. Birds will gather the long, dry blades and "sew" them into their nests.

Mud

Birds have an instinctive understanding of the need to make their nests as waterproof and solid as possible. One of the ways they accomplish this is with mud. You may see birds struggling to fly with pats of mud in their bills, a sure sign that a nest is coming together and is ready for its lining. Mud may be available along the edge of the pond you've installed, or under your birdbath. Let it be through the spring and summer to give birds the water-resistant mortar they need.

Manmade Nest Material

While birds will fare well without any assistance from us, it can be fun and rewarding to help them out. Some household materials make particularly good nest construction aids.

The Cornell Laboratory of Ornithology suggests a list of things most of us have around the house that are safe and useful for birds:

- Yarn or string, cut into 4- to 8-inch pieces
- Human or animal hair, not more than 6 inches long
- Horsehair
- Pet fur, so long as the pet hasn't had a flea or tick treatment
- Sheep's wool
- Feathers
- Cotton batting
- Other stuffing materials
- Thin strips of cloth, no more than 6 inches long

It's a good rule of thumb to avoid offering anything to your birds that has been treated with a pesticide or other harsh chemical. There's a long history of bird species nearing extinction because of pesticides used on plants they ate and chose for their nests. Skip the dryer lint as well: it falls apart when it gets wet, so it won't hold up against rain and wind. Equally important, these fibers may contain concentrated fabric softeners, which can be harmful for birds.

Put your nesting materials out as early as mid-March in the southern states (earlier in South Florida and along the Gulf of Mexico coast) and by early May in northern regions. Most birds begin choosing nest locations and building nests by mid-May, so you'll stay ahead of their schedules if you start early. As you begin to see species you have not seen since the previous summer, you'll know it's time to put out your nesting materials. Watch for birds carrying bits of twig, grass, or leaves in their bills. This is a sure sign that nest building has started. You'll see birds carrying materials well into the summer, as most backyard species produce two or more broods per season, building a new nest for each.

Stuff some nesting material into a mesh bag with a seed bell to make it easy for birds to find

How can you stage these items for optimal use by the birds?

String and Yarn

Drape cut pieces of yarn over the end of a branch, or place it in a mesh bag and hang the bag near your feeders. If you put the yarn in a bush, just let it dangle from the branch—don't tie it or try to secure it. If it falls to the ground in a breeze, the birds will still find it.

Fluff

Some bird feeder manufacturers make molded seed wreaths, cakes, or bells that have tufts of cotton, string, hemp, and/or tree fibers incorporated into the object. It's easy to buy one of these and hang it near your feeders. If you do purchase one of these items, hold on to it when the birds have picked it clean. You can refill it with your own materials next year.

If you're putting out fluffy stuff like cotton batting, animal fur, hair, or strips of cloth, put all of these materials into a spare suet cage. Hang the cage near your feeders, in a nearby tree, or from a fence post or railing. You may see lots of gadgets in your birding specialty store that are made to hold nesting material, but a suet cage, a mesh bag, or a one-cup-sized open container (like the ones berries come in at your farmers' market) will serve the purpose.

WHEN BIRDS NEST

If house wrens started building nests in your boxes last year on April 15, can you expect them to do so at about the same time this year?

Two northern flickers in courtship ritual

The simple answer is that there's no simple answer. Birds' breeding schedules can be as disparate as the number of sunny days you have in one spring versus the next.

The birds themselves will provide plenty of clues to their nesting plans. Resident birds from jays to house sparrows take on brighter mantles as the mating season approaches. Goldfinches slough off their dull winter feathers as bright lemon-yellow growth replaces them. Soon males of every species bicker and peck at one another at feeders and on branches as they establish territories.

Many birds mate for life, including house finches. Even the mated pairs exhibit courtship behavior as a precursor to breeding, however, so you are likely to see some interesting goings-on at your feeders. If you see a male house finch feeding a female, you're witnessing courtship. The female actively solicits food from the male, and the male offers her food and actually feeds her. He may continue to do this for weeks, right through the incubation of the eggs.

Other signs of courtship include males and females chasing one another around your yard, and puffed-up male birds on a twig or feeder showing off their fine features to attract mates. Soon you may witness actual mating, as the male bird mounts the female. Fertilized eggs will not be far behind.

Homes in the south-ernmost United States can expect to see the nesting season begin as early as late February for some resident species. April and May are prime nesting months for the rest of the nation, with most of the activity well underway by the second to third week of May. How-

House sparrows consider nesting in a hole in a garage

ever, harsh weather conditions and lasting cold spells can slow progress, holding migratory birds back from their accustomed breeding grounds.

Nest siting can begin as early as February in most of the country, when a male bird and a female bird begin shopping around for an appropriate cavity or branch. Birds may roost throughout the winter in any number of holes and openings around your neighborhood, but a mated pair is most likely scouting for a spot to build the first nest of the season. If the birds show an interest in a spot they should not, now is the time to seal a crack, mend a screen, or cover a hole in your garage or barn.

Hawks and owls in your neighborhood may accelerate the breeding schedule, starting earlier than smaller species. Most of these larger birds do not build nests of their own, using nests abandoned by other birds, cavities excavated

These house wrens have chosen their nest box

by woodpeckers, or larger nest boxes you provide. Watch for these birds in late February and March, with breeding extending into late April and May.

Some birds—American robins and house wrens in particular—will build several nests at the outset. The birds then choose one nest from these, and the female lays her eggs in that one. If you find a line of nests on a beam or branch, they may be the work of robins. House wrens often build nests in several different nest boxes. They will choose just one for their first clutch, but the male house wren will continue to defend the other nests, chattering and behaving aggressively toward any birds that approach.

WHERE BIRDS NEST

Whether you have a wooded lot with evergreen or leafy trees, an open meadow filled with nodding wildflowers, or a city yard with houses just past the driveways on either side, birds can find places to nest on your property and nearby.

Most birds choose the crotch of a tree or a strong branch higher up on which to build a nest, but many birds pass up trees in favor of depressions in the ground, a convenient "shelf" created by a roof beam, or a sheltered spot under an arbor, bridge, or viaduct.

It seems like it would be fairly easy to find a bird's nest, but here's where the birds are smarter than we might realize. Birds use natural nesting materials like grass, leaves, and lichens to camouflage their nests, making them virtually indistinguishable from the surrounding foliage. You may have a bird's nest nearly in front of your face against the trunk of a pine tree, but the nest may be brilliantly covered by bits of pine needles and twigs, truly hiding it in plain sight.

Not all birds are so crafty, however. The birds in your yard may find their way into your hanging planters, a corner of your garage or porch, a portal created by vines curling around your patio railings, or a cozy spot inside an outdoor lighting fixture.

The best way to locate a nest is to watch the birds from a distance, using your binoculars or scope, to determine if they regularly enter and leave the same tree, shrub, or other shelter. Birds repeatedly entering the same bush at the same spot may very well be building a nest there. By the same token, birds

American robins often nest in dense bushes or trees

spotted slipping through a hole in your garage again and again are undoubtedly in the construction business.

Tree Nesters

Thanks in part to dozens of cartoons and children's picture books, most of us assume that birds nest primarily in trees. Indeed, many of our backyard birds do choose trees, with American robins as the most common backyard tree nesters. Most songbirds (warblers, vireos, and the like) build cup nests in trees as well.

Cavity Nesters

Woodpeckers, sapsuckers, nuthatches, chickadees, and flickers nest in tree cavities. They excavate these holes with their strong bills to make a large enough space for the female and a brood of nestlings. While some of these birds come back to the same cavity year after year, most move on to create a new hole. Check the old cavity anyway, because owls often use abandoned holes in trees for their own nests.

Black-capped chickadee excavating a tree cavity

Birding Tip: Birds in the Wrong Places

As much as we love our birds, sometimes they move into places on our property that may inconvenience us.

If any birds except starlings or house sparrows constructed the nests, the law protects the nest, birds, and eggs. Your best course is to prevent the birds from gaining access before they nest:

- Repair porch screens, cracks in shingles, and small holes in wood trim or door frames.
- Keep garage and shed doors closed.
- Use screen to block any openings in light fixtures.
- Patch holes in roofs.

Shelf Nesters

Swallows and phoebes look for the combination of overhead shelter and surface stability, often building their nests inside manmade structures. If you see a nest on a roof beam or on top of a ledge in your garage, shed, or barn, chances are excellent that it's a barn swallow or phoebe nest. These birds may also choose the shelflike curves of neon signs, beams under bridges, or holes that lead to the attic of your home.

Ground Nesters

Some birds nest in the low branches of shrubs or even right on the ground. Goldfinches and many sparrows prefer low nests, often choosing brush piles, the fallen branches of trees with needles, or the dense lower growth near a shrub's base. Your brush pile may be prime nesting habitat for white-crowned, white-throated, chipping or song sparrows, as well as dark-eyed juncos. Allowing some of your shrubs to keep their natural undergrowth—rather than pruning them to clear the lower story—can provide excellent nest sites for small birds.

NESTLINGS

Here's what happens once the birds finish their nest:

The female begins laying eggs, laying one every day until she's completed the clutch. How many eggs depends largely on the species: Mourning doves, for example, lay just two to three eggs in a clutch, while kinglets may lay anywhere from five to eleven eggs.

Incubation doesn't begin until all the eggs are laid, and then the female bird sits on the eggs until they hatch. Male birds often play a role in the incubation, taking over while the female forages for food.

For most backyard birds, incubation ends in twelve to fifteen days when the eggs hatch. Now all kinds of activity begins! If you listen closely, you're likely to hear the peeping of high voices begging for food. One or both parents are now busy with feeding, keeping their new brood satisfied while they see to their own needs as well. If you haven't spotted the nest itself by this time, watch for

A barn swallow nestling makes its presence known

adult birds carrying food. Follow the bird with your binoculars to get an idea of where the nest and nestlings might be.

Life for newborn chicks is about eating, eating, eating. The parents have more responsibilities than feeding their babies, however—they must also be careful not to give away the nest's location to predators. If you see a bird hopping to branches or other surfaces around its nest for several minutes before approaching, he or she is making certain that no hawks, cats, or other potential threats are watching before she darts in to feed the defenseless nestlings.

Parent birds forage far and wide for appropriate food to feed their nestlings. In some species, including western bluebirds, acorn woodpeckers, and American crows, cooperative groups form to care for the young. Even the previous year's offspring participate, until they reach maturity and begin nesting on their own. For most species, however, the mated pair—or often the female alone—must maintain this constant feeding pace on its own.

Even birds that normally do not eat insects will feed them to their young. Insects provide the protein and other nutrition nestlings need to grow quickly and become strong. They also provide liquid, so there's no need for parents to bring water to the nest.

It's tempting to run up to a nest and peer inside, but your quick movements and proximity will agitate the parent, sending the adult away from the

Birding Tip: Baby Bird 911

What should you do with a baby bird that's fallen out of its nest?

- If it has feathers and it can move around on its own, leave it where you found it. Many nestlings leave the nest before they fly; the parents may know where the bird is and may be feeding it regularly until it matures. This little bird is a fledgling; it will most likely be fine without your help.
- If the bird is too young to have feathers, look around and overhead for the nest. If it's within reach, place the bird back in the nest as quickly as possible. It's a myth that birds will smell human contact—your touching the nestling will not bother the parents.
- If the nest has been destroyed, your last option is to call the nearest animal shelter or bird rehabilitation center in your area. Trained professionals will know what action to take.

nest in the midst of incubating or feeding its young. You can observe the nest from a respectful, nonthreatening distance using a spotting scope. Position your scope behind a tree or shrub. Your concealed presence will keep the adult bird from perceiving you as a threat, allowing feeding to continue.

FLEDGLINGS

How can you tell when the nestlings have made their first forays out of the nest and into the world?

It's easier than you think: they're full grown but fuzzy looking, their markings are not as bold or defined as their parents' plumage, and they perform a constant slapstick routine of tumbling off branches, bumping into one another, and pecking ineffectively at feeders.

Most often, you'll discover the arrival of fledglings by glancing at your feeders and finding seven patchy-colored northern cardinals, for example, where there were just two throughout the spring. Keep watching the comings and goings in your yard, and you'll see American robins with light-colored,

This recently fledged house sparrow is male, but he doesn't yet have the full gray cap with dark brown edges, or the solid black face mask and bib his father sports. The fluffiness remains from his days in the nest, but these feathers will slough off as his adult markings grow in and take shape. You may only glimpse a sparrow with this inconclusive plumage for a few days at your feeders, until he develops to full maturity.

speckled breasts, or dull gray starlings dazedly watching their parents feeding on the ground, occasionally poking with their own bills in imitation of their parents' foraging behavior.

Fledglings often have not yet grown the longer tail feathers their parents sport, so their flying can be off balance at first. Parent birds often feed their young, catching an insect and passing it on bill-to-bill to their offspring. You may see this process at your feeders as the parents bring the fledglings to the food, demonstrate how to pick up seeds, and then drop the seeds from their own bills into the open mouths of their young. Eventually the parents will nudge the fledglings toward the food to encourage them to gather their own seed or suet.

The high-pitched squeaks you heard while the babies begged for food in the nest are now replaced by hoarse or rasping calls that can't approximate the parents' more melodious songs. In particular, immature American crows develop a rough, scratchy call that's not unlike a crow with laryngitis. Listen for new songs and calls that don't quite pass muster, and you'll know that fledglings are nearby.

It's remarkable to watch these young birds change and grow over the course of a few days or weeks as they gain agility, independence, and resourcefulness.

Birding Tip: Puzzling Plumage

If you've never seen a young bird before, you may be baffled to see birds of entirely different plumage suddenly arrive in your yard. Before you run for the phone to report a rarity, check the calendar. Fledglings can begin to arrive in your yard by mid- to late spring, depending on your climate. This fledgling American robin bears only passing resemblance to its parents, but it's a robin and nothing else. A good field guide will show you young ("immature") plumages for many species.

An Eastern tiger swallowtail joins pipevine swallowtails in puddling, consuming nutrients they find in muddy soil

6: What Butterflies Need

We can attract birds to our yards using feeders, water features, and nest boxes, but butterflies are an entirely different story. These tiny winged creatures feed primarily on flower nectar, and their life cycle does not involve building nests, incubating eggs, or raising their own young. How, then, can we capture their interest in visiting our property? The answers are revealed when we have a clear understanding of how butterflies come to be, what they need to go from eggs to flying insects, and how they survive from one season to the next.

THE LIFE CYCLE

The entire life cycle of a butterfly or moth is called *metamorphosis*, a Greek word for transformation. Most insects go through some kind of transformation from egg to adult, but for butterflies and moths, it's a four-stage process.

1. *Eggs.* Adult butterflies and moths lay eggs in the spring, summer, or fall, depending on the species. They lay large quantities of eggs all at once, because many of them will be eaten by birds and other insects, and some simply will not be viable. The more eggs they lay, the more likely it is that some of them will survive and hatch.

Cabbage white butterfly eggs. *Shutterstock #1450753280*

Cabbage white butterfly caterpillar.
Shutterstock #1822861682

2. *Larva.* When the eggs hatch, a larva emerges. For butterflies and moths, we call the larva a caterpillar. The caterpillar has one job for most of its life: it eats, and eats, and eats some more. Eating makes it grow, and as it grows it sheds its skin. Caterpillars will shed their skins four or five times throughout this part of their lives, growing from a tiny organism about the size of a pinhead to as much as one hundred times its original size.

3. *Pupa.* Once the caterpillar reaches its full size, it stops eating, and it puts its energy into forming a pupa: a chrysalis (butterfly) or cocoon (moth). It chooses a twig or branch and makes a silk pad on the underside of it, where it attaches itself using its cremaster, a hook-covered limb on the end of its body. It then sheds its skin for the last time, revealing the opaque container within which it will spend the next few weeks. If the caterpillar is a moth larva, it emits a silk material that it spins around itself, forming a protective silk cocoon.

Cabbage white butterfly chrysalis. *Shutterstock #597451844*

4. *Adult.* When the larva has transformed inside the pupa, it emerges as a butterfly. The change is profound: the butterfly or moth has wings, long legs, long antennae, and eyes with chambers that allow them to see many images, a key factor in defending themselves against predators. They have reached their full size at this point—butterflies and moths do not grow once they have left the pupa. Now they live for the express purpose of mating and laying eggs. Most butterflies and moths have very short life spans, surviving for just a couple of weeks until they have laid their eggs. Some hibernate, however, and a few—most notably the monarch butterfly—migrate to warmer climates for the winter.

Adult cabbage white butterfly

BUTTERFLY VS. MOTH: WHAT'S THE DIFFERENCE?

Butterfly	Moth
Antennae with a ball on the end.	Antennae are straight or feathered.
Most are diurnal.	Most are nocturnal.
Most hold wings upright when at rest.	Most spread their wings wide when at rest.
Forms a chrysalis with a hard shell.	Forms a cocoon with a fibrous shell.

HOW WE CAN HELP

Beautiful, fragile, and short-lived, butterflies and moths perform the cycle of their lives every season, often completely out of view of human beings. They find the nutrition they need in meadows, grasslands, marshes, and woodlands across the country, which also furnish them with the environment they require to lay their eggs and nourish their larvae.

The expansion of human development, however, has curtailed this process for many butterfly and moth species, making it difficult for them to sustain their numbers. They may not recognize the exotic plants from other continents they encounter in cultivated gardens, so they do not understand that the flowers they see can provide them with nectar or with places to lay eggs. Cities with miles of paved roads and parking lots, tall buildings, and landscaped lawns eliminate the formerly open meadows filled with native flowers, making it difficult or impossible to find food and plants for laying eggs and pupating.

How can we help? We can create butterfly paradises in our own backyards by providing trees, shrubs, and flowers for every stage of the life cycle. Gardens of native trees and plants can help to replace what butterflies and moths have lost to human development, giving them the resources they need to thrive and multiply.

HOST PLANTS FOR EGGS AND CATERPILLARS

Caterpillars do not travel very far from the spot where they hatch. With tiny legs and no other means of transportation, they must get their nourishment right where their lives begin if they have any hope of reaching metamorphosis. So they begin eating as soon as they emerge from the egg, and they eat continuously until they pupate. To complicate the process further, each species of caterpillar may eat only one or two kinds of plants, while other kinds may actually be toxic to them. The relationship between caterpillars and these *host plants* has evolved over thousands of years and will not change just because the only

HOORAY! SOMETHING'S EATING YOUR PLANTS!

You will know if you have been successful in attracting caterpillars to your host plants when you see holes in the leaves. This means that caterpillars are eating these plants—which is exactly what you want them to do so that they can grow and metamorphose into butterflies and moths. It may seem contrary to the norm to rejoice when insects are devouring your plants, but you will be delighted when you see lots of butterflies in a few weeks.

plants available are exotic ones from other continents that you may have chosen for your garden. The butterflies will simply go elsewhere to lay their eggs.

Butterflies and moths lay their eggs on host plants, the specific kind of tree or shrub that their offspring must eat to thrive and grow. When caterpillars emerge, they find a ready supply of all the food they need so that they can use their energy to eat and grow.

Host plants may be trees, shrubs, or flowers, depending on the butterfly or moth species that needs them. For the best results, butterfly gardens should contain a wide selection of native plants to attract the widest variety of species: caterpillar food plants to feed the larvae, and nectar plants to feed the butterflies.

Choosing Host Plants for Your Garden

Here are some of the host plant families you can choose to invite butterflies into your yard, and the common butterfly species that use them. Your local nursery or the extensive database at the Lady Bird Johnson Wildflower Center (http://www.wildflower.org/plants-main) can help you find which plants from these families are native to your area.

- **American wisteria** (*Wisteria frutescens*): Horace's duskywing, silver-spotted skipper
- **Aspen** (*Populus*): eastern tiger swallowtail, mourning cloak, red-spotted purple, white admiral
- **Aster** (*Aster*): pearl crescent, painted lady, checkerspot
- **Beardtongue** (*Penstemon*): checkerspot
- **Birch** (*Betula*): mourning cloak, tortoiseshells

Aspen acts as a host plant for eastern tiger swallowtail, mourning cloak, and red-spotted purple butterflies

Asters attract pearl crescent, painted lady, checkerspots, and other butterflies like this clouded sulphur

- **Black-eyed Susan** (*Rudbeckia*): silvery and gorgone checkerspot
- **Cabbage, broccoli, cauliflower, brussels sprouts**: cabbage white
- **Cherry/chokecherry** (*Prunus*): red-spotted purple, hairstreaks, hummingbird clearwing, Io moth, eastern tiger swallowtail, azures, white admiral
- **Clover** (*Trifolium*): clouded sulphur, orange sulphur
- **Coneflower** (*Echinacea*): silvery checkerspot
- **Cottonwood** (*Populus*): eastern tiger swallowtail, mourning cloak, red-spotted purple, white admiral
- **Dill and parsley** (*Antheum*): black swallowtail
- **Dogwood** (*Cornus*): azures
- **Elm** (*Ulmus*): commas, mourning cloak, question mark
- **False nettle** (*Boehmeria*): eastern comma, question mark, red admiral, Milbert's tortoiseshell
- **Golden Alexander** (*Zizia aurea*): black swallowtail
- **Highbush cranberry** (*Viburnum*): azures, hummingbird clearwing
- **Hollyhock** (*Alcea*): painted lady, common checkered-skipper
- **Lupine** (*Lupinus*): Karner blue, silvery blue
- **Mallow** (*Malva*): painted lady, gray hairstreak, common checkered-skipper
- **Meadowsweet** (*Spirea*): azures

- **Milkweed** (*Asclepias*): monarch
- **Monkey-flower** (*Mimulus*): common buckeye, checkerspot
- **New Jersey tea** (*Ceanothus americanus*): spring azure, summer azure, mottled duskywing
- **Paintbrush** (*Castilleja*): checkerspot (several varieties), common buckeye
- **Pipevine** (*Aristolochia*): pipevine swallowtail
- **Poplar** (*Populus*): eastern tiger swallowtail, mourning cloak, red-spotted purple, white admiral
- **Poppy mallow** (*Callirhoe*): gray hairstreak
- **Pussy willow** (*Salix discolor*): mourning cloak, viceroy, Io moth
- **Sage** (*Salvia*): sphinx Moth
- **Sassafras** (*Sassafras*): spicebush swallowtail
- **Sedge** (*Carex*): skippers
- **Spicebush** (*Lindera*): spicebush swallowtail
- **Sunflower** (*Helianthus*): American lady, silvery checkerspot
- **Tuliptree** (*Liriodendron*): eastern tiger swallowtail
- **Vervain and verbena** (*Verbena*): common buckeye, white peacock
- **Violet** (*Viola*): great spangled fritillary, variegated fritillary, falcate orangetip, meadow fritillary
- **Walnut** (*Juglans*): banded hairstreak
- **Wild indigo** (*Baptista*): wild indigo duskywing, eastern-tailed blue, orange sulphur, clouded sulphur, frosted elfin, hoary edge
- **Willow** (*Salix*): hairstreaks, tortoiseshells, duskywing, mourning cloak, red-spotted purple, viceroy, white admiral

Highbush cranberry attracts spring and summer azures and hummingbird clearwing moths

NECTAR PLANTS

Once the butterflies and moths emerge from the pupa stage, they will visit many varieties of flowering plants to feed on their nectar. Here are some of the native plant families that attract many butterfly and moth species. Many of these bloom later in the summer, when butterflies emerge from chrysalises and look for nourishment.

- Aster (*Aster*)
- Bee Balm/Bergamot (*Monarda*)
- Black-Eyed Susan (*Rudbeckia*)
- Blazing Star (*Liatris*)
- Boneset (*Eupatorium*)
- Coneflower (*Echinacea*)
- Goldenrod (*Solidago*)
- Hyssop (*Agastache*)
- Ironweed (*Vernonia*)
- Joe-Pye Weed (*Eupatorium*)
- Milkweed (*Asclepias*)
- Sneezeweed (*Helenium*)
- Sunflower (*Helianthus*)
- Tickseed (*Coreopsis*)
- Wild Geranium (*Geranium*)

The tubular petals of wild bergamot and bee balm work perfectly for nectar-sipping butterflies

In chapter 7, we will talk in more detail about choosing flowers, shrubs, and trees for your garden, which plants attract birds as well as butterflies, and which ones are native to various regions across the country. When you fill your yard with plants that have thrived in your region for thousands of years, you increase the likelihood of birds, butterflies, and other pollinators finding your garden and making it an important part of their cycle of feeding, laying eggs, and raising young.

Many butterflies, including monarchs, seek out goldenrod for its abundant nectar

Aphrodite fritillary

You may see these elaborately spotted butterflies walking on open ground near violets, looking for the right place to lay their eggs. Their hatched caterpillars immediately go into hibernation until the following spring.

- **Wingspan:** 2.5–3.25 inches.
- **Range:** Northern US from Maine to Montana, south through Appalachian and Rocky Mountains.
- **Habitat:** High mountain meadows, barrens, brushy areas, fields, bogs.
- **Host plants:** Violets.
- **Nectar plants:** Milkweed, viper's bugloss.

Aphrodite fritillary

Behr's hairstreak

This tiny butterfly's wings appear almost furry in their streakiness. The brown underside on both the male and female is more often visible than the brighter orange upper side.

- **Wingspan:** 1–1.25 inches.
- **Range:** Western US from Washington to West Texas, including the Rocky Mountain region.
- **Habitat:** Desert landscapes including sagebrush, pinyon-juniper woodland, and chaparral.
- **Host plants:** Antelope brush and mountain mahogany.
- **Nectar plants:** Nectar from a wide variety of flowers.

Behr's hairstreak

Black swallowtail

It takes close observation to differentiate the black swallowtail from its very close cousins. Look for round spots on the outer edges of its wings.

- **Wingspan:** 3.25–4.25 inches.
- **Range:** Eastern and southwestern US.
- **Habitat:** Meadows, fields, parks.
- **Host plants:** Leaves of carrots, celery, parsley, Queen Anne's lace.
- **Nectar plants:** Clover, milkweed, thistle, phlox.

Black swallowtail

Cabbage white

This widely common butterfly was introduced to North America from Europe and North Africa and now makes a nuisance of itself by eating cruciferous crops: broccoli, cauliflower, Brussels sprouts, cabbage, and kale, among others.

- **Wingspan:** 1.75–2.25 inches.
- **Range:** Eastern and western US, with fewer mid-continent.
- **Habitat:** Gardens in cities and suburbs, roadsides, overgrown vacant lots.
- **Host plants:** Mustards.
- **Nectar plants:** Dandelions, red clover, asters, mints, mustards.

Cabbage white

Clouded sulphur

Males are bright yellow with wings edged in black, while females may vary from yellow to greenish white. Look for the pink hindwing edges to differentiate these at a glance from cabbage whites.

- **Wingspan:** 1.5–2.75 inches.
- **Range:** Nationwide except for West Coast.
- **Habitat:** Open fields, weedy edges of roads, lawns, clover fields.
- **Host plants:** Alfalfa, white clover, pea.
- **Nectar plants:** Will visit many different plants.

Clouded sulphur

Common wood nymph

The larvae of this distinctive butterfly hatch in fall and hibernate until the following spring, rather than beginning to feed. Wing colors vary between regions; southern butterflies may have a patch of yellow on the outer forewing, while inland wood nymphs may be more solidly brown.

Common wood nymph

- **Wingspan:** 1.75–3 inches.
- **Range:** Nationwide.
- **Habitat:** Open prairie, well-established fields, bogs.
- **Host plants:** Grasses, including purpletop and others.
- **Nectar plants:** Many flowers; also rotting fruit.

Eastern tiger swallowtail

One of the most common eastern butterflies is also one of the largest and most showy. Females may be quite dark on the underside, with a light bluish wash over the lower interior.

Eastern tiger swallowtail

- **Wingspan:** 2.5–4.5 inches.
- **Range:** Very common in the eastern half of the US.
- **Habitat:** Deciduous woodlands, forest edges, suburban yards with leafy trees.
- **Host plants:** Cherry, magnolia, basswood, tuliptree, cottonwood, mountain ash, willow.
- **Nectar plants:** Wild cherry, lilac, milkweed, Joe-Pye weed.

Giant swallowtail

A larger butterfly with a bold cream-colored pattern across its black wings, the giant swallowtail is virtually unmistakable in the wild.

- **Wingspan:** 4–6.25 inches.
- **Range:** Eastern, central, and southwestern US.
- **Habitat:** Areas with sandy soil and nearby streams, citrus groves, and open fields in towns.
- **Host plants:** Citrus trees, hops, prickly ash, and common rue.
- **Nectar plants:** Goldenrod, Tatarian honeysuckle, lantana, azalea, bougainvillea, swamp milkweed.

Giant swallowtail

Gulf fritillary

While widespread as far north as Ohio and Iowa, this butterfly thrives in warmer climates. It can be seen in South Florida and South Texas year-round and is most plentiful in Mexico and Central America.

- **Wingspan:** 2.5–3.75 inches.
- **Range:** Southern US coast-to-coast.
- **Habitat:** Fields, pastures, gardens, and subtropical forests.
- **Host plants:** Passion vine, purple passionflower.
- **Nectar plants:** Shrub verbena (lantanas), shepherd's needle.

Gulf fritillary

Monarch

Arguably the most recognized butterfly in North America, the widespread monarch is one of only a few species that migrates thousands of miles every fall to hibernate in Mexico and Southern California, laying their eggs on their way south. Tens of thousands of them roost together in trees on their overwintering grounds. Monarchs defend themselves from predators by eating only milkweed nectar, which contains toxins that make birds and animals avoid them.

Monarch

- **Wingspan:** 3.6–4.8 inches.
- **Range:** Nationwide except for mountainous areas in the West.
- **Habitat:** Meadows, weedy lots, fields, marshes, large gardens.
- **Host plants:** Various species of milkweed, especially common and swamp.
- **Nectar plants:** Milkweeds when available; lilac, red clover, lantana, thistle, goldenrods, tickseed, and blazing star when milkweed is not in bloom.

Mourning cloak

This familiar butterfly of wooded areas makes a brief appearance over the summer and then goes into a state of torpor to wait out the warmer months. In fall, they feed voraciously to store energy for winter hibernation, migrating south before the weather turns.

Mourning cloak. *Shutterstock #1296624727*

- **Wingspan:** 2.25–4 inches.
- **Range:** Nationwide.
- **Habitat:** Woods, parks, areas with water, trees, and abundant vegetation.
- **Host plants:** Willow, elm, cottonwood, aspen, birch, hackberry.
- **Nectar plants:** Tree sap, rotting fruit.

Painted lady

Depending on your region, you may find male painted ladies in the eastern United States sitting on open, bare ground waiting for mates to arrive, or perching on shrubs at higher elevations in the west. Instead of the clusters of eggs laid by most butterflies, painted ladies lay single eggs on the top of a leaf.

- **Wingspan:** 2–2.8 inches.
- **Range:** Nationwide.
- **Habitat:** Disturbed ground like vacant lots, roadsides, gardens, sand dunes.
- **Host plants:** Thistle, hollyhock, mallow, and many others.
- **Nectar plants:** Thistle, aster, cosmos, blazing star, ironweed, Joe-Pye weed, milkweed, buttonbush, clover.

Painted lady

Pearl crescent

These tiny butterflies can have highly variable plumage. Look for the dark area around the lower edges of the hindwing, with a fairly bright white crescent.

- **Wingspan:** 1.25–1.75 inches.
- **Range:** Eastern US, as far west as the Great Plains.
- **Habitat:** Open fields, weedy road edges, pastures, open coniferous woodlands.
- **Host plants:** Asters.
- **Nectar plants:** Many flowers, including milkweed, dogbane, shepherd's needle, asters.

Pearl crescent

Pipevine swallowtail

Black and brilliant blue on the upper side with a broken white line along the hindwing, the pipevine's underwing features seven large, bright orange spots.

- **Wingspan:** 2.75–5 inches.
- **Range:** Eastern through southwestern US and California.
- **Habitat:** Edges of wooded areas, as well as open fields.
- **Host plants:** Pipevine (Dutchman's pipe).
- **Nectar plants:** Thistles, bergamot, lilac, azalea, phlox, teasel, dame's rocket, lantana, petunia, and others.

Pipevine swallowtail

Purplish copper

This tiny brownish butterfly gets its name from the male's purply iridescence, as well as the female's coppery upper side. She lays her eggs on the ground in leaf litter below the host plant, where they hibernate until hatching in the spring.

Purplish copper

- **Wingspan:** 1.2–1.5 inches.
- **Range:** Western US, extending as far northeast as Wisconsin.
- **Habitat:** Overgrown vacant lots, open fields, weedy roadsides, meadows, marshes, valleys.
- **Host plants:** Knotweed and other buckwheat relatives, cinquefoils.
- **Nectar plants:** Nectar from many flowers.

Queen

Well known in the southern states, the queen is often mistaken for a monarch because of its similar underside pattern. The queen's scattering of white spots across its solid orange upper wings becomes an important way to tell it from the more common orange species. Its devotion to milkweed makes it inedible to birds and other predators.

Queen butterfly

- **Wingspan:** 2.75–3.8 inches.
- **Range:** Southern states from Florida to California, including the southern Great Plains.
- **Habitat:** Sunny fields and pastures, weedy roadsides, dunes.
- **Host plants:** Milkweed.
- **Nectar plants:** Milkweed, shepherd's needle, fogfruit.

Question mark

The white question mark, found on the under-side in the center of the hindwing, gives this bright orange butterfly its name. Much about this pretty creature raises questions, however. For example, the females do not lay their eggs on host plants, making it a challenge for newly hatched caterpillars to find a meal.

- **Wingspan:** 2.25–3 inches.
- **Range:** Eastern and southwestern US.
- **Habitat:** Woods, parks with trees, suburban areas.
- **Host plants:** Elm, hackberry, nettles, and false nettle.
- **Nectar plants:** Tree sap, rotting fruit, dung; flowers only when they can't find any of these.

Question mark

Red admiral

Long-distance migrants, red admirals congregate in South Texas, South Florida, and other southern states in winter. Caterpillars build tents from the leaves of nettles, their host plants, and form their chrysalises inside this tiny shelter.

- **Wingspan:** 1.75–3 inches.
- **Range:** Nationwide, except in the western deserts.
- **Habitat:** Moist areas, including woods, parks, seeps, and marshes.
- **Host plants:** Nettles, sometimes hops.
- **Nectar plants:** Tree sap, rotting fruit, bird droppings; nectar only when it can't find these.

Red admiral

Red-spotted purple

This dark butterfly hybridizes so readily with the white admiral that they are now considered two forms of the same species. White admiral is found farther north, while red-spotted purple chooses more southerly areas.

- **Wingspan:** 2.25–4 inches.
- **Range:** Eastern US, with a population in Arizona.
- **Habitat:** Deciduous or mixed evergreen woods.
- **Host plants:** Wild cherry, aspen, poplar, cottonwood, oak, hawthorn, birch, willow.
- **Nectar plants:** Tree sap, rotting fruit, dung, carrion, some nectar from spirea and viburnum.

Red-spotted purple

Silvery checkerspot

Large white spots on the underwing give this common butterfly its "silvery" moniker. Its caterpillars stay together in groups as they strip host plants of their leaves, and then hibernate through the winter until they emerge from chrysalises in spring.

- **Wingspan:** 1.6–2 inches.
- **Range:** Eastern, midwestern, and southwestern US.
- **Habitat:** Stream banks, moist forests, boggy meadows.
- **Host plants:** Black-eyed Susans, sunflowers, wingstems.
- **Nectar plants:** Common milkweed, red clover, dogbane.

Silvery checkerspot

Spicebush swallowtail

So united are this butterfly and its host plant that the bug got its name from the shrub. Look for the bright white, round spots on the upper-side edges to differentiate this from the pipevine swallowtail.

- **Wingspan:** 3–4 inches.
- **Range:** Eastern US.
- **Habitat:** Woodlands, fields, gardens, swamps with trees, pine barrens, roadsides.
- **Host plants:** Spicebush, sassafras, tuliptree, magnolia, camphor.
- **Nectar plants:** Tatarian honeysuckle, jewelweed, thistles, milkweed, dogbane, lantana, sweet pepperbush.

Spicebush swallowtail

Variegated fritillary

The many shades of orange throughout the butterfly's wings lend it the elaborate look from which it gets its name. The lacier underside adds some silver.

- **Wingspan:** 1.75–3.2 inches.
- **Range:** Nationwide except for the Pacific Northwest.
- **Habitat:** Open fields, pastures, prairies, landfills.
- **Host plants:** Maypop, mayapple, violets, stonecrop, moonseed.
- **Nectar plants:** Butterflyweed, milkweed, peppermint, red clover, tickseed, dogbane.

Variegated fritillary

Masses of flowers and shrubs create a natural habitat for birds and butterflies

7: Create a Wildlife Garden Paradise

If you were a bird or a butterfly, where would you live: a carefully manicured lawn with exquisitely clipped topiary and sparse plantings of exotic flowers, or a lush carpet of native wildflowers edged with dense, leafy shrubs and berry-laden trees?

If you chose the latter garden, you've already learned something about your feathered guests. Birds need food, water, and shelter, the three factors that a natural garden can provide with ease. Butterflies need host plants—familiar plants on which they can find a mate and lay eggs—and nectar plants that provide plenty of food. While professionally maintained, sculpted gardens may delight the eyes of many gardeners, they may not offer enough of the things that sustain native birds and butterflies.

Planning a garden for wildlife begins with an understanding of what birds and butterflies need, your property's existing elements, and the plants that are native to your area. (Consult appendix B to determine your hardiness zone.)

GARDEN LAYOUT

Begin your garden-planning process by drawing a sketch of your yard and existing plantings. Use your favorite drafting or garden-planning software if you wish, but a piece of graph paper and some colored pencils will do the trick as well.

Measure your property so your drawing will be as true to scale as possible. You don't need special skills for this. Simply decide that each square of the graph paper represents one square foot. If that will make the drawing too large, each square can represent 2 or 3 feet, or whatever makes sense for your garden space.

Once you have the border on paper, add the existing trees, shrubs, and flower beds. Now you can see the spaces between what's already there.

It's common practice in American gardening to plant single, freestanding perennial flowers, as well as individual shrubs and trees. Layers of mulch often extend between them, creating carefully groomed areas in which the individual plantings stand out. This may make a garden neat and orderly, but such a layout does not help you attract birds and butterflies.

Instead, look at these blank spaces and consider how you can fill them. Create a garden in the natural style, one that will look like home to wildlife in your area. Instead of placing one shrub on its own, bring several shrubs of the same species together to create dense foliage and more effective shelter. Lines of shrubs serve a purpose on the edges of your yard, where they help define your space—but an irregular grouping will seem more inviting to birds and butterflies in your area. Planting shrubs in a group can also boost the pollination process, in which butterflies are integrally involved. Shrubs like viburnum, American holly, and blueberries produce more blossoms and fruit when several shrubs are grouped together.

The trees and shrubs already in your yard provide a good starting point. Your next step will be to plant around these established features, making them part of a greater design.

Let's talk about grass—a nonnative monoculture that does more harm than good. Grass's uniformity replaces important habitat with something entirely unnatural: a sweeping carpet that does not support birds or butterflies. Just about all of the grass varieties available in the United States actually come from Europe, and they cannot thrive here without irrigation, fertilization, and chemical herbicides to kill everything that is not grass. Fertilizer and herbicides are unhealthy to birds and butterflies, so maintaining a manicured lawn in the American tradition pleases the neighbors while damaging our wildlife.

So what should you plant instead? Ground covers and vines make excellent alternatives to grass, providing continuous color—often evergreen through the

Dense plantings will pollinate easily, producing lots of blooms that attract birds and butterflies

winter months—and a virtually maintenance-free lawn. These options require little more than a regular trimming around the edges to keep the vines in the territory of your choosing. Native ground covers grow quickly and fill in bare landscapes, remaining hardy for many years.

Your natural garden will feature plants in masses, rather than two or three plants in a small clump. Each area will feature many varieties of perennials and some annuals as you choose, arranging short and tall plants to maximize the show in each season. Most important, the masses overlap, with no breaks between plant varieties.

If you have trees that provide a shape and foundation to your yard, begin to create a leafy understory beneath them with an assortment of low-growing, shade-loving plants. Many bloom with the first touch of spring, while others come into their peaks later in the summer, providing a continuous series of blossoms throughout the growing season.

In addition to floral beauty, the understory provides something important to ground-feeding birds: a safe, sheltered area under which they can forage for insects and invertebrates (like worms and grubs). You'll hear sparrows, thrushes, ground-feeding warblers, and other small birds rustling under the leaves as they search for morsels. Caterpillars enjoy the understory as well, especially if it contains herbs and vegetable plants that supply much of the larval diet.

In some regions, it's entirely acceptable to have no ground cover at all. Landscapes in drier climates may use gravel, crushed stone, or another rock or mineral option, eliminating the struggle with grass altogether. Such a yard can be planted with native shrubs that thrive in sandy soil or drought conditions, filling in the visual gaps while providing plenty of nesting habitat for cactus and canyon wrens, canyon towhees, a variety of western thrashers, and other arid-climate birds.

FINDING NATIVE PLANTS

If your favorite garden center can't supply the native plants you want, look for the Native Plant Society or land preservation society in your state. Many of these societies hold native plant sales every spring, providing you with a wealth of choices that are just right for your climate and soil content. Search on "[your state] native plant society" to learn more. The organization's website may suggest nurseries nearby that specialize in native plants. Land trusts, organizations that preserve green spaces, also hold native plant sales as spring fund-raisers. Search on "[your state] land trust native plant sale" to find one in your area.

FLOWERS BY REGION

One yard's weed is another yard's native flower, whether it's a daisy, an aster, a cluster of wild columbine, or a naturalized daylily. You may wander through your local garden center and marvel at the number of Asian or African species it stocks each spring, but these exotic blooms will not bring birds and butterflies to your yard. It's the native plants—from goldenrod to penstemon—that birds and butterflies will turn to for nutrition, whether they feed on their seeds and fruit in late summer or drink the nectar they produce from spring to fall.

North/Northeast: Flowers

Look around at your garden as it stands today. What flowers do you see? You may already have some native species well established and thriving in your yard—because these flowers are the most suited to your climate, your soil, and the insects and birds that are vital to their successful reproduction.

Make the most of these native flowers as you begin to choose new plants to expand your bird garden. Maybe it's time to add larger numbers of these established plants, creating masses of seed-producing blossoms that will feed your birds throughout the winter.

The eight flower species pictured here are just a few of the hundreds of native blooms that may be right for your garden. These are some of the most popular flowers, well loved by gardeners for their dependable growth and ability to naturalize over time.

Birds arriving during the spring migration will begin looking for food sources as they rest and refuel before continuing north. Seed heads from the previous year's native plants become a valuable source of nutrition, bringing varietal sparrows like fox, Lincoln's, and white-crowned into yards with large areas of plant life. Your wide bed of last year's coneflower and black-eyed Susan seed heads can become a flock's dining room, helping them gather sustenance before they move farther north. As spring and summer blooms arrive like yarrow and Solomon's seal, they will feed your resident sparrows, chickadees, titmice, and other seedeaters.

Butterflies lay their eggs on the underside of leaves or on stems of the plants their larvae (caterpillars) need to eat as soon as they hatch. Trees including aspen, birch, dogwood, maple, oak, poplar, serviceberry, and willow can all provide habitat for the beginning of the butterfly's life cycle, offering nourishment for caterpillars and the right place to spin a cocoon when it's time to metamorphose.

Once the butterfly emerges, flowering plants with trumpet-shaped or thin-tubed blossoms provide nectar. Columbine, bee balm, and dogwood are among the summer bloomers that sustain butterflies, while milkweed—especially for monarchs—and Joe-Pye weed deliver plenty of nectar as summer wanes.

You can watch this entire pageant play out in your own backyard by choosing native flowers, shrubs, and trees for your garden. Ask your local garden center or nursery for the native plants from these families that grow well in your area:

- Aster
- Blazing star
- Bluestem (ornamental grass)
- Cardinal flower
- Columbine
- Daisy
- Goldenrod
- Honeysuckle

- Joe-Pye weed
- Lobelia
- Mayapple
- Penstemon
- Solomon's seal
- Thistle
- Violet
- Yarrow

Purple coneflower (*Echinacea purpurea*)

Officially a member of the daisy family, this drought-tolerant perennial grows wild in prairies and open wooded areas throughout much of eastern North America. Sparrows, titmice, chickadees, cardinals, jays, and other seed-eating birds love the protruding seed heads these flowers offer up, seeking them out almost as soon as the blossoms reach their full bloom. Put in at least a dozen plants to start your garden; add more each year to create a substantial bed.

Purple coneflower

Zones 4–10, full sun, blooms in midsummer

Bee balm (*Monarda didyma*)

A summer bloomer, this red, pink, purple, or white flower attracts both hummingbirds and butterflies. The plants multiply readily, making this a welcome addition to a natural garden. The plants grow to heights of about 3 feet. Bee balm can thrive in wet soil or in drier conditions, depending on the variety you've chosen. The plants are susceptible to mildew if they cluster too closely together, so break apart and separate the plants every other summer to expand your bed and give them breathing room.

Bee balm

Zones 4–9, full sun to partial shade, blooms in mid- to late summer

Black-eyed Susan (*Rudbeckia goldsturm*)

While plants in the rudbeckia family are usually short-lived perennials, black-eyed Susans reseed themselves annually, so you may never notice a gap in the flowers' life span. Once they begin blooming, they keep producing golden-yellow blossoms right into the fall. Many flowers mean many seeds for hungry sparrows, chickadees, titmice, jays, and other seedeaters, which will continue to visit the dead heads throughout the late fall and winter.

Black-eyed Susan

You'll see plenty of these along the roadsides and in open meadows throughout the late summer as well.

Zones 4–9, full to partial sun, blooms midsummer to fall

Wild columbine (*Aquilegia canadensis*)

Whether you choose the red columbine for your hummingbird garden or one of this versatile plant's many other shades, you'll find columbine to be a dependable plant that blooms every spring. Columbine of one kind or another grows in just about every region of North America. Look for it in shades of yellow, red, white, purple, blue-green, or pink. Positioned downward to attract hummingbirds and butterflies, these plants also produce seeds that interest other birds.

Wild columbine

Zones 3–9, partial shade, blooms in mid- to late spring

Swamp milkweed (*Asclepias incarnata*)

Critical to the life cycle of the monarch butterfly, this hardy perennial produces wide, fragrant clusters of tiny flowers from June through August. After the bloom, milkweed continues to produce plump pods of seeds on fluffy stalks that burst open in fall, self-seeding the plant throughout gardens and grassy lots. As persistent as it is, however, the loss of milkweed habitat to commercial and residential development has led to dire consequences for monarchs. More milkweed means more butterflies, so plant plenty of it.

Swamp milkweed

Zones 3–8, full sun to partial shade, blooms in summer

Spotted Joe-Pye weed (*Eutrochium maculatum*)
Monarchs and eastern tiger swallowtails love the shaggy pink flowers of this late summer bloomer. Topping out at over 6 feet tall, it may be the perfect addition to a garden that backs up to a fence or retaining wall. After the blooms are spent, Joe-Pye weed produces seeds that feed sparrows and finches throughout the winter, making it a particularly desirable plant in a year-round garden. It self-seeds and continues to spread if not pruned into place early in the season.

Zones 3–8, full sun to partial shade, blooms in mid- to late summer

Spotted Joe-Pye weed

Blue vervain (*Verbena hastata*)
This tall, spiky perennial blooms with towers of tiny purply flowers, which burst open from the bottom of each spike and work their way up. Bees as well as butterflies—especially skippers—love this continuously blooming plant, but mammals don't care for it, making it popular for gardens in areas with free-range cattle or lots of deer. When the blooms end, nutlets form that provide seed for cardinals, sparrows, and juncos.

Blue vervain

Zones 3–8, full sun to partial shade, blooms midsummer to early fall

Canada goldenrod (*Solidago canadensis*)
Tall, aggressively healthy, and a late summer bloomer, goldenrod pulls all kinds of pollinators into its thick panicles of blossoms. Bees vie with butterflies for the best positions on this plant, and its seeds tumble to the ground once the blooms are spent, feeding juncos, mourning doves, and winter sparrows. Goldenrod works to take over an entire garden, so it's perfectly acceptable to pare it back every spring as the new stalks rise.

Zones 3–8, full sun to partial shade, blooms late summer through fall

Canada goldenrod

South/Southeast: Flowers

Gardeners in the southeastern states have all the luck! Flowers bloom ten to twelve months of the year, and the long growing season makes for some spectacular displays of both native and exotic species throughout the region.

The flowers selected here represent just a fraction of the possible choices for your southern bird and butterfly garden. Watch your garden to see which flowers attract your resident birds all year—but pay particularly close attention in fall and winter, as migrants from as far away as the Arctic Circle arrive and search for food sources. Your garden can play an important role in keeping birds strong and well fueled as they head for Central and South American destinations, and it can feed and host butterflies well into the fall.

Coastal states are part of a Western Hemisphere phenomenon known as the Atlantic Flyway, the route taken by millions of birds during both the spring and fall migrations. Some birds—including the amazing ruby-throated hummingbird—will fly eighteen to twenty hours straight, then drop into wildlife refuges, farmers' fields, and backyards to rest and eat before taking to the skies again.

A century ago, these birds found ample food supplies and resting places along the coastline, but today, with so much choice property now developed for human use, much of this important green space has disappeared.

Your bird garden provides a tremendous service to migrating birds. Make the most of your opportunity to be part of their strenuous journey by selecting plants that offer life-sustaining seeds or nectar, and leaves that shelter exhausted warblers, vireos, and hummingbirds.

How many southern species attract birds? In addition to those profiled here, look for plants in these families:

- Aster
- Cattail
- Columbine
- Daylily
- Grape
- Harebell

- Honeysuckle
- Jack-in-the-Pulpit
- Mistletoe
- Primrose
- Sunflower
- Yarrow

Southern magnolia (*Magnolia grandiflora*)

Choose either the large tree or the low shrub varieties, but by all means, choose this fragrant, abundantly blooming flower for your southern garden. Plants begin to produce seed when they reach about ten years of age. You'll know when this has begun because birds will arrive to devour the bright seed nuggets. Don't be surprised if you find wild turkeys under your magnolia, pecking at the seeds alongside boat-tailed grackles and mourning doves. Locate your magnolia in moist, fertile soil, especially along a stream or near a swampy area.

Southern magnolia

Zones 7–9, full sun to partial shade, blooms in spring and summer

Evergreen rhododendron (*Rhododendron maximum*)

Three varieties of evergreen rhododendron are native to the southeastern United States, but these extravagant white blossoms are familiar as far north as New England. Found in full sun at higher elevations, these plants prefer partial shade in warmer areas. Rhododendron requires soil with good drainage, especially in warmer climates. The blossoms attract hummingbirds with their long pistils and stamens, while the wide evergreen leaves shelter the birds from cold winter winds, rain, and snow.

Evergreen rhododendron

Zones 4–8, full sun to partial shade, blooms in May

Crossvine (*Bignonia capreolata*)

Train this flashy vine up a trellis or over an archway and watch hummingbirds zoom back and forth among its profuse, trumpet-shaped flowers. A strong climber, this vine clings to walls using the strength of clawlike grippers at the ends of its tendrils. In climates that see cold winter nights, crossvine's dark green leaves turn purple.

Zones 4–8, full sun to partial shade, blooms April to August

Crossvine

Lobed tickseed (*Coreopsis auriculata*)

You've seen plenty of this bright yellow flower growing in masses along roadsides—in fact, it's so prevalent that Florida named this bloom its state wildflower. Easy to grow, this coreopsis produces many blooms on a single plant. It readily reseeds itself throughout your garden, making it the perfect plant for naturalizing alongside coneflower and delphinium (larkspur). Seedeaters including sparrows, titmice, juncos, goldfinches, towhees, and more love its seeds and will come to a sizable patch of coreopsis again and again.

Lobed tickseed

Zones 3–8, full sun, blooms from June to fall

Wild blue phlox (*Phlox divaricate*)

Growing up to 18 inches tall, shade-loving phlox's five-petaled blossoms attract butterflies throughout the spring. Some varieties will creep through bare areas under trees and become ground cover, a useful added benefit.

Wild blue phlox

Zones 3–8, partial to full shade, blooms in spring

Common yarrow (*Achillea millefolium*)

Yarrow grows throughout the eastern United States, making it a good choice for gardens as far north as New England, and all the way to southern Florida. It fills in gaps in gardens and thrives in dry areas on the edges of wetlands, in meadows, and in pastures. Adding it to your yard may attract cardinals, grosbeaks, vireos, and finches, as well as common butterflies including eastern tiger swallowtail and black swallowtail.

Common yarrow

Zones 4–8, full sun to partial shade, blooms in summer

Blazing star (*Liatris spicata*)

These four-foot-tall, spiky stalks covered in tight purple, pink, or white flower clusters are unmistakable, making a bold statement in a colorful garden. They are a favorite of hummingbirds, orioles, and butterflies, and some mimic birds (mockingbirds, catbirds, thrashers) visit them as well to enjoy the flower buds. Some gardeners know this perennial as dense gayfeather.

Zones 4–8, full sun, blooms in spring and summer

Narrow-leaf star

Firewheel (*Gaillardia pulchella*)

A standout in any garden, this brilliant orange-and-yellow starburst goes by many names, including blanket flower and Indian blanket. Topping out at just 10 to 12 inches tall, it serves well as a border plant, blooming throughout the spring and summer in the southeastern states (and just in late May and early June farther north). It attracts sparrows, finches, buntings, juncos, and towhees to its seed heads after its blooms have faded, but hummingbirds, orioles, and butterflies take an interest in its nectar. Firewheel prefers dry, sandy soil, making it a great choice for coastal neighborhoods.

Firewheel

Zones 3–8, full sun to partial shade, blooms in spring and summer

North/Northwest: Flowers

Whether your home is high in the Rocky or Cascade Mountains, on the edges of the Olympic rain forest, or in the free-range pastures of Montana, you've seen some stunning wildflowers emerge after the cold, rainy, and snowy seasons end.

You can participate in the seasonal color displays by choosing some of these wildflowers for your own garden. Place them in concentrated masses or allow them to naturalize, letting the flowers' own reseeding process choose the locations of next year's blooms.

Here disparate ecosystems often merge with little preamble, with sudden departures from sagebrush-covered valleys to snow-brushed mountain peaks. High altitudes give way to more temperate zones along the Pacific coast, producing an entirely different set of native flowers, trees, and shrubs that enjoy the benefits of the area's considerable moisture.

In the zones along the edges of these ecosystems, you may find a staggering number of bird species frequenting your garden. Mountain bluebird may cross paths with lark bunting and other grassland birds, while Steller's jays and black-headed grosbeak may vie for seeds with bushtit, varied thrush, and lesser goldfinch. The greater the variety of natural food sources you can supply—from coniferous trees to bright perennial flowers—the more you can persuade these birds to return to your yard every season.

The flowers shown here are just a handful of the possibilities for your garden; your specific location may have its own varieties that represent these plant families. As you choose plants for your garden, keep in mind that some plants that thrive in your state may not do so in the conditions presented by your yard. Your favorite garden center can help you narrow the field, so to speak, to make your garden beautiful and turn it into a haven for the birds in your area.

In addition to the species highlighted, these plant families are native to the northwestern states. See which ones are available from the garden centers or nurseries in your area:

- Aster
- Blazing star
- Campion
- Clematis
- Daisy
- Gilia
- Harebell
- Honeysuckle

- Hyssop
- Larkspur
- Milkweed
- Monkey-flower
- Penstemon
- Primrose
- Sunflower
- Thistle

Giant red Indian paintbrush (*Castilleja miniata*)

Choose from more than two dozen species of this dramatic plant and mass them in your garden to add vibrancy and bright color. The red varieties bring in hummingbirds, and they will linger to buzz from one plant to the next when the flowers reside together. Paintbrush does well in sandy soil or on an alpine hillside, and it holds up nicely in dry conditions.

Zones 1–7, full sun, blooms March to September

Giant red Indian paintbrush

Narrow-leaf fireweed (*Chamaenerion angustifolium*)

This northern beauty is easy to grow in colder climates, with a range that extends all the way to the Arctic Circle and northward. Fireweed's seeds scatter in the wind, so it readily covers hillsides and areas with little vegetation. Its stalks grow to 6 feet in height, and its cheery pink blooms attract butterflies and catch the eyes of hummingbirds. This plant spreads easily and rapidly, so consider harvesting the seeds before they take to the air.

Dwarf fireweed

Zones 1–9, light shade, blooms in midsummer

Glacier lily (*Erythronium grandiflorum*)

Also known as dogtooth violet, this early spring bloomer has the classic downward-facing flower and elongated pistil and stamen of plants that depend on hummingbirds for pollination. Clusters of these push through the forest floor at higher elevations in spring. In your garden, glacier lily may adorn a rock garden or replace mulch under shady trees. At high elevations, watch for calliope hummingbirds when these flowers bloom; broad-tailed and Allen's hummingbirds are also attracted to the flowers' nectar.

Glacier lily

Zones 3–9, partial to full shade, blooms in spring

Nodding onion (*Allium cernuum*)

The oniony fragrance this plant emits attracts mammals as well as butterflies and birds, and its crown of pink or white flowers provides the nectar that butterflies, orioles, and hummingbirds seek. Mockingbirds, thrashers, and vireos may come to these blooms as well. The stalks grow as much as 2 feet high, making this a nice addition to a tall garden.

Nodding onion

Zones 4–8, full sun, blooms in summer

Prairie coneflower (*Ratibida columnifera*)

This showy wildflower goes by many names, including red-spike Mexican hat and thimbleflower, and its velvety-looking petals and high pistil make it a standout in any garden. Butterflies love the blossoms, and once the plant goes to seed, it attracts all manner of seed-eating birds, from sparrows and finches to jays and grackles. It readily reseeds itself, so you can depend on its reappearance from year to year.

Zones 4–8, full sun, blooms in summer

Prairie coneflower

Wild strawberry (*Fragaria virginiana*)

One of several berry-producing plants that attract birds and butterflies, wild "Virginia" strawberry draws in butterflies with the nectar from its five-petaled flowers, and then feeds fruit-loving birds like robins, waxwings, grosbeaks, cardinals, warblers, woodpeckers, and grouse when its berries ripen. This plant provides an excellent base for a large garden, expanding over time to cover the open ground.

Zones 5–9, full sun to partial shade, blooms in spring, berries in early summer

Wild strawberry

California hedge nettle (*Stachys bullata*)

A perennial in the mint family—and neither a hedge builder nor a stinging nettle—this plant draws in hummingbirds and butterflies in wet, boggy places. Its variegated purple blossoms begin to emerge in spring and continue throughout the summer and into early fall, growing on stalks that rise to nearly 3 feet tall.

Zones 4–8, partial to full shade, blooms spring through fall

California hedge nettle

Pearly everlasting (*Anaphalis margaritacea*)

Pearly everlasting

This striking plant's flowers bloom in summer and are short-lived, but they appear readily in areas of recent burn activity, making it a welcome symbol of recovery. It provides caterpillars with shelter and sustenance and then feeds the emerging butterflies with its nectar. Its range extends into Southern California.

Zones 3–7, full sun to partial shade, blooms in summer

South/Southwest: Flowers

Four North American deserts, high mesas, mountains, and river-carved canyons all meet in the southwestern states, making the variety of plants for your garden vast and colorful.

The flowers that will succeed in your garden, however, must be compatible with the specifics of your yard's climate, elevation, soil, and water availability—so the golden columbine that covers mountains in northern Arizona, for example, will wither in the dry climate of the Sonoran Desert.

As you imagine your bird and butterfly garden-to-be, take careful stock of your yard's current attributes. The plants you consider wandering weeds today may be both beautiful and productive when organized in a closely planted mass. Plants that thrive in your neighborhood—along roadsides, in open fields, and in the vacant lots between homes and businesses—are proven performers in your area's climate and soil.

These plants already have a codependent relationship with the birds, insects, and even the lichens and fungi that live in your area. You may not need to look much farther than your own street or community to decide which plants to add to your own garden.

Your choices not only enhance your garden and provide food and shelter options for birds, but they also aid the southwestern environment as a whole. Native plants restore some of the valuable elements of your local ecosystem that have diminished or even disappeared through human development. Even a few native plants in your yard can bring back some resistance to erosion, restore missing nutrients, and reduce water consumption in arid landscapes.

The list of southwestern native plants is vast, but the flowers birds love fall into several specific families. Look for your climate's best matches in these categories:

- Bee balm
- Blazing star
- Buckwheat
- Columbine
- Coreopsis
- Daisy
- Fairy duster
- Gaillardia
- Gilia
- Honeysuckle

- Ocotillo
- Paintbrush
- Penstemon
- Primrose
- Sage
- Sumac
- Sunflower
- Verbena
- Zinnia

James penstemon (*Penstemon jamesii*)

Hardy at elevations between 4,000 and 7,000 feet, this lavender member of the penstemon family thrives in sandy soil. As with all penstemon species, the tubular flowers produce nectar that feeds hummingbirds and butterflies throughout the summer. James penstemon is shorter than some of its siblings, making it a nice border plant in your natural garden.

Zones 4–7, full sun, blooms June to July

James penstemon

Mexican golden poppy (*Eschscholzia mexicana*)

Desert expanses covered with these gorgeous blooms are a sure sign of spring in the Southwest. You can have the same delightful display of yellow-orange blossoms in your own yard without a great deal of effort. The poppies reseed themselves each summer, and seed-eating birds including lesser goldfinches, dark-eyed and yellow-eyed juncos, bushtits, white-winged and mourning doves, and black-throated sparrows help to spread the germination across your yard and in your neighborhood. Think about adding these poppies as a ground cover, letting the emerald foliage take over when the flowers are spent.

Mexican golden poppy

Zones 1–6, full sun, blooms February to May

Indian blanket (*Gaillardia pulchella*)

These vibrant flowers spice up open fields across the Southwest with their dazzling colors. Easy to grow and maintain, Indian blanket can become part of a mixed garden with little effort. The plants grow to about 2 feet tall, keeping the blooms visible even among taller plants. Sandy soil is best for this drought-resistant plant. Leave the deadheads in place to allow black-throated sparrows, canyon towhees, lazuli and lark buntings, grosbeaks and other seedeaters to feed on these in late summer and fall.

Zones 1–6, full sun, blooms May to July

Indian blanket

Desert globemallow (*Sphaeralcea ambigua*)

Vibrant, cup-shaped orange blooms are just the thing to attract attention from many southwestern birds. With more than a dozen species from which to choose, you can find a globemallow that will bring additional color to your garden, as well as height—the stalks grow as high as 6 feet. Leave the faded blooms in place to offer the seed heads to finches and sparrows. Scaled quail are partial to the leaves and stems, and some small birds eat the plant's fruit—watch for bluebirds, grosbeaks, tanagers, and orioles. Here's a bonus: they're also a favorite food of the desert tortoise.

Zones 1–6, full sun, blooms all year

Desert globemallow

Bluebell bellflower (*Campanula rotundifolia*)

You may know this flower by another of its many names: bluebell-of-Scotland, harebell, or witches' thimble. Its bell-shaped flowers attract butterflies and hummingbirds, as well as a wide variety of songbirds. Its range extends throughout the southwestern states and up into the Pacific Northwest.

Zones 3–9, full sun to shade, blooms in summer

Bluebell bellflower

Oswego-tea (*Monarda fistulosa*)

Also known as wild bergamot or bee balm, this lavender version of the hardy perennial attracts butterflies and hummingbirds with its tubular flower petals. It's easy to grow, with stalks up to 5 feet high, each of which produces lots of stems with a pom-pom-like bloom at the top.

Zones 3–8, full sun to partial shade, blooms in summer

Oswego-tea

Butterfly milkweed (*Asclepias tuberosa*)

The ultimate butterfly magnet, this showy, bright orange perennial self-seeds and spreads to fill whatever space it is allowed. Hummingbirds love it almost as much as most butterfly species, so a bed of this flower will be buzzing with activity throughout the summer. It mixes well with a large bed or meadow full of coneflower, black-eyed Susan, and common yarrow, holding its own among these very hardy native plants.

Zones 3–8, full sun, blooms in summer

Butterfly milkweed

Plains coreopsis (*Coreopsis tinctoria*)

Coreopsis varieties are as numerous as the American states; this one's combination of bright red and yellow pulls in hummingbirds and butterflies when it blooms in late summer. When it goes to seed in fall, it attracts sparrows, finches, and all manner of ground-feeding birds to feast as the seeds drop from the spent blossoms.

Zones 5–9, full sun, blooms late summer

Plains coreopsis

Midwestern Plains: Flowers

Great Plains indeed! The open, fertile grasslands and cultivated fields of Iowa, Kansas, Minnesota, and Nebraska not only provide their crops to much of the nation's food supply, but they also support a dedicated ecosystem of birds that thrive in open spaces.

The symbiosis between birds and plants is particularly easy to observe here, as birds glide overhead or perch on fence posts to scan for food sources; land on top of tall, nodding blooms just past their prime; and pull seeds from the center of sun-dried blossoms. Later, these birds excrete during flight, dropping partially digested seeds to earth and planting the following year's food supply, and the cycle continues.

You can attract birds to your heartland backyard by making a conscious choice to become part of this natural process. Flowers with big, showy blossoms that produce plenty of seeds are the best choices for your yard, complemented with flowering shrubs and trees that bring the insects that many grassland birds devour. (We'll talk about shrubs and trees later in this chapter.)

Take a drive or walk along an open pasture or grassy field to see what's already growing there, and on which plants the birds land. You'll see them begin to pick at the center of each flower, a sure sign that tasty seeds reside within. Chances are good that you'll see the birds eating from tall grasses topped with seeds as well; when carefully managed to prevent invasive growth, these can be dramatic additions to your garden.

Moving beyond the most common species, here are some additional plant families that thrive in the midwestern plains:

- Bee balm
- Blazing star
- Buckwheat
- Columbine
- Coreopsis
- Daisy
- Gaillardia
- Gilia

- Honeysuckle
- Paintbrush
- Penstemon
- Primrose
- Sage
- Sumac
- Verbena
- Zinnia

Yellow coneflower (*Rudbeckia triloba*)

Cousin to the familiar purple coneflower (see page 91), this prolific plant produces many blooms on each stalk. Many blooms mean lots of seeds for hungry birds, so leave the spent flowers in place for fall migrants passing through the plains. Easy to grow, drought tolerant, and quick to naturalize, yellow coneflower is a welcome addition to your bird garden.

Zones 4–8, full sun to light shade, blooms June to August

Yellow coneflower

Wild perennial lupine (*Lupinus perennis*)

The tall, abundantly blossomed lupine attracts birds to its nectar and then offers pods of seeds that continue to feed birds including lark sparrows, lark buntings, juncos, goldfinches, and other seedeaters long after the blooms have gone. (The seeds are popular in some European and North African recipes.) Lupines provide another service: they can turn the nitrogen in the atmosphere into ammonia, depositing this into the soil to fertilize itself and the plants around it. It's also the only food eaten by the Karner blue butterfly.

Zones 3–9, full sun, blooms May to June

Wild perennial lupine

Oxeye sunflower (*Heliopsis helianthoides*)

A prairie native, this plant goes by a number of names, including early sunflower and false sunflower, but it is more often mistaken for a black-eyed Susan than a common sunflower. Its seed heads atop 3-foot-tall stalks attract many birds in summer and fall, and pollinators including butterflies and bees during its long bloom time.

Zones 3–9, full sun, blooms late spring to first frost

Oxeye sunflower

Common boneset (*Eupatorium perfoliatum*)

Tiny white flowers in tight clusters make this late summer bloomer easy to confuse with common yarrow or white snakeroot, but its hairier appearance and slender leaves help with identification. It provides a home for caterpillars and feeds the resulting butterflies, and its seeds attract chickadees, migrating warblers, wrens, jays, and other perching birds.

Zones 2–10, full sun to partial shade, blooms late summer to fall

Common boneset

Common milkweed (*Asclepias syriaca*)

The round, snowball-like cluster of pink-to-purple flowers at the top of a milkweed stalk attracts monarch caterpillars and butterflies, making it a must-have addition to gardens and open fields. Monarchs cannot survive without it, so the more milkweed we plant, the better—and it reseeds itself vigorously, popping up all over gardens and in wet areas along roadsides.

Zones 3–9, full sun, blooms early summer

Common milkweed

Great blue lobelia (*Lobelia siphilitica*)

The lobelia's tubular blooms bring all lovers of nectar to them, so expect visits from hummingbirds and butterflies when you add this to your garden. You'll need to keep the soil moist to ensure full blooming throughout the summer and fall, but the result will be worth the effort.

Zones 4–8, full sun to shade, blooms summer and fall

Great blue lobelia

White heath aster (*Symphyotrichum ericoides*)

The North American plants we call asters have been reclassified in a genus of their own, but that doesn't affect your ability to purchase, plant, and raise these easy, dependable flowers. This hardy, creeping perennial goes by many names: prairie, wreath, elongate, dense-flowered, or tufted aster. You may find pink or purple varieties with the same Latin name as well. Whatever form you choose, our native asters produce nectar late in the season, and their late summer arrival warns us that the colder seasons are on their way. Watch for cardinals, grosbeaks, goldfinches, towhees, sparrows, chickadees, and buntings on your asters.

Zones 5–8, full or partial sun, blooms late summer

White heath aster

Common sneezeweed (*Helenium autumnale*)

A member of the daisy family, this bright yellow bloom arrives in late summer and attracts pollinators including bees and butterflies. Its composite blossom contains wedge-shaped petals that expand as they move outward, with a large, almost spherical center disk. It prefers wetter areas like marshes and moist fields, as well as the banks of ponds and streams.

Zones 3–9, full or partial sun, blooms late summer through fall

Common sneezeweed

Exotic Flowers

Not every plant that attracts birds originated here in North America. In fact, thousands of exotic species—so called because they came from places as far away as Eurasia, the Pacific Rim, and Africa—fill garden centers and adorn lawns from the Northwest Territories to the tip of South Florida.

Exotic plants can take more effort to raise and maintain because they did not evolve under the conditions found in North America. Their requirements for specific temperature ranges, soil types, water availability, nutrients, and sun or shade can be very different from the garden in South Dakota's Black Hills or the subtropics of Louisiana. Choosing nonnative plants only begins with reading the labels at your favorite nursery; it's important to understand the commitment you may be making to this plant's care.

That being said, many exotic plants have become so commonplace in North American gardens that we no longer see them as exotic at all. We can observe that our summering or resident birds have adapted to these plants, finding sustenance deep within their blossoms or cleaning up fallen seeds as the growing season ends.

Choose your exotic plants carefully to be sure your choice will augment your bird garden without driving you wild with the plants' delicate needs.

DOES "EXOTIC" MEAN "INVASIVE"?

Not every time. Many exotic plants available at nurseries are self-contained, making it fairly easy to keep them from spreading throughout a garden and beyond.

Invasive plants take over your garden or whatever green space they encounter.

- Prolific reseeders like purple loosestrife crowd out the native plants on which birds, butterflies, and other animals depend.

- Crawling vines like black swallowwort and English ivy choke plants, shrubs, and trees in their path, eventually killing whatever foliage they encounter.

- Invasive ornamentals like bush honeysuckle dominate trees and shrubs in forests and block the sun from reaching plants on the forest floor. In some areas, oak trees have ceased reproducing because of this interloping vine.

The result: destruction of the positive, symbiotic relationship between birds and plants.

Petunia (*Petunia*)

A South American native closely related to tobacco, tomato, and potato plants, petunias are a staple in North American gardens. Pink, red, purple, white, or variegated, they easily fill in gaps between garden plants, give shape to a border, or fill hanging baskets. The large, trumpet-shaped blooms attract nectar-eating birds and butterflies, and birds eat their seeds as well. In warmer climates, you may find that the birds have "planted" some additional petunias for you later in the season.

Zones 3–11, full sun, blooms all summer into fall

Petunia

Impatiens (*Impatiens*)

You may know these hardy little flowers as jewelweed, touch-me-not, or balsams. Annuals throughout most of North America, impatiens fill flowerpots, finish hanging baskets, or provide elegant edges between your garden and lawn. While the red and pink varieties help bring hummingbirds to your garden, the seeds will convince your sparrows, goldfinches, juncos, grosbeaks, towhees, cardinals, and chickadees to stay. Watch out for the seed pods, which break open and spray seeds across your yard.

Impatiens

Zones 1–11, full sun to partial shade, blooms early summer to first frost; blooms year-round in zones 10 and 11

Snapdragon (*Antirrhinum*)

Whether or not you see the resemblance to a dragon's mouth when you look at this annual, you certainly can see how snapdragon's shape and bright color attract birds. Choose from more than thirty-six species. Planting a number of plants together creates a mass of blossoms, an area of your garden that hummingbirds will consider an all-day buffet. Beyond hummingbirds, cliff swallows and woodpeckers have been observed eating the blooms. Deer, squirrels, raccoons, and small burrowing animals like a snapdragon snack as well.

Snapdragon

Zones 4–11, full sun to partial shade, blooms in summer

Foxglove (*Digitalis*)

With its pink or purple elongated tubes that fit over your finger, foxglove brings drama to your garden. It loves acidic soil, making it a good complement to any conifers in your yard. It's fairly easy to grow, although a new plant won't produce any flowers until at least its second year. Foxglove is at home on mountain slopes, on cliffs facing the ocean, and in open woods. Let your hummingbirds enjoy this

Foxglove

plant's nectar, and watch the sparrows, chickadees, and finches go for the seeds, but don't try foxglove for yourself—every part of digitalis is toxic to humans.

Zones 4–8, partial sun to deep shade, blooms in summer

TREES AND SHRUBS BY REGION

As you choose the trees and shrubs that will become the anchoring features in your garden, remember some of the key elements birds need: food, shelter, and places to rest and nest. Trees and shrubs that provide fruit, nuts, or seed-filled cones quickly rise to the top of the list, while trees with dense foliage that masks nesting birds' location from predators are excellent choices for your backyard birds.

At the same time, think about your own needs as well. You want to be able to see the birds that arrive in your yard, so place trees and shrubs where you can view them from your window during winter months, and from your deck, porch, or patio in the warmer months. Equally important, you want your trees and shrubs to be positive additions to your yard, bringing beauty as well as bird activity.

North/Northeast: Trees and Shrubs

The northeastern states and provinces enjoy a substantial list of long-lived, highly productive trees and shrubs, many of which produce fruit from late summer through the fall. In addition to the four species highlighted here, look for winterberry, spicebush, baneberry, cherry, chokecherry, and wild grape. Nut-bearing trees like oak, walnut, and hickory will bring in the birds, especially acorn-loving blue jays.

A word to the wise: be careful to avoid berry-producing vines that are not native to your area. For example, American bittersweet is an endangered, self-regulating plant that produces yellow and orange berries in fall, creating a fine spectacle in your garden. Oriental bittersweet, however, looks very similar but is highly invasive, strangling or blocking out other plants in its path. If you're not sure what you're buying, ask at your favorite nursery or garden center. (Many nurseries are committed to native plants and will not stock or sell invasive species.)

WINTER BRINGS TIPSY BIRDS

As winter arrives, you may be surprised at the amount of fruit that still lingers on your trees—but have no fear that the birds have rejected your offerings. Many bird species wait until freezing temperatures begin the fermentation process in the fruit, bursting the berries and allowing wild yeast to convert the natural sugars into alcohol. You may suddenly find yourself with a flock of cedar waxwings or robins that can't retain their perches, flopping out of shrubs and trees and bumping into one another. While it's alarming (and amusing) to see drunken birds, it's a natural part of a northeastern winter.

Common wild rose (*Rosa virginiana*)

A pink rose with five petals and a yellow center, the truly wild rose is a native of the eastern United States—but the rose you may be able to acquire for your yard may not be strictly "wild." Many cultivated species have been developed based on the native, while roses you may see in the wild can be remnants of residences long gone. In fall, this rose produces bright orange-red hips that contain seeds. House, purple, and goldfinches flock to devour these over the winter.

Zones 5–10, full sun, blooms in June

Common wild rose

American holly (*Ilex opaca*)

Glossy, dark green leaves that stay green all winter, and shiny, cherry-red berries—it's no wonder that this iconic plant has become a symbol of the winter holidays. This holly requires at least one male shrub for every small group of females. Without a male plant, the females will not produce berries. Both male and female plants bloom, covering themselves with small white flowers in spring. By midsummer, the berries appear on the female shrubs. Look for mockingbirds, catbirds, thrashers, robins, and bluebirds eating the berries in winter.

Zones 5–9, full sun or partial shade, blooms in spring

American holly

Shadblow serviceberry (*Amelanchier canadensis*)

One of the first trees to produce flowers in spring, this tree will grow to 20 to 25 feet. Its fuzzy grayish leaves led to its other common name: downy serviceberry. Its round, purple and red berries are edible for humans as well as birds; they may attract squirrels as well as cedar waxwings, robins, mockingbirds, cardinals, and many others. In addition to its berries, shadblow turns yellow, gold, orange, and red in fall, a welcome ornament in your yard before the winter snows.

Zones 4–7, full sun or partial shade, blooms in early spring

Shadblow serviceberry

Northern highbush blueberry (*Vaccinium corymbosum*)

From Nova Scotia to Alabama and from Maine to Wisconsin, people and birds love northern blueberry. You may be reluctant to share the abundant fruit with your resident waxwings, robins, mockingbirds, and bluebirds, so plant several shrubs. You'll have plenty of berries for everyone, and the additional bushes will aid the pollination process, increasing the yield. Keep the soil moist, and you should have good luck with this hardy native shrub.

Zones 3–8, full sun or partial shade, blooms in late spring/early summer

Northern highbush blueberry

South/Southeast: Trees and Shrubs

Whether they cultivate beautyberry and yaupon holly among the live oaks on the Florida Panhandle, or the silvery-white berries of the southern wax myrtle on the South Carolina shore, gardeners in the Southeast can present a veritable smorgasbord of tasty choices to resident and migrating birds.

Berries become an important energy and calorie booster for birds heading south in fall, bringing northern flycatchers, waxwings, finches, warblers, and many others into southern backyards. The yard with the greatest variety and quantity of berries could even experience a fallout, that most thrilling of migration season experiences, when hundreds or even thousands of birds of many species descend on a small area to rest and feed before heading farther south. What would you do if a dozen orioles or scarlet tanagers arrived in your yard at once? It can happen to the gardener who's been generous, planting many trees or shrubs that produce life-sustaining fruit.

Equally important, the dense foliage offered by holly and bayberry helps to shield resting birds, while the hawthorn's spiky thorns keep spent birds from being ravaged by hunting hawks or overly curious cats.

In addition to the selections highlighted on pages 114–115, broaden your shrub choices with black chokeberry, blackhaw or arrowwood viburnum, sweet pepperbush, and any of the dozens of dogwood varieties, each with exuberant blossoms and plenty of fruit. Virginia sweetspire, a shrub that usually grows wider than it is tall, produces berries that some songbirds enjoy as well.

Nut trees are big hits with jays, nuthatches, woodpeckers, thrushes, and creepers—and with wild turkeys when the squirrels allow some nuts to make it to the ground—so consider increasing your bird activity with shagbark hickory, American beech, black walnut, or white oak.

Yaupon holly (*Ilex vomitoria*)

Birds flock to this evergreen shrub and its bright red fruit. You can expect to see anything from northern bobwhite to eastern bluebird devouring this southern staple. Prune the shrub if you want it small, or let it reach its full potential height of 20 to 25 feet. You'll need a male plant as well as a female to produce fruit; ask your garden center to help you choose the right ones.

Yaupon holly

Zones 8–10, full sun to shade, blooms in early spring

American beautyberry (*Callicarpa americana*)

There's no mistaking these bright violet berries for anything else. Add beautyberry to your garden, with its candy-pink flowers in spring and its astonishing berries, and your backyard may become the talk of the neighborhood. Robins and mockingbirds gobble up the cold-sweetened berries over the winter. You may see deer at your beautyberry bush as well. Folk wisdom says that the plant's leaves, when crushed, provide an effective mosquito repellent. Science confirms that an isolated compound called callicarpenal has been found in beautyberry, and the USDA has patented its use as a repellent.

American beautyberry

Zones 6–10, full sun to partial shade, blooms mid-spring to midsummer

Southern wax myrtle/bayberry (*Myrica cerifera*)

One of the South's most popular landscaping plants, southern wax myrtle grows from multiple trunks, producing a rounded, open canopy of olive-green leaves. Only the female trees produce the silvery-blue berries so prized by yellow-rumped warblers, so you'll need two trees—one male, one female—to complete the pollination process. While landscapers prefer to prune away all the lower branches, your birds will thank you if you allow the low foliage

Southern wax myrtle

to remain, where it can provide cover and nesting opportunities.

Zones 7–10, full sun to partial shade, blooms early spring

Hawthorn (*Crataegus*)

A member of the rose family (from which it gets its thorns), America's native hawthorns grow wild in wooded areas and protected lands across the country. Hawthorn blooms in early spring before its leaves appear, creating quite a spectacle with its cloud of white flowers. Its second act arrives in summer as big berries with red dots burst into production. Look for cedar waxwings, robins, bluebirds, and red-winged blackbirds eating these berries.

Hawthorn

Zones 6–11, full sun to partial shade, blooms late spring

North/Northwest: Trees and Shrubs

In the valleys, deciduous trees create leafy canopies with plenty of places for birds to build well-hidden nests.

In the mountains, aspen, maple, and dogwood trees make way for conifers as the elevation increases.

Together, native trees create a mixed wood that offers food and shelter to the birds, while gracing your backyard with spring blooms, summer berries, fall cones and colors, and winter evergreen.

The four species described here are meant only to point you in a series of useful directions, toward trees and shrubs that will make your yard a place of interest for migrating and resident birds. Mixing deciduous and coniferous trees draws a significantly wider variety of birds, from varied thrush in the Pacific Northwest to Clark's nutcracker at Rocky Mountain altitudes.

Your backyard habitat has the potential to be at its most exciting in winter, when so-called winter finches come looking for food as natural supplies dwindle in northern Canada. Possibilities abound for visits by common and hoary redpolls, red crossbills, rosy finches, evening and pine grosbeaks, Bohemian waxwings, and other unusual and much-coveted birds.

Many of these birds look for cones that have not yet been plundered by resident birds, or berries and nuts left behind by your area's robins, cedar waxwings, thrashers, and thrushes. When you supply the habitat and preferred dining for each species, they may surprise you with their cheery colors and industrious cone raiding in the middle of January or February.

Red elderberry (*Sambucus racemosa*)

The bright red berries this flowering shrub produces bring wrens, grosbeaks, thrashers, mockingbirds, and vireos to your garden. Make plenty of room for this treelike plant, as it can expand to as much as 20 feet tall if space allows—a healthy haven for caterpillars. Spring blooms are cone shaped and pale pink or white, attracting butterflies and hummingbirds until the flowers give way to clusters of fruit.

Red elderberry

Zones 3–8, full sun to full shade, blooms in spring, fruit in summer

Woods' rose (*Rosa woodsii*)

Blooming continuously from May to July, this simple rose of the woodlands grows on shrubs 2 to 5 feet high. Its remarkable hardiness makes it a favorite for cultivated gardens, forming small hedges or standing on its own as the anchor for a larger flower bed. Butterflies, warblers, crows, jays, and orioles visit the blossoms, while nuthatches and woodpeckers appear as the petals

Woods' rose

fall and the remaining stems produce bright red rose hips. Woods' rose also provides a home for many species of caterpillars.

Zones 3–8, full sun to shade, blooms in spring and early summer

Western chokecherry (*Prunus virginiana*)

Growing to just 20 feet tall, chokecherry can be found in the wild in hedgerows, on the edges of fields, and in open woods. The bright purple-red cherries—smaller than a conventional cherry—follow masses of white flowers that cover the tree in spring. You'll find that they're not sweet like the cherries we bake into pies. Instead, they have an astringent quality that makes humans pucker. Waxwings, titmice, bluebirds, robins, and mockingbirds wait for the fruit to ferment before they arrive to enjoy it.

Zones 2–6, full sun to partial shade, blooms mid-spring

Western chokecherry

American cranberry viburnum (*Viburnum trilobum*)

Big, splashy, 4-inch white flowers pre-cede clusters of small, bright crimson berries that last well into the fall—because thrashers, mockingbirds, titmice, robins, sparrows, bluebirds, and other fruit eaters will wait until late winter to devour them. By fall, the berries turn blue-black, and the shrub's foliage turns from green to a maroon that borders on purple, making this a stunning addition to your yard's autumn spectacle. This viburnum grows to 8 to 10 feet, making it a candidate for a hedge or privacy border.

Zones 3–7, full sun to partial shade, blooms mid-spring

American cranberry viburnum

South/Southwest: Trees and Shrubs

Nowhere in North America is it more important to take the climate into account than in the Southwest, where the low humidity, sandy soil, and intense spring and summer sun can ruin exotic trees and shrubs.

Stroll through a desert landscape and see what's growing there. If you're new to the Southwest, you may be amazed at the overall green color of this virtually waterless space. Many shrubs and small trees thrive in the well-drained, sandy soil, producing blooms and fruit for the resident birds and animals. From spring through early summer, the desert blooms—but not like an open meadow of nodding wildflowers. The most spectacular flowers actually burst from the tops of cacti, adding their vibrant pinks and yellows to an already fascinating vista.

You can bring this same kind of desert magic to your own yard by choosing shrubs and cacti that reflect the landscape southwestern birds understand. As birds arrive in spring from their Central American wintering grounds, they know exactly how and where to find the food they need—and many of them flock to backyards and feeders throughout South Texas, Arizona, New Mexico, and Southern California.

Turn your own backyard into a migration stopover for the birds, and you may find some of them setting up housekeeping and raising their young inside your cholla tree or prickly pear.

Rocky mountain juniper (*Juniperus scopulorum*)

You'll find Rocky Mountain juniper in areas from 500 to 2,700 feet in elevation throughout Utah, southern Colorado, and northern New Mexico. This small tree (or large shrub) sports bluish-gray berries—actually seed cones—at the ends of its tiny branchlets. To produce the berries, you'll need two plants—a male and a female. Robins will be the first to find these berries, but mockingbirds, waxwings, titmice, and woodpeckers will soon follow.

Zones 2–9, full sun, no bloom

Rocky Mountain juniper

Cane cholla (*Cylindropuntia imbricata*)

Brilliant magenta flowers, 3 inches in diameter each, manage to emerge from the ends of each spiny cholla cane. Cholla also produces a yellow fruit, but birds generally prefer to use this cactus as a nesting site instead of a source of food. Cactus wrens, mourning and white-winged doves, and other birds take up residence in the cholla, the plant's spines serving as excellent protection for nestlings.

Zones 8–11, full sun, blooms late spring/early summer

Cane cholla

Prickly pear cactus (*Opuntia*)

Easy to spot in deserts because of their flat, rounded stems, prickly pears produce a bright yellow flower that's followed by a pink-to-red, spiny fruit—which does indeed look like a pear with prickles. Like most cacti, prickly pear covers itself with long spines—but its arsenal also includes shorter spines, like lots of little hairs, which easily stick into skin. Cactus wrens, curve-billed thrashers, and greater roadrunners readily make prickly pear their home.

Zones 8–11, full sun, blooms late spring/early summer

Prickly pear cactus

Mesquite mistletoe (*Phoradendron californicum*)

If you have mesquite trees in your yard already, watch for the arrival of mistletoe—a parasitic plant that feeds off its host. Over a long period of time, it will kill the tree in which it resides. The story is not all bleak, however: in the ensuing years, mistletoe provides an important source of nutrition to a slender black bird called a phainopepla, which eats the red berries the plant produces. The birds then excrete the seeds into other trees, and the parasitic process begins again. More common berry-eating birds including robins, bluebirds, towhees, and house and Cassin's finches will find their way to mistletoe as well.

Mesquite mistletoe

Zones 8–11, no care required, no bloom

Midwestern Plains: Trees and Shrubs

With incomparably fertile soil, more than enough rain, and sparkling sunny days, the midwestern states are the home of hundreds of native tree and shrub species. Your backyard habitat can become a very exciting place with seasons-long color, from spring flowers blooming in abundance to fall's leafy brilliance and multitoned berries.

Both deciduous and coniferous trees thrive in the Midwest's climate and soil, widening your options from dogwood, hornbeam, and maple to eastern red cedar and white pine.

Add oak, hickory, and Ohio buckeye to provide nuts and fruit that squirrels and jays can share. Serviceberry, elderberry, mountain ash, and hawthorn provide berries that birds will snap up in winter.

Sumac, with its bright red towers of fruit and its scarlet autumn leaves, can become a freestanding, two-story tree in the middle of your yard or a border shrub along a fence or lawn edge. Virtually ubiquitous in nature preserves and woodlands, it becomes a striking addition to a backyard, signaling birds that you're serious about creating a true natural habitat.

Red osier dogwood (*Cornus stolonifera*)

One of the most distinctive shrubs in the dogwood family, red osier's construction involves dozens of bright red canes rising from a central source. The canes produce clusters of tiny, fluffy white flowers in spring, which give way to snow-white berries. The red stems and white berries make red osier a pleasure to see in frigid winter months. Mockingbirds, waxwings, robins, and grosbeaks devour its berries in late winter, when fruits with higher sugar content have been depleted.

Red osier dogwood

Zones 3–8, full sun to partial shade, blooms in late spring

Pagoda dogwood (*Cornus alternifolia*)

This sun-loving dogwood makes a large shrub or a small tree, producing white flowers in late spring. Blue-black fruit follows the flowers in late summer, hanging on long after the leaves have turned purple-red as winter approaches. Virtually all fruit-eating birds love dogwood berries, so watch for grosbeaks, waxwings, bluebirds, jays, towhees, and other overwintering species.

Pagoda dogwood

Zones 3–8, full sun to partial shade, blooms in late spring

Smooth sumac (*Rhus glabra*)

Spreading easily from the initial plant to cover a fence or wall, sumac produces greenish flowers in tall, upward-pointed clusters. When the flowers fade, the real show begins: the cluster turns scarlet with fruit, maturing to a rusty red as fall approaches. But wait, there's more: now the leaves turn as red as the fruit, giving you a spectacular fall show. Chickadees, robins, and bluebirds will feast on this fruit all winter, while your long-lasting sumac seeds may attract such

Smooth sumac

wonders as ruffed grouse, ring-necked pheasant, gray catbird, wood and hermit thrushes, and eastern phoebe. Watch out for American crows and European starlings plundering your sumac as well.

Zones 4–8, full sun to partial shade, blooms in late spring

Common elderberry (*Sambucus nigra* L. ssp. *canadensis*)

Keep the soil moist under this shrub, and it will reward you with clouds of white blossoms and plenty of purple berries. You'll have birds all winter as long as the fruit lasts, with visits from robins, waxwings, chickadees, finches, mockingbirds, grosbeaks, titmice, and woodpeckers. Be sure to choose the elderberry species named here, which produces purple or blue berries. The red berries of other species are toxic to humans. Other parts of this plant are edible: dip a flower cluster in batter and fry it up for breakfast, or add the petals to batter for pancakes.

Common elderberry

Zones 3–9, full sun, blooms in late spring/early summer

Exotic Trees and Shrubs That Work

If you would like to add exotic plants to your garden—that is, plants that are not native to North America—make careful selections that will be best for your yard, the birds and wildlife, and your area's environment.

Remember that when birds eat berries, they excrete the undigested seeds in places beyond your yard. When these seeds hit the ground, they have the potential to germinate, spreading seedlings of the exotic fruit shrub to fields, woods, or your neighbor's yard.

Watch out for invasive plants that take over a portion of your yard, weakening or even killing your carefully tended flowers and shrubs. Keep vines at bay by trimming them regularly, and pull new suckers off your walls and foundation—and off the trunks of your trees and shrubs. These aggressive plants require aggression in return, so don't be shy about ripping unwanted tendrils off their targets.

The shrubs detailed on pages 122–123 are both beautiful and self-contained, the kinds of plants that bring pleasure to gardeners without forcing us to pay an ongoing price for their charms.

In use across the continent and widely available, these plants attract birds with their blooms or fruit, while providing shelter and nesting opportunities.

Japanese wisteria (*Wisteria frutescens*)

There's an American wisteria that's native to the southeastern states, but it's the Japanese variety that grows in gardens across the continent. This gorgeous vine climbs fences, deck railings, trellises, and archways for a dazzling effect. Shiny, forest-green leaves and elongated clusters of purple-blue flowers give any deck or garden a sense of romance. Robins often build nests in the strong, clockwise-winding vines.

Zones 3–9, full sun to partial shade, blooms in spring

Japanese wisteria

Cotoneaster (*Cotoneaster*)

A noninvasive shrub that produces thousands of small red berries each year, this relative of the rose family grows well at high altitudes or in scrubby areas. Flowers may be white, creamy, light pink, or dark pink, attracting several butterfly and moth species that eat from the blooms. The fruit brings in thrushes, blackbirds, and many of the birds that switch to berries in winter to keep their energy levels high.

Zones 4–9, full sun, blooms in late summer

Cotoneaster

Weigela (*Weigela*)

With varieties that produce blooms in a wide range of pink shades, this Asian native is easy to grow, noninvasive, and dazzling in late spring. Its tubular flowers cover its branches, drawing the attention of flocks of hummingbirds. This shrub doesn't bear fruit, but it can be coaxed into a second bloom in late summer by careful pruning.

Zones 4–8, full sun to light shade, blooms in spring to early summer

Weigela

Lilac (*Syringa*)

A hummingbird magnet, the lilac's mid-spring bloom can stop traffic with its clusters of lavender, white, pink, or deep purple flowers. Get closer, and the plant's perfume will make you linger to inhale as deeply as possible. Lilacs don't bear fruit, but their forest-green leaves conceal birds within, making these hardy shrubs a good choice for backyards.

Zones 3–7, full sun to light shade, blooms in mid-spring

Lilac

GROUND COVERS

Ground covers present a host of opportunities to reduce the maintenance required in a garden or yard while providing shelter and hiding places for birds. They also provide an easy, thorough way to cover sizable areas of lawn with a permanent solution. Best of all, a native ground cover will block falling weed seeds, keeping them from germinating in your garden.

Choose a different ground cover for each area of your garden if you wish, or mix several as replacements for your lawn. Over time, the plants will take advantage of the gaps between your trees, shrubs, and perennials, establishing the ground cover as the foundation of your garden.

Even these self-sustaining carpets of green require some maintenance as they grow. Most ground covers are invasive, extending their territory beyond the space you may have allotted for them. Regular pruning and trimming will keep your lush greenery in check—but keep an eye out for one ground cover sending shoots out into another. If you don't want your covers to mix, add low stone walls between one plant and the next, and trim each species along the edge of the stone.

As you choose ground covers, check with your garden center or online to see if your choice is deciduous or coniferous. Some ground covers die back completely in winter, while others remain green year-round. Some also produce flowers, adding another dimension to your spring color.

Virginia creeper (*Parthenocissus quinquefolia*)

This common plant is native to eastern North America and now grows wild as far west as Utah and South Dakota. It produces small, greenish flowers in late spring, and berries in late summer (that are great for robins and mockingbirds, but toxic to humans). The vines also produce a sap that can cause skin irritation in some people. Left to its own devices, this plant climbs trellises, poles, and trees. It makes a hardy ground cover on slopes and in wide-open areas. In fall, its leaves turn brilliant red.

Virginia creeper

Zones 3–9, partial shade to full sun, blooms in spring

Stonecrop (*Sedum*)

Stonecrop, more popularly known as sedum, can be found in a wide variety of forms. Its slow-growing but hardy hold on your garden's soil makes it both attractive and useful as it wanders between rocks or edges around tree roots. Sedum protects your garden from erosion, especially on hillsides, growing low and close to the ground in compact clusters. Its flowers form tight bunches of seeds when the bloom is over, making them a good source of food for ground-feeding sparrows, juncos, thrushes, and doves.

Stonecrop

Zones 4–8, partial shade to full sun, blooms in spring

Allegheny spurge (*Pachysandra procumbens*)

The native cousin to the exotic pachysandra so many people plant in their yards, Allegheny spurge grows more slowly than the Japanese version. Its leaves add fall color to northern landscapes, then drop off and grow again in early spring. In its lower territory in the southern states, the leaves remain green year-round. Separate the plants in spring or fall to spread the ground cover more quickly. While the plant does not provide food for birds, its broad leaves give

Allegheny spurge

cover to ground-feeding birds including sparrows, thrushes, and thrashers.

Zones 5–9, partial to full shade, no flowers

Juniper (*Juniperus*)

Low-growing, tolerant of bad soil, drought resistant, and not especially tasty to your neighborhood deer, this plant makes the perfect western ground cover. The bluish green foliage remains throughout the year, turning a little bit purple in colder climates. For homes near the Pacific Ocean, juniper is comfortable in sandy soil and remarkably resistant to salt spray. Juniper produces berries that are particularly attractive to waxwings, mock-

Juniper

ingbirds, and robins, as well as grosbeaks and bluebirds in winter.

Zones 4–9, full sun to light shade, no flowers

The blue jay easily dominates
this house sparrow

8: Bird Identification

In a field guide, birds look distinctly different from species to species. Arrows and call-outs help draw your attention to the distinguishing field marks, and multiple drawings or photos help you learn how to tell one bird from another.

In real life, with birds hopping behind leaves or standing directly between you and the sun, identification becomes much more complex. Brown, gray, and brightly colored birds swoop in and out of your field of vision, disappearing as quickly as they came.

Before your eyes cross, here's the number-one rule for improving your bird identification skills: *Look at the bird before you look it up.*

Start with the bird's basic shape. Generally, the species in the same family of birds—warblers, vireos, doves, hawks, ducks, geese, and so on—have a similar, fairly recognizable shape from head to tail. It may take some time to learn these, but you will soon see that a sparrow has a short, heavy bill, while a wren has a longer, sharper bill. By the same token, the wren's tail stands perpendicular to its body, differentiating it from a sparrow, which has a long, usually fan-shaped tail.

Look at the bird's size. Warblers and vireos are smaller than sparrows, for example, and sparrows are smaller than towhees. If your bird is smaller than a robin but larger than a warbler, you know something about what kind of bird it may be. Bigger birds are easier to see, so you may learn the larger birds—robins, towhees, jays, phoebes, kingbirds, and the like—faster than the smaller birds. Birds of the same family may differ slightly in size—a house wren, for example, is significantly smaller than a cactus wren, and some warblers are larger than others. When you look from one bird to another in your backyard, however, you can make a size comparison in no time.

What is the bird doing? A bird creeping up the side of a tree may be a woodpecker, nuthatch, or brown creeper. A bird sorting through leaves on the ground is more likely a towhee, thrush, or sparrow than an oriole or flycatcher. Behavior can tell you enough about the bird to guess its family, even if its wing patterns or tail colors are obscured from your view.

FIELD MARKS

Ever since Roger Tory Peterson introduced the world to the concept of field marks in 1934, the process of identifying the bird in your binoculars became much easier. We owe much of bird watching's popularity to Peterson, who published the very first field guide. Captivated by birds in seventh grade, Peter-

Goldfinches and house finches are both in the finch family

son developed a passion for identifying species, sketching birds in the field, and noting the characteristics he called "field marks." When his first book sold out its entire printing in two weeks, modern birding was born, and today, tens of millions of birders around the world rely on field marks for bird identification.

The concept is simple: look at as many of the bird's markings as you can in the time you see the bird. Each part of the bird becomes important: head, chest, wings, tail, underbody, and feet. Ornithologists and hard-core birders divide each of these parts into dozens of subsections with names like supraloral, tibial feathers, malar, and coverts, but we'll start here with the basics.

Here's the most important advice we can give you: Look at all the field marks, not just one or two. Many woodpeckers have red on the backs of their heads, for example, but only a couple of these have black and white horizontal stripes running from their shoulders all the way down their backs. One field mark is rarely enough to identify any bird species, but a collection of observations—along with the bird's size, shape, behavior, diet, habitat, and range—will help you narrow down the possibilities.

Birding Tip: One Family, Many Colors

Both of the birds in the above photograph are finches, but their plumage varies significantly from one species to the next. How can you tell they're both finches? Start with the silhouette. Each of these birds is about the same size and has a fairly short tail and a bill that looks like a tiny triangle. Next, consider their behavior. Both the house finch and the goldfinch love nyjer seed. They fly with a very distinctive bobbing, dipping motion.

Field marks are a terrific identification tool, but they are just one tool in your bird identification kit. Use them all to learn what new arrival has found its way to your yard.

Head

- Birds' heads can be the most boldly marked parts of their bodies.
- Look at the top of the head (crown) for its color and shape. Is there a crest?
- Look at the eye. Is there a ring around it? What color is it? Does the bird have a visible eyebrow?
- The bill shape and color are important. Is there a spot of color between the eye and the bill (lores)?
- What color is the bird's cheek? How about the back of its neck (nape)?

The house sparrow, shown in all six of these identification keys, is the most common bird on the continent. Its bold markings make it a good subject for examination.

Breast

- Is there color on the throat? Some birds have lines that divide the throat area into sections; others have a single-color throat, or the throat blends into the breast.
- Look at the breast. Is it clear, spotted, or streaked? Is there a single spot, or a wide band of color?
- What about the bird's sides? Are they clear, spotted, or streaky? Is there color, and is it different from the breast color?
- Is the entire bird a single color (more or less)?

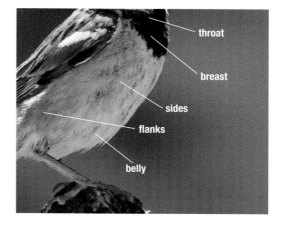

Underside

- It's not always easy to see what's going on under the bird's belly, but this area can be important to identification.

- Are there markings on the underbelly, or is it clear? What color is it? Many birds have yellow or rosy feathers here—this is one of the ways you can tell some flycatchers apart.

- What color are the bird's legs and feet? This is less important for feeder birds, but critical for shorebirds and gulls.

Now that you're thinking about a bird's size, shape, and the clear variations in the color of its head and body, it's time to add the wings and tail into the equation.

Wing patterns are particularly tricky parts of bird identification. Sometimes the most obvious field marks on the wings are hidden from view when the bird is standing and feeding. A northern mockingbird, for example, looks like a fairly plain gray bird while perching on a utility wire, easily confused with a gray catbird or even a kingbird. When the mockingbird extends its wings and takes flight, however, its bright white wing patches make the species unmistakable.

Wing patterns and colors can differ from adult birds to young ones, from male to female birds, and from winter to summer. Some birds have very complex tones on their wings, as their plumage changes several times on each feather.

As a result, serious birders have a specialized vocabulary that labels each segment of the wing. While this may seem far too complicated for the birds in your backyard, you may find it useful to begin to consider birds' wings (and tail) as having a myriad of colors, with subtle shading that can help you differentiate one species from another.

Wing

- Wings are divided into three sections:
- Primaries: the ends of the wings, often extending to the tail. This is the lowest part of the wing when the wing is folded.
- Secondaries: the largest part of the wing, just above the primaries.
- Tertials: the top part of the folded wing.
- Next, the wing parts below the bird's shoulder are called coverts.

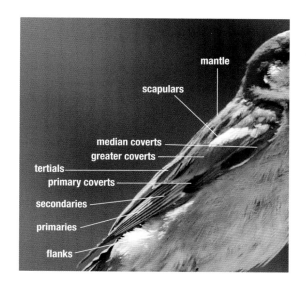

These break into three sections as well: primary, greater, and median.

Extended Wing

- When the wing is extended, you can see the primary coverts more easily.
- The secondary coverts become much clearer as well. If a bird has a shoulder patch, it's most likely on one of the secondary coverts.
- A bird in flight may reveal a well-defined wing bar or a big patch of white, black, or another color.

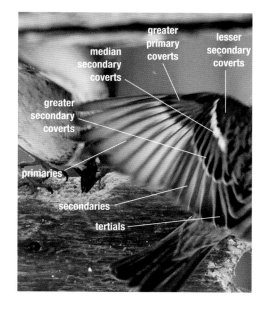

Tail

- Like the wings, the tail may not reveal all of its secrets until the bird flies—but even on the ground, a bird's tail can flash a lot of detail at eager observers.

- Is the tail a solid color, or are there stripes, spots, or markings like leaded stained glass (color outlined in black)? Does the tail have white edges, or a different color in the middle?

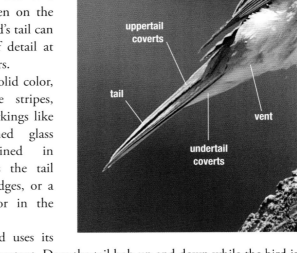

- How the bird uses its tail is also important. Does the tail bob up and down while the bird is feeding or perching? Does it fan out when the bird flies?

FIELD MARKS CHECKLIST

❏ Crown	❏ Belly
❏ Eyebrow	❏ Legs and feet
❏ Nape	❏ Mantle (back)
❏ Eye ring	❏ Wing primaries
❏ Eye color	❏ Wing secondaries
❏ Bill	❏ Wing tertials
❏ Cheek	❏ Underwings
❏ Throat	❏ Tail
❏ Breast	❏ Upper base of tail
❏ Sides	❏ Undertail

MIGRATION PATTERNS

The movement of millions of birds across the continents twice a year comes as seasons change, often beginning well before the weather has turned warmer or colder. Birds respond instinctively to factors beyond temperature—most notably, the length of days and the angle of natural light as the earth's Northern Hemisphere tilts toward the sun in spring and begins to pull back from the sun in late summer and fall.

The result is a regularly changing pageant at your feeders and in your trees and shrubs, bringing an assortment of birds that spend the warmer months in North America.

Birds habitually return to the same general breeding grounds from year to year, so you are likely to see the same birds at your feeders—many of which remember exactly where you placed the food the year before. New birds will come as well, including some species you may not have seen in previous years.

As you riffle through your field guide to find the new bird, how can you narrow down the search?

Just about every field guide provides a map of North America on the page with the photos or illustrations of the birds. This map is color coded to help you understand where the bird lives at different times of the year, where the species nests and breeds, and where occasional or rare individuals have popped up unexpectedly.

A Baltimore oriole arrives at a familiar feeder in spring

Know the birds that live in your region, and those that come to visit. Is the bird in your meadow an eastern or western meadowlark? Is that a Hutton's vireo in your tree, or a female ruby-crowned kinglet? The answer may be simpler than you think—it starts with your own location and the birds that live and breed in your region.

Each bird species lives in an established range, a section of the country or continent that is most conducive to the species' needs.

Many birds enjoy a very wide range, covering the entire United States and beyond. Most, however, are more limited in their geographic area, choosing only the regions that offer them the food, shelter, climate, and habitat they prefer for healthy living and breeding.

EAST: Jays come in many colors, but this strikingly marked blue jay rules the roost east of the Rocky Mountains.

Most North American field guides include a map for each species, with colors that indicate where the bird lives in winter, during migration, and in summer. If the bird is nonmigratory, its permanent range is indicated as well.

WEST: This Woodhouse's scrub-jay is in the same family as the blue jay of the East but lives in the deserts and scrublands of Utah, Colorado, New Mexico, and northern Arizona

The best maps also note where the species has made an occasional appearance, and where one or more individual birds may show up on a fairly regular basis (annually, for example).

It's very important to understand a bird's established range before you decide what species it is. Many birds have similar plumage but very different ranges. If you live in New York State, for example, the bird you are certain is a female lark bunting—a bird of the Great Plains grasslands—is far more likely to be a song sparrow, a bird that bears the same facial pattern, streaked sides, and large black spot on its chest. Song sparrows are widespread, especially in New York State; lark buntings are rarely seen east of Nebraska.

Checking a bird's range can help you avoid some fairly embarrassing moments. There's nothing like texting experienced birders and announcing that you've got a bananaquit in your backyard—a tropical bird that does not live in the United States—and having them explain that it's just a red-breasted nuthatch!

NORTHWEST: The Steller's jay prefers the rugged northwestern states and western Canada. You're not likely to see one of these much farther east than the northern Rocky Mountains, although their range does cover the higher elevations of southern Utah.

SOUTHWEST: The Mexican jay has a completely different range. You'll find the Mexican jay only in the southeastern corner of Arizona, with a bit of overlap into western New Mexico.

It's important to understand that not every species can be seen all over America. In fact, only a tiny fraction of the continent's nine-hundred-plus bird species live in every state and province.

Knowing which birds live in your area year-round, which ones migrate through in spring and fall, and which ones nest in your region will help you identify new species more quickly.

HABITAT

While people can adapt to just about any environment by building high-tech protective shelters and augmenting our clothing, most living things—especially birds—are adapted to specific environments. Birds need to live in the right habitat to thrive, based on the foods they eat, the kind of shelter they know how to construct, and the amount of water they require to maintain their own health.

Travel the country, and you'll see well over a dozen different kinds of ecosystems. Wetlands attract water-loving birds like long-legged waders, shorebirds, ducks, and geese. Grasslands are perfect for upland game birds and foraging blackbirds and hawks. Deserts become home to birds that make small lizards and crawling insects part of their diet, the arid open land serving as their hunting ground. Forests are home to dozens of cavity-nesting species that devour the insects they find under tree bark and in the air, making the most of the trees as sturdy, reliable shelter.

This cactus wren, one of the most common birds in the Chihuahuan and Sonoran deserts of Texas, New Mexico, and Arizona, bears a striking resemblance to a Carolina wren, a bird of the eastern United States—and that's not surprising, as they're both in the same bird family

White-breasted nuthatch lives on the abundant supply of insects found under the bark of mature trees

As you consider the birds you'd like to attract to your backyard, take into consideration the habitat that surrounds you and your home. No matter how many purple martin houses you put up in a desert environment, for example, you won't get a single one of these water-loving, mosquito-eating birds. If your home is surrounded by dense forest, you're not likely to see grassland birds like meadowlarks and savannah sparrows.

Focus on birds that are native to your habitat, and you'll have far more luck in attracting these birds to your yard.

PLUMAGE

How many different bird species visit your feeders regularly? If you're new to the birding game, you may assume that every bird that looks a little different is a species unique from the others around it. The facts may be just the opposite, however: each species may have as many as half a dozen different plumage variations, based on the gender and age of the bird, the time of year, and the speed of the change from one season's feathers to another.

Male and Female Comparisons

Everyone loves to see brightly colored birds in the backyard, so there's considerable excitement when an American goldfinch, summer tanager, or Bullock's oriole arrives at the feeder. As you watch these gorgeous birds, however, you may see that they bring their gray, brown, or olive friends that are not so striking to the eye.

In most bird species, the males have showy, well-defined markings in bold or bright colors, and some go so far as to produce an iridescent shimmer in the sun. Their ornamental tones have one specific purpose: female birds are attracted to the flashiest males. The brighter and more defined the male's colors, the more interesting he will be to a potential mate.

Producing all that color takes energy, especially for birds with spectacular tails or crests. If you've ever seen a displaying wild turkey, with his fanlike tail unfurled and his head turned bright blue, you know that some significant exertion is involved to create these effects. Most backyard birds expend many calories producing their spring coats, so they eat more—making your feeders the hot spots for male activity and female observation.

There's another reason that female birds wear more muted tones: they require the camouflage to stay out of sight while they sit on their nests for weeks at a stretch in spring and summer. In fall, when birds begin the migration southward, many of the males lose their pretty colors and turn nearly as drab as their mates. This strategy helps them hide from predators as they rest and feed during the long flight to warmer climates.

Here are four side-by-side comparisons.

Western Bluebirds

The male western bluebird's spectacular cobalt shade catches our attention every time one flies by. In contrast, the female bluebird wears a grayish coat with just a hint of a blue wash. Look at her breast as well—it does not have the bright ruddiness of her male counterpart. The same difference in coloration is true of eastern and mountain bluebirds.

Female (left) and male (right) western bluebirds

Red-Bellied Woodpeckers

At first glance, you might miss the difference between the male and female red-bellied woodpecker. The subtle difference is on the forehead. The male's forehead carries a bright red streak all the way down between the eyes to the bill. The female's red cap stops at the top of her head, leaving her with a grayish separation between her crown and her bill.

Female (left) and male (right) red-bellied woodpeckers

Northern Cardinals

These are probably the most easily recognizable mated pair in the backyard bird world. The male cardinal is a bold, vibrant red, dimming down to a deep, velvety red in winter. The female's plumage is quite striking on its own, featuring a soft golden-brown mantle and red highlights on the wings, under the tail, and along the crest. Her orange bill makes her unmistakable in a crowd of winter birds.

Female (left) and male (right) northern cardinals

Red-Winged Blackbirds

The dynamic male red-winged blackbird flashes his red and yellow epaulets, which contrast sharply with his black head, wings, and body. On first glance, you might guess the female red-winged to be a large sparrow. A dull brown bird with buff-colored stripes above its eye and along its throat, the female has dark brown streaks from the throat to the undertail coverts.

Male (left) and female (right) red-winged blackbirds

Seasonal Plumage

Once the breeding season ends, you may notice that the male birds in your backyard start to look a little less flashy and vibrant.

Many beginning birders become concerned when they spot a goldfinch that appears to be molting. The bird may still bear much of his lemon-yellow coloration, but patches of color have given way, revealing olive-brown areas that look as though the bird might be ill.

There's no need for concern, though—these birds are healthy and are going through a very normal process. Over the summer months, birds' flamboyant feathers wear away, and are replaced with a more practical layer of earth-toned colors. These provide the disguise birds need to blend in seamlessly with brush piles, leafless tree branches, and shrubbery as they make their trip south to their overwintering grounds.

Not all birds lose their fine feathers in the fall, but most male birds dull down a bit at least, especially if their spring plumage is very bright. Female birds don't need to make any kind of transformation in fall, as most are already cloaked in subdued shades throughout the spring and summer.

Male American goldfinches are bright yellow through spring and summer to attract a mate, and a duller yellow in the fall and winter for migration

The change in plumage from one season to the next serves another important purpose for birds. Fragile feathers can break off or splinter, impairing their ability to protect birds from precipitation, sun, heat, and cold. When birds go through their late summer molting process, they slough off feathers that may be damaged. The new, less ostentatious feathers help birds gain back the protection they need.

Seeing birds change their colors in late summer and early fall signals the approaching cooler seasons, often long before the leaves of deciduous trees transform to their spectacular fall tones.

Other Plumage Variations

Every once in a while, something truly strange shows up at a backyard feeder. You may recognize the bird as a house finch, red-winged blackbird, cardinal, or some other common species, but there's something up with its plumage.

Some birds have lighter or darker plumage than others in their species based on the region of the country in which they live. Red-tailed hawks, for example, have a light phase and a dark phase, and birds of each phase tend to be found in localized populations.

You may see birds with other kinds of color variations, well beyond appearing lighter or darker than normal.

This leucistic robin lacks melanin in some areas of its body

If a bird is completely white from head to tail, with pink-to-red feet, bill, and eyes, it's an albino. An albino bird has no melanin, the substance in the body that creates color in skin, hair, and feathers.

True albino birds are very rare, but birds that are leucistic—partially white from a birth defect that blocks the melanin in its body from working properly—can turn up much more frequently. Some of these birds may look like their species, but they appear pale or washed out, as if they're wearing a white film over their true colors. Others may have white patches on their bodies, with areas of normal color as well.

Not all birds with aberrant white patches are leucistic. When a bird has a narrow escape from a predator, it may lose some feathers—particularly tail feathers—in the battle. These feathers may grow back white, changing back to normal plumage next season when the bird goes through its usual molt.

SONGS

Stand in your backyard and listen. Beyond the roar of lawn mowers, the neighbor kids' laughter, and the music from contractors' radios, sweet sounds reach your ears: the chirps and whistles birds use to announce their territories, attract mates, and warn of potential dangers from predators.

You may already know which birds go with many of the songs you hear. The harsh caw of an American crow permeates neighborhoods of every size, while the nearly constant single cheep notes belong to house sparrows. Keep listening, and you may pick out an oriole's syrupy song, a blue jay's piercing

HOW RARE ARE RARITIES?

It's very exciting to be a beginning birder! Every bird is new, and every season brings a wonderful new assortment of colorful, fascinating little creatures.

There's one rite of passage every birder goes through on his or her way to birding maturity: the wrong call.

Here's how it happens. Something lands at your feeder that you don't recognize. You feverishly flip through your field guide and land on a bird that looks pretty much like what you have. But in your haste to identify the new arrival, you neglect to look at one or more of several important things: the bird's normal range, the habitat in which the bird lives, the behavior it exhibits at your feeder, or what it actually eats.

Certain that a rare bird from the opposite side of the country has arrived in your backyard, you dial up an expert birder to spread the word, or you post a photo to your birding community's Facebook page.

If you're lucky, a kindly birder with considerable experience will look at your photo and explain why it's something fairly common, or at least seasonal. Your embarrassment at the wrong call will dissipate quickly, and the next time something unusual lands in your backyard, you'll take more time identifying it.

If it happens to you, take heart—we've all had that moment, and we are better birders for it.

With that said, every year a few lucky people in the United States find themselves with a truly rare bird at a backyard feeder. If you really believe you have a rarity for your region, start by calling the most experienced birder you know to come over and check it out. If your sighting is the real deal, you may want to broadcast your find to the area birding community. Understand that birders may come from all over the region to see it, some traveling hundreds of miles for this opportunity.

Sound like fun? Then join your local birding club's Facebook page or listserv, as well as the page for your state's rare bird sightings, and post a photo of your rare bird. That's all you will need to do; the birders will spread the word.

There are no wild canaries in the United States or Canada. There are, however, several predominantly yellow birds with sweet voices like this yellow warbler. It appears completely golden from a distance, making it easy for new birders to guess mistakenly that someone's canary has escaped and needs rescuing.

cry, a house finch's astonishingly loud cascade of notes—always ending on a rising "vrrrreet"—or the multidimensional song of the wood thrush, so like music being poured from a bottle.

The northern cardinal's boisterous, clear-as-a-clarinet song often drowns out the more subtle buzzes and trills of warblers, vireos, and sparrows, but it's the most welcome song you will hear in the northern states. Usually the cardinal acts as the first herald of approaching spring. Limited to chip notes throughout the fall and winter, the cardinal will begin to sing just as the days become noticeably longer—as early as mid-February in some areas.

The common yellowthroat's "witchity-witchity-witch" song becomes one of the first that beginning birders can identify without help. The yellowthroat, a resident of wetlands and reedy areas around ponds, eagerly perches at the top of a cattail or tall stalk in spring and sings in full view. If you have a water feature in your yard, you may have the opportunity to attract these beautiful little birds and enjoy their song in early spring.

One of the best things about singing birds—and also one of the most confusing—is that many birds have more than one song. The northern mockingbird serves as a prime example of this. Mockingbirds get their name from their ability to mimic the sounds they hear. As a result, they can sing any number of different songs, imitating other birds, sirens, mobile phone ringtones, or even car alarms. If you hear a tumble of different songs all coming from one tree, shrub, or bird on a wire, it's most likely a mockingbird.

Identifying birds' individual songs and call notes is not required for backyard birding, but knowing the songs definitely will enhance your experience. Imagine waking up on a spring morning and hearing birdsong coming through your window. How much more exciting would that moment be if you could pick out the song of a yellow warbler, a white-throated sparrow, or a hermit thrush? Hearing any of these birds would tell you that the spring migration has begun and that you're about to have exciting new guests at your feeders and in your trees.

Singing western meadowlark

Birding Tip: Learning Birdsongs

- Many bird identification apps for your smartphone contain birdsongs and calls. These can help you narrow down the birds you hear, but you will need to have some idea of what bird you are hearing before looking it up.
- Merlin Bird ID, the amazing photo identification app developed by the Cornell Laboratory of Ornithology, now has a birdsong component. With the touch of a button, you can record the song you hear and have Merlin identify it for you in seconds. Other background noise can be confusing for the app (just as it is for the human ear), but it can sort out multiple birdsongs and chip notes and tell you what bird may be making them. Best of all, it's free!
- There's no substitute for learning and remembering birdsongs, however, so that you can recognize them quickly in the field. Apps including Larkwire, Chirp!, and iKnowBirdSongs all help you learn the most common and not-so-common songs.

Cedar waxwings congregate
in flocks in fruit trees

9: Most Common Backyard Birds Nationwide

Each region has its own assortment of backyard birds, but the birds in this chapter can be seen in virtually any region of the country.

Widespread because of their adaptability to many climates and conditions, these birds are quite accustomed to foraging for food in areas inhabited by human beings. They come readily to new feeders, helping you to get the word out through the bird world that there's a new, continuous supply of food to be found in your backyard.

SMALL PERCHING BIRDS

These common birds are likely to build nests in areas they share with people, and they're just as likely to scold you loudly if you come too close to their nest site. Watch for fledglings at your feeders by mid-June, or earlier in southern regions, as the parent birds teach their young to become the next generation of feeder birds in your yard.

Chickadees and goldfinches can perch or cling to your feeders, as they are just as comfortable feeding in a vertical position as they are upright. Song and chipping sparrows, two of the smaller birds in the family of sparrows known by the Latin name *Emberizidae*, may feed voraciously on seeds in the winter and then switch to insects and grubs when they become plentiful in summer.

Birding Tip: The Four Most Common Birds

Data from eBird tells us which undomesticated birds are the most common in the world, with more than a billion individuals each. Chances are good that at least one of these species will frequent your yard.

- House sparrow
- European starling
- Ring-billed gull
- Barn swallow

American goldfinch

The only bird in North America with an all-yellow body and black wings, the male goldfinch is one of our easiest birds to spot. The female has a grayish mantle and streaky sides, with a yellow wash over her breast and throat.

American goldfinch

- **Habitat:** Open fields, orchards, suburban and rural backyards.
- **Food:** Very partial to nyjer seeds; also some insects.
- **Nest:** In the fork of a horizontal tree branch. The female incubates the eggs; they usually hatch in twelve to fourteen days.

Black-capped chickadee

Each quadrant of the United States has its own chickadee species, but these cheeky little birds call the northern half of the country and most of Canada their home. The male and female are identical.

- **Habitat:** Any area with a lot of trees, including neighborhoods in any environment.
- **Food:** Sunflower and safflower seeds, peanuts, suet.
- **Nest:** Chickadees are cavity nesters that excavate their own holes. They will use nest boxes stuffed with wood shavings or sawdust, allowing them to dig their own cavity. The eggs hatch in twelve to fifteen days.

Black-capped chickadee

Chipping sparrow

Smaller than a house sparrow, with a rusty cap and clear breast, this little bird arrives in flocks and stays throughout the season. The male and female are identical; they live year-round in the southern states and migrate in spring to breed in the rest of the country and Canada.

Chipping sparrow

- **Habitat:** Suburban neighborhoods and any other buildings with lawns.
- **Food:** Sunflower and safflower seeds, mixed seed blends. These birds will perch on feeders, but they prefer the ground.
- **Nest:** Usually in pine trees or other conifers, 3 to 10 feet off the ground. The female incubates, and the male joins her to feed the nestlings. Eggs hatch in eleven to fourteen days.

Song sparrow

You'll hear this bird's jubilant song before you see one. A small sparrow with a streaky breast and a big black dot in the center of its chest, song sparrows can vary by region from dark brown to a reddish shade.

- **Habitat:** Suburban yards, in vegetation near water, farm fields.
- **Food:** Sunflower and safflower seeds, mixed seed blends. These birds will perch on feeders, but they prefer the ground.
- **Nest:** On the ground, often in a brush pile or under a bush. The female incubates, and the eggs hatch in twelve to thirteen days.

Song sparrow

Pine siskin

A winter visitor throughout the United States and a year-round resident in much of the West, siskins reveal their identity through the yellow streaks on their wings. They usually arrive in small flocks to feed on cones in your evergreens.

- **Habitat:** Open woodlands, especially coniferous forests; also well-treed suburban areas.
- **Food:** Seeds from cones, especially pine; also many other kinds of seeds. At feeders, they prefer nyjer and sunflower chips.
- **Nest:** Midway up a conifer, at the end of a branch.

Pine siskin

Purple finch

Washed with pink as if the bird has bathed in raspberry juice, the purple finch is not as common as the closely related house finch, but its voice and habits are essentially the same. The purple finch lacks the streaky sides of the house finch, but the female makes up for this with bolder, darker breast streaks and a bright white eyebrow.

- **Habitat:** Areas with many trees and shrubs.
- **Food:** Naturally occurring seeds including maple, ash, sycamore, and weeds, as well as some berries and insects.

Purple finch

- **Nest:** In a conifer with dense needles, often as much as 60 feet off the ground. The female incubates the eggs, which hatch in about thirteen days.

LARGER PERCHING BIRDS

Not all of these birds will frequent your feeders, but you will know that they are in your yard when you hear their songs. Some may stop at your platform feeder—especially if you're feeding with raisins or other small fruits—for an energy pick-me-up as they migrate to their breeding grounds.

Insects and invertebrates play a critical role in attracting these birds to your yard. Mockingbirds, red-winged blackbirds, and catbirds catch flying insects, while robins pull worms and grubs out of the ground. Blackbirds have expanded their range significantly because they are opportunistic feeders, plundering farmers' fields for corn left behind after the harvest or snacking on millet at your feeders.

If you really want catbirds and mockingbirds in your yard, plant berry bushes like holly and hawthorn. Mockingbirds also are very partial to the fruit of the multiflora rose, an exotic species that grows wild in many areas of the country. These birds, along with robins and blackbirds, will supplement their high-protein diets with berries when the weather is too cold for insect activity.

Robins' nests are the most common nests to find in your backyard or near your home. These birds prefer to nest on a shelf of some kind—a flat surface like a roof beam, a corner under your porch ceiling, at the top of a trellis, or anywhere else that offers a stable support.

They may be harder to find, but you may come across a mockingbird or catbird nest in your yard. Both of these species choose tall shrubs for nesting, and catbirds have shown a preference for bushes in suburban gardens.

Red-winged blackbirds are secretive nesters, hiding their nests in masses of last year's reeds and cattails in marshes or at the edges of ponds.

Gray catbird

Named for its mewing call that sounds eerily like a cat, this velvet-gray bird wears a showy black cap and flashes ruddy undertail coverts. You may see a lot of gray birds in your yard, but this is the only one with a black cap.

- **Habitat:** In shady, wooded areas, particularly along hedgerows and among large shrubs.
- **Food:** Catbirds eat insects and invertebrates, and they have a special taste for Japanese beetles. Berries are also on the menu.
- **Nest:** Catbirds nest deep in a bush 3–10 feet from the ground. The eggs hatch in twelve to thirteen days.

Gray catbird

Northern mockingbird

The mockingbird's rapid-fire series of disparate calls often confuses new birders; this bird can have as many as fifty different melodies in its repertoire. An all-gray bird with a long tail that points upward when it perches, the mockingbird flashes large white wing and tail patches when it flies, making it particularly easy to identify.

Northern mockingbird

- **Habitat:** Suburban areas with lots of trees and shrubs, as well as city parks.
- **Food:** Mockingbirds eat insects and love fruit, often defending a berry-laden tree from all comers for hours at a time.
- **Nest:** Look in trees and shrubs, or even in thick masses of vines between 3 and 10 feet from the ground. The eggs hatch in twelve to thirteen days.

American robin

The harbinger of spring across the northern states, the robin can be found in every state and is one of America's most widely recognized birds. You'll see them scattered across mowed lawns, cocking their heads and listening for earthworms moving just below the surface.

- **Habitat:** Cities and suburbs, parks and wooded areas.
- **Food:** Invertebrates are the favorite, but robins eat berries in winter. They may come to mealworm feeders.
- **Nest:** Often on ledges or beams of buildings, or in the crotch of a tree. Eggs hatch in twelve to fourteen days.

American robin

Red-winged blackbird

A year-round resident in every state except in the Northeast, to which it migrates in spring, this bird's flashy red and yellow epaulets make it a perennial favorite. Its "onk-or-REEE" call signals the beginning of warmer weather.

Male red-winged blackbird

- **Habitat:** Any area with water and brushy or tall grasses and reeds.
- **Food:** Seeds and invertebrates; the red-wing readily comes to feeders until grubs and bugs are available.
- **Nest:** Low in bunches of reeds, sedge, grasses, or other tall vegetation, often in colonies. The eggs hatch in ten to twelve days.

TREE-CLINGING BIRDS

Birds that travel up and down the sides of trees remain a novelty even after you've seen thousands of them. The fact that these birds are comfortable hanging by their feet from the underside of a branch makes them a marvel as well as a curiosity.

The prerequisite for attracting these birds is a stand of trees, particularly aspen or poplars, that become hollow as they decay from the inside. Nuthatches prefer dead trees, either with natural cavities of their own or with holes previously excavated by woodpeckers.

If you see a lot of woodpecker activity in your area and you can't spot the nesting cavity, try looking at the undersides of the largest tree branches. Downy woodpeckers often excavate a hole in this position, shielding the inside from spring rain while hiding the opening from predators.

Generally, our most common woodpeckers do not use nest boxes except to roost in winter. White-breasted nuthatches may choose a nest box, presumably if no suitable excavated cavity can be found.

One of the tricky things about attracting woodpeckers to your yard is their propensity for drumming a rhythm on buildings and wooden structures. Drumming is a territorial behavior, letting all the other woodpeckers in the vicinity know that this individual claims this area as his breeding ground. The birds often choose their drumming sites based on how loud their pounding sounds—so you may hear persistent tap-tap-tapping on your metal storm drain or chimney cap. In the worst cases, the bird can actually drill holes in your wood siding.

Brown creeper

These little birds' plumage makes them tough to spot on tree trunks, so watch for their rapid upward movement as they search for bugs under the bark—and then fly all the way to the bottom of the trunk to start their upward journey over from the beginning.

- **Habitat:** Densely wooded areas with a mix of conifers and leafy trees.
- **Food:** Insects and spiders; in winter, they may come to suet and seed feeders.
- **Nest:** Behind the bark of a tree, wedged between the bark and the trunk.

Brown creeper

Downy woodpecker

America's smallest woodpecker, the downy's squeaky call often announces its approach—but it's the white stripe down the center of its back that makes it easy to identify. The male sports a bright red patch on the back of his head, while the female is virtually identical except for the lack of a red patch.

- **Habitat:** Wooded areas, neighborhoods with trees, riparian areas.
- **Food:** Insects found under the bark of trees, nuts and suet from feeders.
- **Nest:** In a cavity it excavates in a tree or stump, or in a fence post or other tall wooden pole. Male and female share the incubation; birds hatch in twelve days.

Male downy woodpecker

Hairy woodpecker

Nearly identical to the downy wood-pecker, but larger and with a bill twice as long, the hairy woodpecker prefers mature woods for foraging and nesting. These woodpeckers occupy a territory for life, so you will see the same bird in every season.

- **Habitat:** Wooded areas, neighborhoods with mature trees.
- **Food:** Insects found in live trees, sunflower seeds, peanut butter, and raw suet.
- **Nest:** In a cavity it excavates in a live or dead tree or stump. Male and female share the incubation; birds hatch in twelve days.

Male hairy woodpecker

Northern flicker

With its spotted breast, striped wings, and gray head—adorned with a red spot in males—flickers confuse many beginning birders. Look for the white rump as it flies.

- **Habitat:** Open areas, including suburban lawns. You'll find flickers in woodland areas and parks as well.
- **Food:** Ants and beetles are favorites; flickers dig in the ground for them.
- **Nest:** In tree cavities that they excavate, sometimes returning to the cavity they used the year before. Eggs incubate for eleven to thirteen days.

Northern flicker

Red-breasted nuthatch

With its bright white eyebrow and sharp little bill, this tiny bird quickly catches your eye when it lands on your suet. It's most often seen in winter throughout most of the country, and year-round in the coldest states and in mountainous areas.

Red-breasted nuthatch

- **Habitat:** Mixed woods, including evergreens and leafy trees.
- **Food:** Sunflower seed, suet, insects, and peanuts.
- **Nest:** In a dead tree cavity; the birds smear the entrance with wood resin (pitch) to keep out insects and other predators. Birds hatch in twelve days.

White-breasted nuthatch

You'll see this bird moving down the trunk of a tree upside down and head first. Larger than the red-breasted nuthatch, this bird's bright white head and dapper black cap make it easy to spot against tree bark.

- **Habitat:** Anywhere with mature trees.
- **Food:** Sunflower seed, suet, peanuts, insects.
- **Nest:** This nuthatch will take advantage of an existing cavity, so you may find them in your nest box. Eggs hatch in twelve days.

White-breasted nuthatch

GROUND-FEEDING BIRDS

Many birds decline to perch on a feeder, choosing instead to keep both feet firmly underneath their bodies while they search for seeds or bugs on the ground or on a platform feeder.

Doves, cowbirds, and sparrows also will perch on a utility wire or clothesline while they survey the availability of food on the ground. Looking at birds on a wire is a great way to learn to distinguish birds by shape, as they become silhouetted against the bright sky.

In the northern states, the arrival of juncos on snow-covered lawns is a herald of winter's end, while the white-crowned sparrow migration signals the beginning of the spring season. Mourning doves remain resident across the country throughout the year except in the northern Great Plains states, to which they return in spring.

Backyard birders share mixed feelings about the arrival of brown-headed cowbirds. These birds do not build nests of their own but lay eggs in the nests of other birds, often rolling the other birds' eggs out of the nest to insert their own. Yellow warblers and song sparrows bear the brunt of these parasitic breeders—in many cases, birders discover multiple cowbird eggs in the nests of these much smaller birds. Some American robins and gray catbirds now recognize the dark, heavily speckled cowbird eggs as different from their own and throw them out of their nests. Most birds, however, do their best to incubate the eggs and raise the young, even though the cowbird eggs and chicks are often several times the size of the birds' own. The result is devastating: the smaller nestlings perish while the young cowbird dominates, devouring all the food the parent birds provide.

The Migratory Bird Treaty Act of 1936 protects cowbirds, so it's against the law to remove cowbird eggs from other birds' nests.

American crow

Big, loud, and clearly smarter than average, these all-black birds are highly adaptable to their surroundings, making them regular visitors to neighborhoods. They feed readily on the leavings of humans, making them common in parks, on beaches, near landfills, and around restaurants.

American crow

- **Habitat:** Wherever there are trees and food, frequently the wooded edges of fields, parks, and neighborhoods.
- **Food:** Seeds, nuts, berries, mice and other tiny rodents, insects, small fish, shellfish, carrion, and bird eggs and nestlings, as well as human food found in trash.
- **Nest:** High in trees, usually evergreens.

Mourning dove

With their gray-brown plumage and a series of dark gray spots on their wing coverts, mourning doves come in pairs or small flocks, frequenting the same feeders for months on end. Listen for the somber cooing that gives them their name—and also for the whistling sound their wings make as they take flight.

Mourning dove

- **Habitat:** Open lawns with sheltering woods or shrubs close by.
- **Food:** Many kinds of seed.
- **Nest:** A tangle of loose twigs mashed flat, well above the ground in trees. Both male and female birds incubate the eggs, which hatch in thirteen to fourteen days.

White-crowned sparrow

Bright black-and-white head stripes make these little birds stand out in a flock of ground-feeding sparrows. Note the long tail and clear, unmarked breast. First-year sparrows have buff-colored stripes instead of white.

White-crowned sparrow

- **Habitat:** Forest and habitat edges with brushy shrubs; they forage at the boundaries of meadows and under feeders.
- **Food:** Seeds and insects they find by scratching on the ground.
- **Nest:** Cup-shaped nests are built in shrubs, from 1½ to 10 feet from the ground. Incubation is ten to fourteen days.

White-throated sparrow

The slow, plaintive, "Oh Sam Peabody-Peabody-Peabody" call announces this sparrow's arrival. Watch for a bird with a black-and-white striped head, bright yellow lores (at the base of the bill), and a white throat.

White-throated sparrow

- **Habitat:** Normally these birds prefer forests, where they rustle through leaves on the ground for food. In migration, they drop into backyards and feed along field and forest edges.
- **Food:** Natural seeds and fruits, supplemented with black oil sunflower seeds from feeders.
- **Nest:** On the ground in an existing depression, surrounded by dense vegetation. Incubation lasts twelve to fourteen days.

Fox sparrow

One of the largest sparrows, this ground forager gets its name from its fox-red plumage (which may be browner in western birds). It migrates through the Northeast and Midwest, breeding in the northwestern states and in Canada; in winter, fox sparrows congregate in the mid-Atlantic and southeastern states and along the Mexican border.

Fox sparrow

- **Habitat:** Some prefer underbrush in wooded areas, while others choose thickets of leafy shrubs and fruit-bearing trees. Still others migrate to chaparral, especially in Southern California.
- **Food:** Insects, invertebrates, fruit, plant buds, seeds. Look for them on the ground under feeders in winter.
- **Nest:** In underbrush on the ground, or low in shrubs and trees.

Brown-headed cowbird

The male's shiny, iridescent blue-black body creates a distinctive contrast with the dull brown head. The female is entirely slate gray with some subtle wing markings.

Brown-headed cowbird

- **Habitat:** Stands of trees, open areas on the edges of forests.
- **Food:** Seeds and insects found on the ground; cowbirds will come in flocks to graze through a lawn.
- **Nest:** Cowbirds do not build nests. As parasitic breeders, they lay their eggs in other birds' nests and leave the young for the other species to raise.

Dark-eyed junco

With plumage variations by region, this little dark bird is the most reported feeder bird in America, according to Project FeederWatch. Eastern "slate-colored" birds (top) are dark gray with pink bills and white underbelly. Western "Oregon juncos" (bottom) have gray or black heads, reddish flanks, and white underparts, while other variants in the Southwest and Rocky Mountains have lighter or darker heads and brighter white bellies.

Dark-eyed junco

Dark-eyed junco, "Oregon" race

- **Habitat:** Open woods with clearings or areas of bare ground.
- **Food:** Seeds and insects found on the ground; these birds are frequent feeder visitors in winter.
- **Nest:** Often on the ground, hidden by grasses, weeds, and low shrub branches. Eggs hatch in twelve to thirteen days.

Wild turkey

There's no chance that you'll mistake this bird for anything else. Females are fairly uniformly brown with white-tipped feathers, while males feature extraordinary blue heads and red wattles when displaying.

Wild turkey

- **Habitat:** Normally open fields; more recently, turkeys wander into backyards in rural, suburban, and even urban areas.
- **Food:** Turkeys are omnivores, eating nuts, fruits, seeds, new spring buds, and the occasional amphibian.
- **Nest:** On the ground, usually in an existing depression. It may take as long as twenty-six to twenty-eight days to incubate the eggs.

INTRODUCED SPECIES

When house sparrows descend on your feeders and clear out several pounds of sunflower seeds in the space of a few hours, blame some misguided individuals in the mid-nineteenth century for their lack of foresight in bringing these birds to America.

In 1852, the commissioners of New York City's Central Park released fifty pairs of house sparrows they had imported from England. These birds were meant to help eradicate a variety of insect pests and met with enough success that organizations in other states began importing them as well. The birds brought insects to their nestlings, but generally ate seeds—and they began to thrive on natural seed sources. Now this "English" sparrow has become the most abundant bird in North America.

The same goes for European starlings, birds that did not exist on the North American continent until 1890, when Eugene Schieffelin, a Shakespeare enthusiast, released eighty to one hundred birds in Central Park. Reportedly, Schieffelin planned to introduce into the United States every bird species mentioned in the Bard's plays and sonnets. Perhaps we can be thankful that his attempts to introduce skylarks, nightingales, chaffinches, and bullfinches were unsuccessful, as our feeders might be loaded with these species at the expense of our bluebirds, warblers, and other songbirds. As it happens, more than two hundred million starlings now crowd onto our utility wires and cover our open fields and backyards.

The house finch's story seems far less galling in comparison. These birds are native to America's western states and were brought to the eastern states in captivity, to be sold as pets on Long Island. When the federal government enacted migratory bird protections in the 1930s, a shop owner released perhaps thirty pairs of house finches into the wild—and they bred successfully, creating the eastern population we enjoy today.

Rock pigeons—the soot-covered city birds we all know so well—came here with European farmers in the 1600s as domestic birds. Wild rock pigeons live in the cliffs of the Himalayas and other Asian mountain ranges, so it's no surprise that our own pigeons choose tall buildings and window ledges as their homes in the United States.

House sparrow

Familiar because of their ability to find new feeders before any other birds do, house sparrows dominate the cities and suburbs. The male's black bib and gray and rufous cap differentiate him from the more drably marked female.

- **Habitat:** Cities, suburbs, and anywhere where people congregate.
- **Food:** Seeds and suet from feeders; table scraps and crumbs left by humans.
- **Nest:** In a store sign, on a window ledge or beam, inside an open pipe, or in any other manmade structure.

House sparrow

House finch

With its bright red (or sometimes orange) face and streaky sides, the male house finch brings welcome color to a winter feeder. The female's streaky breast and sides make her easy to spot. Finches usually forage in pairs.

House finch

- **Habitat:** Woods and other areas with lots of foliage, suburban yards and parks.
- **Food:** Seeds and suet from feeders; seeds found in the wild.
- **Nest:** Nest boxes, tree cavities, in small sheltered places near human structures (inside an outdoor light fixture, in a hanging planter).

European starling

Numerous and widespread, starlings dominate suburban roadsides and open fields, foraging in large, tight flocks that seem to move in perfect synchronization. Thousands may appear in one place on utility and guide wires.

European starling

- **Habitat:** Cities, suburbs, and anywhere people congregate.
- **Food:** Seeds and suet from feeders; insects, grubs, and natural seeds on the ground; also berries and other fruit.
- **Nest:** Nest boxes; in small holes in houses, barns, and other outbuildings; or in pre-excavated holes in trees.

Rock pigeon

The bird with the iridescent throat and nape, gray wings and back is the original domestic pigeon; the other shades we see in city parks are the result of interbreeding with many other pigeon species.

Rock pigeon

- **Habitat:** Cities, suburbs, and anywhere people congregate.
- **Food:** "Feed the birds, tuppence a bag . . ." or bring your own seed or breadcrumbs, and pigeons will crowd around you in the middle of an intersection. These birds live entirely on what they scavenge from humans.
- **Nest:** Nest boxes; in small holes in houses, barns, and other outbuildings; or in pre-excavated holes in trees.

Eurasian collared-dove

This transplant from Europe came to North America by way of the Bahamas and has expanded its range throughout the continent except for the northeastern states (though some individuals are found as far northeast as New York). The black stripe on the back of the neck and the lack of spots on its wings differentiate this bird from the more common mourning dove.

Eurasian collared-dove

- **Habitat:** Towns and cities, as well as open farms and fields.
- **Food:** Seed, especially millet and sunflower. This dove relies heavily on feeders.
- **Nest:** On buildings or in trees, at least 10 feet off the ground.

Many birds that do not visit feeders still will come readily to backyards, drawn by the availability of water, the opportunities for sheltered nesting, and the busy bird activity already in evidence.

For example, an open meadow may attract phoebes and kingbirds—and phoebes may stay to nest if there's an open lean-to, barn, or shed that provides a suitably shadowy, hidden environment.

Warblers, kinglets, and vireos all eat tiny insects, making a yard that attracts gnats and no-see-ums just the place for these birds to stop for breakfast. The aptly named gnatcatchers may join them, and the resulting show of tiny, colorful birds hopping rapidly from branch to branch will provide you with plenty of spring entertainment.

Shrubs and trees that produce berries will bring in another entire crop of birds, including the fruit-loving cedar and bohemian waxwings. Cedar waxwings travel in great flocks, making it easy to see when a host of them descends on your mountain ash or serviceberry trees in late summer. Their high-pitched call notes pierce the top of our audible range, but when they sing in chorus, their voices become unmistakable.

Cedar waxwing

One of the most striking birds in North America, this smoothly colored, masked bird sports a silky crest, red spots on its wings, and a yellow tail tip. Be sure to plant berry-producing shrubs and trees to draw flocks of these in winter.

Cedar waxwing

- **Habitat:** Mixed woodlands throughout the continent, including suburban yards and parks.
- **Food:** Fruit, especially from serviceberry, winterberry, juniper, strawberry, and many others.
- **Nest:** In leafy trees, usually well hidden on a horizontal branch.

Eastern or western meadowlark

If you're fortunate enough to live near an open meadow, or even if you have a large property with some acreage you allow to grow without mowing, you may attract meadowlarks to your extended backyard. The eastern and western species are virtually identical except for some additional white or yellow facial color, but they can be distinguished along the overlapping edge of their regions by their markedly different songs.

Eastern meadowlark

Western meadowlark

- **Habitat:** Open fields, prairies and meadows with tall vegetation, and cultivated fields with tall crops.
- **Food:** Insects, worms, and natural seeds or those left from harvested crops.
- **Nest:** In a depression on the ground, lined with grasses and horsehair. Incubation lasts thirteen to fourteen days.

American tree sparrow

A winter visitor to most of the United States, this little sparrow nests in northern Canada. The black dot in the middle of a clear breast, coupled with the rusty cap, makes this an easy bird to pick out from a winter sparrow flock.

American tree sparrow

- **Habitat:** Shrubby areas, woods with brushy edges, frozen swamps in winter, tundra in summer.
- **Food:** Naturally occurring seeds; these sparrows will come to feeders as well.
- **Nest:** In a natural depression on the ground or just off the ground in a low shrub; incubation takes twelve to fifteen days.

House wren

If it seems like all your nest boxes are filling up with twigs and grass but you don't see any birds inside, you've probably got a pair of house wrens. The tiny, loquacious males build several nests to impress a mate, who chooses just one for her brood. Look for a brown or grayish bird with a striped tail held upright and a long, slightly sloping bill.

House wren

- **Habitat:** Wood edges, shrubs and brush piles, as well as dense bushes in gardens; you'll hear the house wren long before seeing one.
- **Food:** Exclusively insects, from beetles to spiders.
- **Nest:** Busy cavity nesters, building a cup nest in a wren house (with a 1⅛-inch entrance hole). Nestlings hatch in fifteen to seventeen days.

Ruby-crowned kinglet

Tiny, greenish, and moving every second, kinglets are even more frenetic than most warblers. Watch for the tiny cream-colored eye ring, the bright white wing bar, and the raised, bright red crest on the male kinglet.

Ruby-crowned kinglet

- **Habitat:** High in trees and down in low shrubs in wooded areas.
- **Food:** Gnats and other tiny insects.
- **Nest:** Usually in spruce trees or other conifers with dense needles; the nest can be as much as 100 feet off the ground. Eggs hatch in about two weeks.

A northern flicker of the eastern variety shows off its yellow shafts

10: Most Common Eastern Backyard Birds

With its abundance of green areas, heavily wooded mountain ranges, high annual rainfall, and a wealth of major rivers, Great Lakes, and smaller waterways, the eastern United States attracts a distinctive and plentiful collection of birds to its residents' backyards.

SMALL PERCHING BIRDS

Some of the smallest of these eastern birds are also the most prolific, bringing many individuals into neighborhoods and delighting feeder watchers with their bright colors, easily recognizable songs, and regular patterns of behavior.

Each of the birds pictured here has its equals in the western United States. The East's tufted titmouse is the more colorful cousin of the bridled, juniper, and oak titmice of the West, while the Carolina chickadee is closely related to the nationwide black-capped chickadee and the chestnut-backed chickadee of the West Coast. The purple finch is often confused for the house finch, and vice versa, while the Carolina wren, one of the East's most prodigious songsters, is related to the rock, cactus, canyon, and Bewick's wrens of the western states.

If you're already feeding birds, you may have noticed the peculiar feeding habits of the tufted titmouse and black-capped and Carolina chickadees. Each of these birds will take a single seed from a feeder and fly off with it, landing on a branch and grasping the seed with its feet while pecking at it furiously. They eat the seed and instantly return to the feeder to start the process again.

Carolina chickadee

Barely distinguishable from its nationwide counterpart, this southeastern specialty is a little less brightly marked than the black-capped and has a slightly shorter tail.

- **Habitat:** Wooded areas, parks, trees near water, and yards with seed feeders.
- **Food:** Insects found in tree bark, switching to seeds found at feeders in winter.
- **Nest:** Carolina chickadees excavate their own cavities in trees and fence posts. They readily use nest boxes as well.

Carolina chickadee

Carolina wren

This large wren announces itself loudly with its "teakettle-teakettle-teakettle" call. Watch for its quick movements, straight-up tail, and bright white eyebrow stripe.

- **Habitat:** Woods, parks, marshes, areas with lots of shrubs, and neighborhoods. This wren's range has expanded northward into the mid-Atlantic and southern New England.
- **Food:** Strictly an insectivore.
- **Nest:** A dense cup that seems to lean on its side, often found in hanging plants, flowerpots, and other small, sheltered places.

Carolina wren

Tufted titmouse

Small and sleek, this little gray-mantled bird displays rosy flanks, a black eye and forehead, and a white chest and face.

Tufted titmouse

- **Habitat:** Wooded areas with broadleaf trees, including parks, orchards, and neighborhoods. Titmice prefer elevations below 2,000 feet.
- **Food:** Bugs, spiders, and snails, as well as berries, nuts, and seeds.
- **Nest:** Natural or previously excavated holes in trees, in which they build cup-shaped nests. Titmice also use nest boxes.

Field sparrow

With a song that sounds like a bouncing ping-pong ball, field sparrows are far more easily heard than seen. They love weedy meadows, fields, and Christmas tree farms, but shy away from suburbs and densely populated areas. If you have an expansive backyard or your property backs up to fields and farmland, you may find this sparrow at your feeders.

- **Habitat:** Former farm fields with brushy overgrowth, pastures, fields of small trees, orchards.
- **Food:** Insects in spring and summer, small seeds from various grasses in winter.
- **Nest:** At ground level in a shrub or in a mound of grass. Nestlings emerge in ten to seventeen days.

Field sparrow

Pine warbler

Most warblers feed on insects and larvae, but pine warblers eat seeds as well. These little yellow birds live year-round in the southeastern states and migrate northward in early spring, breeding from Tennessee to Maine.

- **Habitat:** Pine trees of just about every species.
- **Food:** Caterpillars, insects, spiders, fruit, and pine seeds; also peanuts, sunflower, millet, and suet from feeders.
- **Nest:** High in pine trees, usually completely obscured by needles.

Pine warbler

LARGER PERCHING BIRDS

When we place bird feeders in our backyards, what are we hoping to attract? House sparrows and grackles may be the first visitors, but it's the arrival of gorgeously adorned cardinals, jays, grosbeaks, and orioles that send us scrambling for binoculars to get a closer look.

The nation's eastern half has its fair share of colorful beauties, some of them so abundant that we forget how striking they are. The extraordinary shading of a blue jay's wing and tail feathers, the rose-breasted grosbeak's dazzling magenta chest, and the flame-colored brilliance of a male northern cardinal or Baltimore oriole in the sun—all of these are easy to take for granted when they arrive at our feeders on a daily basis. Entertain a visiting bird enthusiast from the other side of the country, however, and we suddenly remember that these birds can be some of the most exciting in North America.

While cardinals remain year-round residents throughout much of the eastern states, blue jays, grosbeaks, and orioles migrate south in the fall, generally bypassing the southern states and continuing to South America. Plentiful food sources—especially feeders—in the Northeast will keep some jays in place throughout the winter, but a day comes in early spring when northern woods fill with the high, harsh calls of returning jays—often by the hundred—to signal the beginning of the spring migration season. Grosbeaks and orioles follow weeks later, with the first arriving in the northern states in late April, and establishing their nesting territories by mid-May.

If you're feeding orioles with jelly and orange halves, put your feeders out in mid-April for the southeastern region, by late April in the mid-Atlantic states, and by the first week of May in the North and Northeast. You'll find that orioles will come back to yards where they have fed on jelly or fruit before, and they'll go right back to the spot where you had your feeder the previous year. An area with a large number of fruit trees and shrubs may attract orchard orioles, the more rust-colored relative of the East's Baltimore oriole. Orchard orioles often share jelly feeders with the brighter Baltimores, taking turns at the feeder when the others have flown off.

If your home is fairly near a body of water like a pond or lake, you may see flocks of swallows darting through the sky at night, devouring the mosquitoes (and we're so glad they do!). Purple martins may join the swallow flight, as these birds establish their colonies near water and feed on the same insects their swallow cousins require.

Northern cardinal

The only all-red bird in the eastern states, the cardinal's bright color, tall crest, and black face are unmistakable. The female's soft brown mantle, red-edged wings and tail, and bright orange bill make her equally easy to identify.

- **Habitat:** Woods, dense shrubs, tall trees, thickets, and other areas that offer concentrated cover and high perches.
- **Food:** Sunflower and other seeds, berries, fruit on trees, and occasional insects.

Male northern cardinal

- **Nest:** An elaborate cup with several layers of material, usually in the middle of a dense shrub. Incubation takes eleven to thirteen days.

Blue jay

The most prevalent jay east of the Mississippi River, this bold, aggressive bird can dominate a feeder. Nonetheless, its intricate color patterns, sharp crest, and bold facial markings make it a backyard favorite. Listen for the jay's gurgling alternate call, one that confuses many a beginning birder.

Blue jay

- **Habitat:** Forests, particularly around the edges.
- **Food:** Jays are particularly fond of acorns. They forage for seeds, nuts, and insects from trees and come to feeders for sunflower seeds. They are also known to eat eggs and nestlings from smaller birds' nests.
- **Nest:** A mass of entwined twigs in the crotch or branches of a tall tree. It takes seventeen to eighteen days for the eggs to hatch.

Rose-breasted grosbeak

Easy to spot with its vivid magenta breast, white front, black head, and startlingly large gray-white bill (the "gross beak"), the grosbeak arrives in the states in late April to early May. You may not recognize his mate, a streaky brown-and-white bird too large to be a finch.

Rose-breasted grosbeak

- **Habitat:** Forests of mixed deciduous and coniferous trees, young woods and parks, on the edges of moist areas, and in suburbs with mature trees.
- **Food:** Seeds and fruit at feeders, as well as insects.
- **Nest:** In a leafy tree or shrub with dense foliage. The nests tend to be loosely constructed—you may see the eggs right through the bottom. Incubation takes twelve to fourteen days.

Baltimore oriole

What could be easier to see than a bright orange bird with black head and wings? This stunning creature announces itself with a song that crosses the robin's warble with a cardinal's clear notes. The female's head is more shaded than solid black, and she wears a less vibrant shade of orange.

Baltimore oriole

- **Habitat:** Open areas with clusters of leafy trees, neighborhoods with mature trees, and woodland edges.
- **Food:** Orange halves, nectar, and grape jelly at your feeders, as well as insects, caterpillars, and fruit on trees.
- **Nest:** Famously sack shaped, carefully fastened to a supportive angle in a tree branch. Eggs hatch in eleven to fourteen days.

Orchard oriole

More of a burnt orange shade than its brighter counterparts, the orchard oriole is otherwise marked very much like a Baltimore oriole—but it's at least an inch shorter in length. Females are yellow with gray wings.

- **Habitat:** In woods near streambeds, and near open fields and parks.
- **Food:** Insects and spiders provide protein, while nectar and jelly from feeders give the bird its energy.
- **Nest:** A suspended cup much like the Baltimore's, but not as long or deep. Incubation lasts about twelve to fourteen days.

Orchard oriole

Purple martin

The largest member of the swallow family, this distinctly purple bird has a heavier chest, larger head, and longer body than most swallows. Females have grayish underparts and appear more blue than purple.

Purple martin

- **Habitat:** Along the edges of large bodies of water, usually seen in flight.
- **Food:** Martins fly over water to catch insects in midair.
- **Nest:** Famous for their colony nesting behavior, martins nest almost exclusively in multi-hole houses provided by humans. The house must be placed near water. Incubation takes fifteen to seventeen days.

Brown thrasher

Singing a similar song to the northern mockingbird but in couplets instead of elongated phrases, the East's only thrasher visits platform feeders and the ground beneath them for stray seeds. Its yellow eyes, rust-colored mantle, and streaked breast and sides make it surprisingly easy to spot.

- **Habitat:** The edges of deciduous woods, as well as in hedgerows and open areas overgrown with new shrubs and young trees.
- **Food:** Insects, grubs, larvae, fruit on bushes and trees, nuts, seeds.
- **Nest:** Low in a shrub with thorns; occasionally on the ground in a well-concealed spot under a shrub. Eggs hatch in about fourteen days.

Brown thrasher

GROUND-FEEDING BIRDS

While some birds battle for a spot on a perch, others prefer to forage on the ground for whatever may drop from the feeders above. These birds may find their way to platform feeders, especially if they are placed low to the ground, but they are just as content to pick through what falls from the tubes and hoppers overhead.

You may find sparrows of several varieties at different times of the year, each choosing solid earth instead of waging war with the domineering house sparrows for perches. White-throated sparrows often join the more ubiquitous white-crowned sparrows in mixed flocks under feeders, sometimes combined with Lincoln's or fox sparrows in early spring.

Common grackles mix with starling flocks under feeders, or use their larger size to intimidate others into giving up their perches. You may see grackles on your suet feeder or foraging on the ground for grasshoppers and caterpillars. If you have a large water feature, look for grackles there as well—they like a frog, salamander, or fish as a more substantial meal.

The startlingly all-blue bird making its way through your grass is an indigo bunting, arguably one of the most beautiful birds in North America. Smaller than a bluebird and more uniformly cobalt, this bunting visits your yard to dig for insects or devour strewn seed. You may also spot this bird in your berry bushes in late summer and early fall.

The bright blue bird will certainly catch your attention, but nothing makes a suburban backyard birder sit up straight and take notice like a visit from a wild turkey. Once a bird of open meadows and forest edges, the turkey has expanded its range as its natural habitat disappears under the bulldozers of eager developers. Today you may find turkeys bringing their newly hatched poults to your yard for mouthfuls of seed (and corn, if you choose to supply it).

Indigo bunting

Usually found in open fields, this brilliant bunting may appear in yards in rural or sparsely developed areas. Its small, light-colored bill and solid coloring make it easy to identify. Look for the drab brown female bird nearby.

Male indigo bunting

- **Habitat:** Fields and farmland with little human activity, hedgerows, and brushy roadsides.
- **Food:** Almost exclusively insects, with berries and seed when the bugs are scarce.
- **Nest:** Close to the ground in a shrub or thick, leafy plant. Incubation takes twelve to thirteen days.

Common grackle

Glossy purple-black with an iridescent blue head, the common is the smallest North American grackle. It's easy to spot this bird in flight, with its rudder-shaped tail creating a distinctive silhouette.

Common grackle

- **Habitat:** Left to their own devices, grackles prefer open grassland, meadows, and marshes. Highly adaptable to human development, these birds now thrive in city and suburban neighborhoods.
- **Food:** Grackles are notorious for stealing corn and other grains from farmers' fields. They do well with sunflower seed and berries from your shrubs, but they will forage through your trash given the opportunity.
- **Nest:** High up in a pine or other conifer, often with easy access to water and open land for foraging. Eggs hatch in eleven to fifteen days.

Eastern towhee

This brightly colored sparrow dodges human eyes by skulking on the ground, making its way through the brushy understory in search of food. Its "drink your tea-tea-tea-tea-tea" song alerts you to its hiding place, but despite its rusty sides and bright white belly, it rarely comes out to give you a good look.

Eastern towhee

- **Habitat:** Underbrush, usually in fields with forested edges or beneath hedgerows.
- **Food:** Fruit, insects, seeds of open fields, flower buds, and sunflower or other seeds fallen from feeders, if the feeders are close to a brushy area.
- **Nest:** On the ground in a pile of last year's leaves, or very low in a shrub.

TREE-CLINGING BIRDS

If your backyard suddenly erupts in a series of cackles that sound like laughter, you'll know that the woodpeckers have arrived in force.

Lucky you! Loaded with personality and strikingly colored plumage, these birds can be a delight to watch. Four of the most common eastern species depend on the suet offered by backyard birders in winter, making your feeder a regular stop on the daily food-finding circuit.

Perhaps the most baffling bird to new birders, the northern flicker almost defies description with so many different patterns and colors on a single bird. The American Ornithologists' Union chose to combine the eastern yellow-shafted flicker and its western counterpart, the red-shafted flicker, into one species many years ago, but many birders still think of them as two separate entities, making a sighting just that much more interesting. When the bird takes flight, look for the feathers' yellow shafts on the underside of its wings.

Larger than any other living woodpecker, the pileated (a fancy word for crested) woodpecker appears almost prehistoric when it lands on the raw suet you've spread on a tree's bark. This is the bird that served as the model for the cartoon *Woody Woodpecker*, and its call certainly harkens back to that character's staccato laughter. Watch for this bird toward sunset if you live near a forest or if you have large trees in your yard.

New birders often mistakenly call the red-bellied woodpecker "red-headed," as the bright red stripe from the nape of its neck to its forehead seems like a red head. Once you've seen an actual red-headed woodpecker, however, you'll never make the error again. The all-red head, well-defined blue-black back, and bright white wing patches quickly dismiss any thoughts of the red-bellied woodpecker's simple stripe.

Red-bellied woodpecker

It's a bit of a mystery to new birders how this bird got its name, as its "red" belly is barely pinkish. Its smooth tan breast and face make it unique in the eastern states.

Red-bellied woodpecker

- **Habitat:** Wooded areas, including neighborhoods with mature trees.
- **Food:** Insects are first on the menu, with nuts, pinecones, and fruit all tied for second. Seeds and suet supplement the bird's winter diet.
- **Nest:** In tree cavities that they excavate, building the nest on the wood chips that remain in the hole. Eggs incubate for twelve days.

Pileated woodpecker

Big and bold, this woodpecker's arrival feels like a special event. Watch for the all-dark body, the white underside of the wings, and a well-defined red crest on both the male and the female.

Pileated woodpecker

- **Habitat:** Wooded areas with large, mature trees.
- **Food:** Partial to carpenter ants and other bugs that bore into wood. You may attract this bird with raw suet.
- **Nest:** Pileated woodpeckers excavate large holes in living trees to find food, and do the same for nesting. Eggs hatch in about eighteen days.

Red-headed woodpecker

The all-red head and white chest make this bird easy to identify. You may discover a cache of insects or seeds stashed behind tree bark, stored by this woodpecker for later use.

Red-headed woodpecker

- **Habitat:** Areas with deciduous trees, whether an orchard, a stand of trees in an open field, or dead trees in a marsh.
- **Food:** This bird eats everything: seeds, nuts, insects, berries, other birds' eggs, and small rodents.
- **Nest:** In a hole in a dead tree, sometimes used repeatedly for a whole season. Eggs hatch in about fourteen days.

Yellow-bellied sapsucker

Sapsuckers find food by using their bills to drill horizontal rows of holes in a tree trunk, quickly devouring the sap that runs out—and the insects that come with it. While they rarely come to feeders except for the occasional suet snack in winter, they may linger on a tree in your yard for some time.

Yellow-bellied sapsucker

- **Habitat:** Areas with many trees, especially dense forests.
- **Food:** Sap from trees with high sugar content, ants, spiders, fruit.
- **Nest:** In a tree cavity with an opening about 1½ inches wide.

OPEN-LAND BIRDS

If you've just moved into a newly built house and your landscaping consists of a mowed lawn and a few saplings, you may have an exciting birding opportunity ahead of you.

Some birds prefer wide-open spaces instead of trees, using grasslands and fields as easy places to catch flying insects. Kingbirds, phoebes, and some of the many birds in the flycatcher family establish residence on the edges of new suburbs, especially if the developer has included natural wetland areas in the neighborhood's overall design.

Northern bobwhite—the only eastern member of the quail family—chooses open fields with tall grasses, where it can be heard but not seen. Remarkably, these secretive birds can adapt to humans in their midst, suddenly putting in an appearance under a feeder and supplementing their plant-based diet with seeds.

Eastern bluebirds, the species most desired by backyard birders, require open fields that provide a long, wide view of the area around their nest box. The spaciousness makes foraging for food an easier task, while discouraging predators from approaching the nest box. It's highly unlikely that bluebirds will be attracted to a nest box in your yard unless you have this kind of habitat to offer them.

If you have the right environment for bluebirds, place the nest boxes at least 100 yards apart to give each mated pair enough room to establish its own territory. Your bluebird box may attract an unwelcome guest: house sparrows. These invasive birds actually throw the young out of the nest boxes so they can build their own nests inside. The sparrows construct their nest right on top of the bluebird nest, and they often excavate a larger entrance hole as well. If house sparrows move in, it's legal to open the box and discard their nest.

Eastern phoebe

It's surprisingly easy to differentiate this bird from the rest of the flycatcher family: the phoebe is larger, with a darker head and tail, and it bobs its tail continuously. Listen for its "PHEE-bee" call.

Eastern phoebe

- **Habitat:** Open areas including the edges of fields, forests, and hedgerows.
- **Food:** Watch the phoebe catch flies in midair—these are its staple diet.
- **Nest:** Check your garage, shed, or other outbuildings for nests close to the ceiling, on a beam or shelf. Eggs incubate for about sixteen days.

Northern bobwhite

Round and rust colored, these secretive birds run from place to place. The white strip above the eye and whitish throat can help you spot this bird, but the "Bob-WHITE" call is a bigger help in finding their location.

- **Habitat:** Open tall grassland or woodlands, and marshes with tall vegetation.
- **Food:** A plant eater, the bobwhite will occasionally visit a feeder, usually returning to the same one for a season.
- **Nest:** On the ground, often with a woven hood of grasses to conceal it. Incubation takes about twenty-four days.

Northern bobwhite

Eastern kingbird

Solidly gray on top with a white cheek, chest, and underbelly, the eastern kingbird sports white tips at the end of its dark tail feathers. This bird ranges as far west as the foothills of the Rocky Mountains.

Eastern kingbird

- **Habitat:** Open fields, grass-lands, and the edges of wooded areas.
- **Food:** Insects caught in midair by fly catching.
- **Nest:** On a sturdy tree limb or in the crotch of a tree. Incubation takes twelve to thirteen days, but this kingbird raises only one brood per season, caring for the young for nearly two months.

Eastern bluebird

With its blue head, wings, and back, and its orange breast and throat, the bluebird differentiates itself from the indigo bunting or blue jay with ease. Watch for one on a fence post or overhead on a wire. Females are grayish with blue highlights.

Eastern bluebird

- **Habitat:** Open fields, pastures, farmland, and marshes. Look for them at your local golf course.
- **Food:** Crawling insects including larvae, caterpillars, and mealworms are favorites. Overwintering birds eat all kinds of berries.
- **Nest:** If no nest box is suitable, bluebirds nest in cavities in trees high off the ground. Eggs hatch in eleven to nineteen days.

Mountain bluebirds are a welcome sight in western backyards in spring and summer

11: Most Common Western Backyard Birds

The widely diverse habitats found in the West provide homes to an equally wide variety of birds—with the mountains, grasslands, desert, and seashore each producing its own finches, orioles, woodpeckers, and sparrows.

SMALL PERCHING BIRDS

Some of the most common birds find habitat throughout the western states and provinces, with individuals or flocks popping up whenever the birds can find a few deciduous trees, or just enough water for bathing and soothing thirsty throats.

Nyjer seed feeders in the western states play host to the lesser goldfinch, the black-mantled counterpart of the American goldfinch. Both finches may vie for feeder perches in the Southwest and along the California shoreline, delighting residents with their bright yellow tones and gregarious nature.

House finches abound across the continent, but only the western half is home to Cassin's finch, a very similar bird with the same magenta wash over its head and breast. If you manage to see both on the same feeder, the difference comes to light: Cassin's finch has a clearer breast with little or no streaking, and the feathers on top of its head stand up in fair imitation of a bright pink crest. The female Cassin's, in contrast, actually has a streakier breast than the female house finch—but with a much whiter base shade.

Many a new birder finds the pine siskin entirely confusing. This light brown, streaky, sparrowlike bird can be tough to recognize; look for the darkly streaked breast, the yellow wing bars, and the light yellow at the ends of its wings (the primaries).

Smaller than a bluebird but quite similarly marked, the lazuli bunting can stump a new birder. On close examination, however, the differences become clear: the lazuli bunting has strong white wing bars and a pointier head than either the eastern or western bluebird, and the rusty shade on the lazuli's breast is shorter than the bluebird's showy color.

Lesser goldfinch

The smallest of the four North American goldfinches, the lesser presents many variations in its plumage. Birds in Arizona and west have an olive-green mantle and yellowish wing bars (shown here), while Texas birds have a black back and wings and bold, white wing markings.

Lesser goldfinch

- **Habitat:** Wooded areas, riparian woods, and forested areas on the edges of deserts and mountains.
- **Food:** Goldfinches are partial to nyjer seed at feeders, as well as seeds they find naturally.
- **Nest:** Tree nesters, lesser goldfinches nest in colonies, masking their nesting sites with leaves. Incubation takes twelve to thirteen days.

Cassin's finch

Larger than either the purple or the house finch, Cassin's finch is less pervasive than the house finch it resembles. Look for the clear white belly with faint streaks or no streaking at all to be sure you have a Cassin's finch.

- **Habitat:** In the foothills or mountains, generally in coniferous forests.
- **Food:** Fruit, seeds, and berries. Cassin's finch is a regular visitor to many backyard feeders.
- **Nest:** On a horizontal branch in a conifer, usually in the mountains. Incubation lasts twelve to fourteen days.

Cassin's finch

Lazuli bunting

The deep blue head and reddish breast of this little songbird may make you think "bluebird," but the white wing bars are strictly lazuli bunting. The much drabber female is grayish with a warm, slightly rosy breast.

Lazuli bunting

- **Habitat:** Brushy fields and woods edges, particularly in the northern badlands and southwestern deserts.
- **Food:** Fruit, seeds, insects, as well as feeder seed. These buntings may gather in flocks in a backyard.
- **Nest:** Low in a shrub; incubation continues for twelve to fourteen days.

Bushtit

If this tiny bird stops moving long enough to give you a close look, you may spot its yellow-ringed pupils and dull brown cap on an otherwise grayish body. Further inland, bushtits are primarily gray with a paler breast. The good news is that they tend to move in small flocks, so you may have many chances to glimpse one in a group.

- **Habitat:** Densely packed shrubs, as their name implies.
- **Food:** Insects, spiders, caterpillars; suet during the winter.
- **Nest:** A sack-shaped nest, hung by spiderwebs from a tree branch.

Bushtit

Bewick's wren

This western wren's white eyebrow makes it distinctive when you spot one, but its long, cheery series of musical trills and whistles will alert you to its presence long before you focus your binoculars on it. You won't see it at your feeders, but a hedge filled with berry bushes may attract wrens throughout the year.

Bewick's wren

- **Habitat:** Areas with thick shrubs, low brush, chaparral, or forests of mixed conifers.
- **Food:** Larvae and eggs of insects, seeds, fruit.
- **Nest:** A cup nest atop a pile of grass and leaves, inside a cavity or on a ledge.

Chestnut-backed chickadee

This handsome chickadee with its rich brown shawl is particularly easy to find in the Pacific Northwest, but its range stretches down the Pacific coast into California. It usually forages in flocks, sometimes mixed with black-capped chickadees—so watch for the rusty shoulders and brown cap.

- **Habitat:** Densely wooded areas, especially near water; also suburban parks.
- **Food:** Primarily insects, supplemented with seeds and fruit.
- **Nest:** In a cavity in a rotting tree or stump, or in other soft wood; they also use nest boxes.

Chestnut-backed chickadee

Juniper titmouse

A year-round resident of pinyon-juniper woodlands in the lower western states, this little gray bird is one of two of the former "plain titmouse" species. If you position your feeders near shrubs and trees, you may make this titmouse a regular visitor.

Juniper titmouse

- **Habitat:** Open woodlands with substantial stands of pinyon pine and juniper, at elevations above 2,250 feet.
- **Food:** Insects, spiders, pinyon seeds, sunflower seeds, suet.
- **Nest:** In a tree cavity or a nest box, within 12 feet of the ground.

LARGER PERCHING BIRDS

If you like birds that are blue, you've chosen the right side of the continent—not only are there plenty of bluebirds and lazuli buntings, but the roster is also crowded with brilliantly sapphire jays and the solid markings of the black-billed magpie.

Woodhouse's scrub-jay dominates feeders in the southwestern states, giving way to Mexican jay in southeastern Arizona but ruling the roost to the north. In the Rocky Mountains, Steller's jay takes over, willingly coming to picnic tables in backyards and parks to scavenge for crumbs dropped by amused tourists.

The black-billed magpie, formerly known as the American magpie (renamed by the American Ornithological Society when scientists determined it was closely related to another American bird, the yellow-billed magpie), soars from one open field to the next, posing on fence posts and waving its ultralong tail to onlookers' delight. Usually found in small flocks, these dynamic birds may turn up in parking lots and on city streets as well as in backyards, making the most of what humans have left behind.

A quieter, less showy bird, the Say's phoebe follows the habits of its flycatcher family, preferring habitat near water and nesting on ledges or in the eaves of sheds and barns. Easily distinguished from kingbirds and other flycatchers by its salmon-colored underbelly, this bird frequents backyards near open prairies, fields, and desert flats.

Say's phoebe

The gray head and back, sharp crest, and long tail distinguish this bird as a phoebe, but it's the rusty belly that makes it distinctly Say's. You'll find this bird as far north as Alaska.

Say's phoebe

- **Habitat:** Any open space in the West, from sagebrush prairie to deserts. Like other phoebes, these birds like to be near buildings.
- **Food:** Insects in flight or on the ground; you'll see this bird fly catching.
- **Nest:** All phoebes nest on ledges, beams, or natural shelves. Look for nests in your shed or barn, under a bridge, or on a windowsill or other ledge. Eggs hatch in twelve to fourteen days.

Black-billed magpie

You won't miss this glorious bird if it puts in an appearance on your fence post—its large size; bold black, blue, and white patches; and long, sweeping tail make it a showstopper. Watch out, though, as magpies are known to steal eggs and nestlings from other birds' nests.

Black-billed magpie

- **Habitat:** Open grassland, meadows, fields of sagebrush, and sparse woodlands. Magpies are well adapted to human-populated areas as well.
- **Food:** True omnivores, magpies eat small animals, field grains, acorns, road kill, and other carrion.
- **Nest:** In trees, on utility poles, and in thick shrubs. Incubation takes sixteen to eighteen days.

Woodhouse's scrub-jay

Deep blue with a brownish gray patch on its back, this jay may look slightly different if you live along the Pacific coast—its white throat stripes may be bolder, and its color may be more royal than cerulean.

Woodhouse's scrub-jay

- **Habitat:** Oak and juniper woodland in brushy areas, from deserts to foothills.
- **Food:** Insects, nuts, and seeds from feeders in winter.
- **Nest:** In oak or pinyon trees, just above human head height. Incubation takes seventeen to nineteen days.

California scrub-jay

With its bright-blue head, blue breast band, and clean white throat, this jay is easy to differentiate from the equally prevalent Steller's jay in the Pacific coastal states. Telling a California from a Woodhouse's scrub-jay can be tricky, but their territories do not overlap much; the California's shade of blue is somewhat brighter than Woodhouse's, and California has a shorter, stouter bill. The much rarer pinyon jay is more uniformly light blue.

California scrub-jay. *Shutterstock #1670478616*

- **Habitat:** Oak woodlands, coastal chaparral, some pinyon woodlands.
- **Food:** Insects, fruit, some small animals, acorns, sunflower seeds, peanuts.
- **Nest:** Up to 14 feet high in a tree, or behind vines, leaves, or mistletoe in a tall shrub.

Clark's nutcracker

Using their long, sharp bills to crack open pinecones and a pouch under its tongue to carry the nuts away to store for the winter, these large gray, black, and white birds announce themselves with a harsh squawk. They live near the tree line in western subalpine forests, and are fairly easy to find in campgrounds and human-inhabited areas in the Rocky and Sierra Mountains, as well as in the North Cascades.

Clark's nutcracker

- **Habitat:** Pine forests at elevations above 3,000 feet.
- **Food:** Pine seeds and some insects, as well as peanuts and suet from feeders.
- **Nest:** At the end of conifer branches, within the territory where they have stored their pine seeds.

Varied thrush

For such a flashy bird, with its bright orange throat trimmed with a black stripe, black mask, orange wing bars, and rusty belly, varied thrush makes itself very hard to see. If you are not lucky enough to get one searching for seeds on the ground under your feeders, you'll need to stretch your neck backward to glimpse one at the very top of a tall conifer.

Varied thrush. *Shutterstock #1850735509*

- **Habitat:** Dense forests of the Pacific Northwest and California coast, especially among redwoods, Douglas fir, hemlock, and cedar.
- **Food:** Insects in spring and summer; fruit and nuts in winter.
- **Nest:** Near the trunk of a conifer, often quite out in the open.

Black-headed grosbeak

Widespread throughout the western states during breeding season, this lyrical-voiced grosbeak makes itself easy to spot with its orange body, black wings with wide white stripes, and long black tail. They come readily to feeders and linger to devour your sunflower seeds.

Black-headed grosbeak. *Shutterstock #702572560*

- **Habitat:** Forests near water, especially where there's a healthy understory of smaller plants.
- **Food:** Insects, spiders, fruit, seeds, sometimes nectar from hummingbird feeders, and monarch butterflies.
- **Nest:** In deciduous trees about 25 feet up, usually hidden from view.

Steller's jay

With its black head and crest and royal blue body, this may be the most stunning of America's jays. They're bold birds that willingly steal a bite of food out of your hand at a picnic.

- **Habitat:** Coniferous woods, often with access to parkland and areas where people congregate.
- **Food:** Whatever it finds: bugs, nuts, seeds, fruit, and food in feeders. Steller's jays will take other birds' eggs and nestlings, or food left behind by people.
- **Nest:** Usually high in a conifer, close to the trunk. Eggs hatch in sixteen days.

Steller's jay

Bullock's oriole

Bright yellowish orange with a black cap and the definitive eye-line, this oriole makes its home in wooded areas—including neighborhoods with mature trees.

- **Habitat:** Leafy woods throughout the West.
- **Food:** Caterpillars, insects, fruit, and nectar.
- **Nest:** The characteristic oriole pendulous nest, hung from a tree branch. Eggs hatch in twelve to fourteen days.

Bullock's oriole

Curve-billed thrasher

Grayish brown above and spotted below, this medium-sized thrasher's long, sloping bill and bright orange eye make it easy to identify.

- **Habitat:** Mesquite desert woods, or gardens with lots of vegetation in cities and suburbs.
- **Food:** Insects, cactus seeds, fruit and berries.
- **Nest:** In a thorny plant like a cactus or other shrub. Eggs hatch in twelve to fifteen days.

Curve-billed thrasher

GROUND-FEEDING BIRDS

When quail arrive to browse through the seeds on the ground under your feeders, their burbling voices and round bodies create a sense of occasion—and comedy. Always appearing a little bit startled, a condition perhaps aggravated by the single plume rising from their foreheads, these quick little birds arrive in groups and do a thorough job of clearing the ground of wanton seed.

Gambel's quail and California quail are the most prevalent in backyards, although homes in the Chihuahuan deserts of Texas and New Mexico will see scaled quail dashing across the bare ground. If you don't actually see quail, listen for their voices—a chorus of warbles will rise from your tall grasses or your vegetable garden as a covey of quail pass through.

Backyards in the southwestern states will see white-winged dove, in addition to the mourning doves found in every part of the country. Hooting a call that's disturbingly close to a barred owl's "who cooks for YOU-all," these doves have little fear of humans and will join you on your deck to clear up stray crumbs after your lunch.

The great-tailed grackle dominates in the lower West, while the northwestern states have no dedicated grackle species. The nation's largest grackle, the great-tailed, is every bit as aggressive as its smaller cousins in the eastern states, and equally noisy—you'll hear flocks of these in your trees well before they knock the sparrows off of your feeders.

At the other end of the spectrum, the comparatively diminutive lark sparrow provides one of the West's visual treats. Wearing a harlequin mask of brown, black, and white stripes across its head and face, this bird stands out between the chipping and white-crowned sparrows in your yard, but it can also shield itself from view in dry grasses and brush. Its larger size, clear breast, and dark center spot differentiate it easily from chipping sparrows.

Lark sparrow

A plentiful western specialty, lark sparrows usually arrive in groups and walk, rather than hop, across your lawn. Watch for the white outer tail feathers when these birds fly.

- **Habitat:** Open areas including grassland, desert scrublands, sagebrush, and on the edges of fields and parklands.
- **Food:** Insects when available, and seeds at any time of year.
- **Nest:** On the ground or low in a shrub. Eggs hatch in eleven to twelve days.

Lark sparrow

California quail

If you see one California quail, keep an eye out for the rest of the covey, as these roly-poly-looking birds live in colonies. Their burbling song often precedes a sighting. It would be easy to mistake these for Gambel's quail, their close cousin—but the two species' territories barely overlap, so location can inform your identification of the quail under your feeders.

California quail

- **Habitat:** California and northwestern deserts, as well as coastal chaparral.
- **Food:** Seeds, flowers, leaves, some nuts and berries; sunflower and other seeds in ground feeders or spread on the ground.
- **Nest:** On the ground under a tree or concealed by brushy shrubs. Eggs hatch in about twenty-two days.

Gambel's quail

Closely related to the California quail of the West Coast, this ground bird appears at feeders throughout the southwestern states. The chestnut cap and sides are strictly Gambel's; California quail have a dark brown cap and sides.

Gambel's quail

- **Habitat:** Brushy areas with dense cover, in which birds can run from one stand of shrubs to the next. Farmers' fields are a favorite.
- **Food:** Seeds and berries, and insects in a pinch.
- **Nest:** On the ground. When nestlings hatch in twenty-one to twenty-three days, they can leave the nest immediately.

Great-tailed grackle

If the blue-black head and iridescent body don't signal a great-tailed's arrival, the flag-like, triangular tail certainly does. The female grackle is a dark brown bird with a lighter brown breast; her tail is lengthy but short in comparison to the male.

- **Habitat:** Open rural and suburban areas including parks, fields, farms, and backyards.
- **Food:** Insects, caterpillars, small fish and reptiles, and plants. These grackles are known to attack other birds' nests for eggs and nestlings.
- **Nest:** In trees or shrubs, or in or on manmade structures. Eggs hatch in thirteen to fifteen days.

Great-tailed grackle

White-winged dove

Nearly as common as mourning doves in the Southwest, the white-winged dove's range is expanding steadily northward and eastward. Look for the bright white leading edge of the wing, both in flight and at rest.

- **Habitat:** Open woodlands, picnic areas, parks, and backyards.
- **Food:** Natural seeds and those provided by people.
- **Nest:** In a tree or low bush. Eggs hatch in thirteen to fifteen days.

White-winged dove

Band-tailed pigeon

A year-round resident in Southern California and a summer breeder northward into Canada, this pigeon differs from its rock pigeon cousins with its predominantly uniform gray plumage, yellow bill, and a light-colored band at the end of its tail (though this is only visible in flight). Look for the white mark at the nape of its neck as well.

Band-tailed pigeon

- **Habitat:** In the northwest, they prefer temperate rainforests; southwestern birds are found in dryer forests at high elevations.
- **Food:** Seeds, fruits, and nuts; these pigeons regularly come to feeders.
- **Nest:** In trees, often high in the treetops of the tallest conifers. Eggs hatch in two to three weeks.

Golden-crowned sparrow

A winter visitor from Washington State to Baja California, this sparrow's sweet, four-note song and bright yellow forehead patch make it fairly easy to identify. Despite their melancholy "I'm-so-tired" sound, they delight backyard birders—that is, until these little bandits help themselves to bites from their vegetable gardens.

- **Habitat:** Thickets, chaparral, backyard hedges.
- **Food:** Seeds, plant buds, insects found on the ground.
- **Nest:** On the ground, hidden behind grasses or under low-hanging shrub branches. Nesting takes place in western Canada and Alaska.

Golden-crowned sparrow

Harris's sparrow

A midwestern migrant and winter resident in the Great Plains, this showy sparrow—pictured here in winter plumage—is the largest sparrow on the continent, except for towhees. It frequents backyards in the coldest months.

- **Habitat:** Fields, roadside hedges, pastures, and backyards with shrubs.
- **Food:** Seeds from feeders, including sunflower and millet; berries, insects.
- **Nest:** On the ground under a short tree, in northwestern Canada. Harris's sparrows do not nest in the United States.

Harris's sparrow

Spotted towhee

Jet black above and brightly rusty on its flanks, the spotted towhee looks much like its eastern counterpart, but the white on its wings comes in spots instead of stripes. A master of camouflage, this towhee's movements are clear as it hops and scrapes among the leaves on the forest floor, but it can be much more difficult to get a good, solid look at its brightly colored profile.

- **Habitat:** On the ground in fields, forests, and brush, or foraging along the edge of hedges or foundation plantings in a backyard. Watch for them in mulched areas.
- **Food:** Insects and invertebrates, acorns, fruit, and seeds.
- **Nest:** Somewhere between the ground and about 12 feet up, in a tall shrub or behind a screen of grasses.

Spotted towhee

TREE-CLINGING BIRDS

If you've got big trees on your property or nearby, your chances are excellent for attracting some of the western states' and provinces' most impressive backyard birds. Add an acorn-bearing oak tree, and your prospects grow immediately brighter.

Acorn woodpeckers, so named because of their favorite food, readily come to backyards and establish colonies in stands of oaks. Not only do they eat acorns, but they store them as well, carefully putting them in holes they excavate in trees or utility poles. If there's a pole with a series of holes in or near your yard, check inside—you may find a storehouse of nuts, each in its own crevice, waiting for the woodpeckers to return.

The little black-and-white woodpecker in your tree is most likely a ladder-backed woodpecker, distinctly different from the more common downy and hairy woodpeckers in that it has no white stripe down the center of its back. A desert-loving bird, the ladder-backed generally feasts on insects, but it comes readily to suet and nuts in backyards.

Acorn woodpecker

With a facial pattern that brings circus clowns to mind, the acorn woodpecker becomes immediately visible as it clings to a tree. If you see one, there must be more, as these birds live in colonies with complex social strata.

- **Habitat:** Oak forests, usually at higher elevations; in parks with lots of oak trees.
- **Food:** In addition to acorns, these birds eat insects and fruit.
- **Nest:** An excavated tree cavity; the eggs are laid on wood chips at the bottom. Incubation lasts eleven to fourteen days.

Acorn woodpecker

Ladder-backed woodpecker

One of the smallest western woodpeckers, the ladder-backed prefers desert habitat from Texas to Southern California. The male flashes a red stripe on his head, while the adult female has no stripe.

- **Habitat:** Desert scrub and dry areas with suitable trees for nesting.
- **Food:** Generally an insect eater, the ladder-backed also visits suet feeders.
- **Nest:** In a hole in a tree or cactus, usually excavated by the bird. Eggs hatch in thirteen days.

Ladder-backed woodpecker

OPEN-LAND BIRDS

From Iowa's cornfields to Idaho's pastures, wide-open fields have their own selection of resident birds. The desert expanses from Texas to California also attract species that thrive on open spaces, feeding on insects that are easy to see against flat plains filled with bright sunlight.

Meadowlarks (see page 166) and bobolinks are fixtures in the Nebraska and Kansas grasslands, rarely venturing out of the tall grasses or cultivated fields—although meadowlarks readily perch on fence posts to fill the air with their song. Lark buntings join them, coal-black birds with white wing patches that catch the sunlight as the birds take flight. If your new suburban yard backs up to a farmer's field, you may see these birds around the edges of your property, their wings flashing as they dart here and there.

Brewer's blackbirds can be just as numerous as their red-winged counterparts. Purple-black and sleeker than grackles, these birds forage on the ground for food but often pose for extended periods on utility wires or balance on wire fences. They're eager to check out your yard for stray seeds or to hop up onto your patio table to clean up whatever crumbs you've left behind.

Ponds and streams invite yellow-headed blackbirds—these gorgeous creatures are one of a kind in the North American bird annals, with their bright yellow hoods extending down to their shoulders and breast. While they thrive on insects and seeds, it's not uncommon to see these birds clobber a slice of bread left unattended by an unwary picnicker.

If your yard provides scrubby cover in an arid landscape, or if it's a riparian oasis in the midst of a desert, watch for the vermilion flycatcher, a fiery red bird with a black mask and wings. Perched conspicuously on a dead snag or open branch, this showy bird delights visiting birders from every corner of the continent.

Yellow-headed blackbird

If you see one, you'll soon see a flock of these brilliantly colored birds. Listen for their scratchy, squeaky-door call, different enough from other blackbirds to alert you that they're part of a mixed flock.

Yellow-headed blackbird

- **Habitat:** Marshy areas and prairie wetlands, including ponds in the middle of farmers' fields.
- **Food:** Seeds from natural sources, and wetland insects.
- **Nest:** Deep in the reeds, always balanced over water. Incubation takes eleven to thirteen days.

Brewer's blackbird

One of the western states' most common birds, this blackbird's iridescent feathers shine purple, green, and blue in the sun. Females are fairly uniformly brown with a dark eye.

- **Habitat:** In colonies of up to one hundred birds, in many different kinds of habitat. Near humans, they like parks, golf courses, and large lawns.
- **Food:** Grain, seeds, and insects.
- **Nest:** Always in groups, but the location may vary—low shrubs, high in trees, or somewhere in between. Eggs hatch in eleven to seventeen days.

Brewer's blackbird

Lark bunting

Closely related to the sparrow, this bunting's markings are unique among North American birds. In fall and winter, its plumage changes to a sparrow's streaky black and brown.

Lark bunting

- **Habitat:** Grasslands and prairies of the Plains states and southern Saskatchewan and Alberta.
- **Food:** Grain, seeds, insects, and berries.
- **Nest:** On the ground, usually under a low shrub or other cover. Incubation ranges from eleven to twelve days.

Vermilion flycatcher

Stunningly red or reddish orange, this bird is the nation's most conspicuous flycatcher. Vermilions like to show off their gorgeousness by sitting at the top of a dead or open shrub. Females are gray and white with pink underparts.

- **Habitat:** Desert scrub, the edges of riparian woodlands, and plowed fields.
- **Food:** Strictly insects and spiders.
- **Nest:** In the crotch of a tree branch, anywhere from 8 to 50 feet off the ground. Incubation ranges from fourteen to fifteen days.

Vermilion flycatcher

Black-crested titmouse

12: Backyard Specialties Near the Borders

The closer you live to the US borders with Canada and Mexico, the more likely you are to have some very special birds visit your backyard gardens and feeders.

Boreal species are birds of the northern forests, where winters are long and summers go by in a few weeks. These birds have unique adaptations that allow them to thrive when snow deepens: cleverly evolved bills that can pry open seed cones in seconds and extract the goodness within, or large, heavy bills that crack a tough nut wide open. Red and white-winged crossbills can hang upside down to plunder all sides of a cone, while evening and pine grosbeaks can pulverize seeds that smaller birds have to pass up. Canada jays, as gregarious as they are elegant, horde seeds and berries throughout the summer so they can feast all winter.

On the border between the United States and Mexico, birds ignore fences, walls, and the Rio Grande to enjoy the bounty in the backyards of Texas, New Mexico, and Arizona. The stunning green jay, bright blue Mexican jay, dapper black-crested titmouse, and charismatic plain chachalaca are just a few of the fascinating species that show up at feeders. This slim birding region has its own share of woodpecker varieties as well, including the boldly patterned Arizona woodpecker and the golden-fronted and gila woodpeckers, their more subtle hues helping them blend into the desert landscape.

Gulf Coast and South Florida residents also have their share of exciting backyard birds, including a wide range of exotic species that have established small colonies in cities like Miami/Fort Lauderdale and New Orleans. The most common of these, monk parakeet and nanday parakeet, are brilliantly green birds that have no business living in North America. They have, however, demonstrated extraordinary resilience in adapting to their situation, and backyard birders are more than happy to help support this. In addition, the southeastern coast enjoys one of the most sought-after feeder birds in America: the painted bunting, a bird with plumage ready for Mardi Gras.

Boreal chickadee

A brown cap and rufous sides set this far northern bird apart from the more common black-capped species. If you live in northern Maine or along the US/Canada border, watch for it in summer as it visits feeders to collect seeds for the winter months.

Boreal chickadee

- **Habitat:** Coniferous forests in the north country.
- **Food:** Insects and their larvae, spruce seeds, feeder seeds like sunflower.
- **Nest:** In a cavity of a dead tree, close to the ground or as high as 35 feet up.

Canada jay

Friendly and fearless, this most northern of the jays readily comes to an outstretched hand if it contains peanuts or sunflower seeds. It nests and raises young in winter, bringing its young to feeders long before other birds have even started breeding.

- **Habitat:** Boreal forests with aspen, birch, cedar, and/or spruce trees.
- **Food:** Invertebrates, berries, fungi, seeds, carrion, and human scraps.
- **Nest:** In a tree, usually facing south to get as much warmth from the winter sun as possible. The nest may be low in the tree or about midway up.

Canada jay

Common redpoll

Usually these pink-and-brown birds with their red caps confine themselves to the northernmost areas, but every few years, an irruption occurs—an influx of winter finches pushing farther south in search of food. Redpolls flock to feeders as far south as Virginia, Nebraska, and Utah when the seed crops in Canada do not yield enough to support them.

Common redpoll

- **Habitat:** Open boreal woodlands (aspen, birch, cedar, spruce, and so on).
- **Food:** Seeds from birch trees, nyjer seed, and sunflower chips.
- **Nest:** In the crotch of a tree, fairly close to the ground; or on a rock ledge. Nesting takes place near and above the Arctic Circle.

Evening grosbeak

For all of its grosbeak bulkiness, this bird's bright yellow body, black-and-white wings, and thick yellow eyebrow stands out strongly against the snow when it puts in a winter appearance. These birds move south in large flocks during irruption years, when there's not enough food up north to sustain them through the winter.

- **Habitat:** Mature forests of fir, spruce, juniper, pine, pinyon, and oak.
- **Food:** Invertebrates, seeds, berries and other fruits, plant buds.
- **Nest:** In trees, usually conifers, mostly in Canada and some parts of northern Maine.

Evening grosbeak

Red crossbill

Crossbills get their name from the shape of their bill, which has evolved to give the bird access to conifer seeds even when the cones are firmly closed. The red crossbill needs conifer seeds to survive, so it will wander very long distances—sometimes across the continent—to find enough food to sustain itself and its young.

Red crossbill

- **Habitat:** Coniferous forests with plenty of cones, especially Douglas fir, pine, spruce, and hemlock.
- **Food:** Seeds from cones; insects in summer. In winters with low availability of seed cones, they will come to bird feeders.
- **Nest:** In trees in open woodlands, usually about 60 to 70 feet up.

White-winged crossbill

Easily distinguished from the red crossbill by the bright white patches on its wings, the white-winged crossbill confines itself to spruce and tamarack forests—unless it can't find food there. In winters with low cone production, these crossbills may wander as far south as Kentucky and Missouri in search of enough spruce seeds.

- **Habitat:** Spruce forests.
- **Food:** Spruce and tamarack seeds; in a pinch, they will come to bird feeders.
- **Nest:** In a spruce tree, near the trunk and concealed by needles. Nestlings emerge in fourteen to sixteen days.

White-winged crossbill

Black-crested titmouse

A South Texas specialty, this dressy titmouse's sharp black crest and peachy flanks make any sighting of one a treat. It readily comes to feeders, announcing itself loudly with a trill not unlike a chipping sparrow, or a "peer, peer" song like its eastern counterpart, the tufted titmouse.

Black-crested titmouse

- **Habitat:** Anywhere with woods, whether deciduous or coniferous.
- **Food:** Insects, larvae, seeds, acorns, berries, and other fruit.
- **Nest:** In cavities excavated by woodpeckers in years past—just as likely in fence posts or utility poles as in trees.

Cactus wren

Highly visible and always busy, cactus wrens are easy to spot in the arid region from South Texas to southeastern California. Look for them standing on top of a cactus or fence post, craning their necks and singing their rattling song almost continuously, or hopping across open ground.

Cactus wren

- **Habitat:** Desert scrub with a variety of cacti and sage.
- **Food:** Insects, spiders, butterflies, fruit from cacti, sunflower seeds, and suet from feeders.
- **Nest:** Three or more feet off the ground in a cholla or other short desert tree.

Arizona woodpecker

While its range is restricted to southeastern Arizona, this woodpecker makes daily appearances in backyards and woodlands throughout the area. Its chocolate-brown markings make it distinctly different from all other western woodpeckers. The male sports a bright red spot on the back of its head.

- **Habitat:** Wooded areas, particularly those with oak trees.
- **Food:** Insects, including beetle larvae; this woodpecker also enjoys fruit and may show up at half an orange in your backyard.
- **Nest:** In a tree cavity; incubation takes about fourteen days.

Arizona woodpecker

Gila woodpecker

The only western woodpecker with a black-and-white barred back and a gray-to-brown head, this bird is a southern Arizona backyard staple. Look for the red forehead spot in males; the females are identical except for the lack of a red spot.

- **Habitat:** Deserts with trees or large cacti, particularly the saguaro.
- **Food:** Fruit and seeds, insects, and some small reptiles. These birds readily come to suet feeders.
- **Nest:** In a tree or saguaro cactus. Eggs hatch in twelve to fourteen days.

Gila woodpecker

Golden-fronted woodpecker

A bright yellow nape and yellow belly area sets a golden-fronted woodpecker apart from other species; the male also adds a yellow dot above the bill and a red spot on top of its head. Otherwise, these pale woodpeckers sport black backs covered with white horizontal stripes.

Golden-fronted woodpecker

- **Habitat:** Arid forests in South Texas; they also frequent parks and backyards.
- **Food:** Insects, spiders, berries, nuts, prickly pear, and many other fruits, as well as food from feeders: sunflower seeds, peanuts, oranges, corn, and even bananas.
- **Nest:** In a cavity excavated in a tree, utility pole, or fence post.

Green jay

At the farthest point south in Texas, startlingly gorgeous green jays dominate feeders—in fact, feeders at wildlife refuges and along the border are the best way to spot them. Large flocks of these birds can be found along the Rio Grande in Brownsville and McAllen, and a little farther north in Harlingen.

- **Habitat:** In mesquite woods near water, in thickets, and in palm trees along the border.
- **Food:** Insects, invertebrates, seeds, fruit.
- **Nest:** About 8 feet up in a tangle of brush and vines.

Green jay

Inca dove

This dove looks like it's covered in drab, beige scales, but when it flies, it reveals rufous "armpits" that glow with color. Inca doves are largely acclimated to sharing their space with people and now show up in city parks and in vacant lots where plenty of human activity takes place.

- **Habitat:** Suburbs, parks, open farmland, other places with bare ground.
- **Food:** Seeds, especially millet and sunflower, making them frequent ground feeders in backyards.
- **Nest:** On houses and buildings, as well as in trees. Nests may be on the ground or as high as 50 feet up.

Inca dove

Plain chachalaca

Big, loud, and charismatic, plain chachalacas have come to dominate feeders along the southern tip of Texas. You may see them high in trees, strolling along the side of a road, or scouring the ground under feeders for seed the green jays dropped.

Plain chachalaca

- **Habitat:** Brushy areas, as well as all kinds of forests with tall trees and a thriving understory.
- **Food:** Fruit, insects, invertebrates, and milo or cracked corn under feeders.
- **Nest:** In a big shrub or tree, usually near water, at least 5 feet up.

Pyrrhuloxia

The hotter it is, the more pyrrhuloxia thrives, choosing desert scrubland with plenty of cacti for its year-round home. This member of the cardinal family bears a striking resemblance to the northern species, but its gray mantle and bold red face, breast, belly, and tail distinguish it from the rest.

Pyrrhuloxia

- **Habitat:** Southwestern deserts, as well as mesquite savannas and woodlands near water.
- **Food:** Insects, seeds, and fruit, including offerings at backyard feeders.
- **Nest:** At least 5 feet off the ground in mesquite or other shrubs.

Mexican jay

A southeastern Arizona specialty, this jay is more uniformly bright blue than Woodhouse's scrub-jay and brighter than pinyon jay, with which it shares part of its range.

- **Habitat:** Mountain woodlands up to about 7,000 feet, preferably with pine, juniper, and oak.
- **Food:** Acorns, insects, pine nuts, fruit, berries, caterpillars, moths, jelly from oriole feeders.
- **Nest:** In a tree, about 30 feet up.

Mexican jay

Scott's oriole

With its black head and brilliantly yellow body, further augmented by black wings with white wing bars, Scott's oriole is one of the brightest birds in the southwestern desert region. Its clear song and its propensity for sipping nectar and eating jelly from oriole feeders make it a backyard favorite along the southern Arizona and New Mexico borders.

- **Habitat:** High deserts in mountainous areas, usually above 1,000 feet.
- **Food:** Insets, fruit, nectar from plants and from feeders.
- **Nest:** In a tree, 5 to 7 feet up from the ground.

Scott's oriole is a common sight in dry southwestern states

Florida scrub-jay

Florida's endangered jay is the only bird that lives in this state and nowhere else. Found exclusively in central Florida and in limited areas of the East and West Coasts, it restricts itself to sandy patches of scrub oak and is particularly easy to find at Merritt Island National Wildlife Refuge, where it is quite

Florida scrub-jay

comfortable approaching hikers on trails. Its offspring stay close by for the following breeding season to help their parents raise young, an unusual behavior among jays. While it's generally not a feeder bird, gregarious individuals do visit backyards with the right environment, especially if there are oak trees.

- **Habitat:** Scrubby areas with sandy soil.
- **Food:** Insects, berries, acorns, snakes, small rodents, and lizards.
- **Nest:** Hidden under vines or leaves at the base of a shrub, usually about 3 feet off the ground.

Boat-tailed grackle

Where common and boat-tailed grackle territories overlap, you can tell the difference between the two by the length of the grackle's tail: the boat-tailed has a much longer and wider tail than the common. Female grackles are brown with darker wings.

Boat-tailed grackle

- **Habitat:** Along banks and shorelines including oceans, lakes, marshes, and the Intracoastal Waterway.
- **Food:** Grackles eat whatever they can find, from seeds and berries at your feeders to picnic scraps and trash.
- **Nest:** In reeds or shrubs near water, often just above the water line. Incubation lasts about thirteen days.

Painted bunting

One of the most sought-after backyard birds in America, this summer resident of Texas, Louisiana, and parts of Arkansas also overwinters in South Florida. Maintain a healthy understory of vines and brush in your backyard to create a habitat they will enjoy.

- **Habitat:** Woods on the edges of fields, open scrubland between hedgerows, overgrown roadsides, backyards with brushy areas.
- **Food:** Seeds year-round, with insects during breeding season.
- **Nest:** Between 3 and 6 feet off the ground in a low shrub or short tree.

Painted bunting

Monk parakeet

These South American natives began their US residency as far back as the 1960s, as pets released by their owners. Now established in colonies in many cities throughout the continent, they congregate in areas with tall poles, trees, or structures that can support their massive nests.

- **Habitat:** Normally residents of open, arid lands with a few tall trees, these parakeets manage to thrive in city parks from South Florida to Connecticut. A colony in El Paso, Texas, inhabits the

Monk parakeet

  electrical power substation there, building large nests on utility poles.
- **Food:** Seeds, berries, and buds. They are most likely to arrive at feeders in winter, when natural food sources are scarce.
- **Nest:** Large stick nests at the tops of trees, poles, or buildings, in which an entire colony can gather.

Nanday parakeet

This gorgeous green-and-blue bird with a black face and hood comes from the interior of South America and arrived in the United States as a pet. Escaped or released from captivity, these parakeets formed colonies along the coasts of Florida, in Los Angeles, and in Phoenix, Arizona. They are most likely to come to feeders that offer fruit, as well as to a birdbath.

Nanday parakeet

- **Habitat:** Palm trees and other tropical perches, often along roadsides and open fields.
- **Food:** Seeds, fruit, nuts, berries, plant buds.
- **Nest:** In a tree cavity, usually 20 feet up or higher.

Brown-headed nuthatch

A chorus of delightful squeaks—like a dog's chew toy—announces a cadre of these tiny nuthatches, which usually arrive in groups. In you live in the southeastern United States, planting pine trees in your yard may invite them to become year-round residents.

- **Habitat:** Mature forests of pine trees without much brush or plant activity below.
- **Food:** Insects, spiders, and larvae found under tree bark; they also come to suet feeders.
- **Nest:** In a cavity high in a dead or nearly dead tree, or in a nest box with the appropriately sized entrance (1 to 1½ inches).

Brown-headed nuthatch

A Rivoli's hummingbird feeds on nectar from tubular flowers

13: The Magic of Hummingbirds

Attracting hummingbirds to your yard and garden is not nearly as tricky as it may first sound. It's important to understand a few fundamentals about these jewels of the bird world—and, not surprisingly, they're the same things you need to know about any bird you hope to bring into your yard.

Hummingbirds need food: natural nectar from tubular flowers, additional nectar you might provide in a feeder, and protein they gain from eating tiny insects they can catch with their amazingly threadlike tongues. Offering just one of these things may bring you a few hummingbirds, but creating a garden that offers all three will convince hummingbirds to stay once they've arrived and to bring their friends and families.

Your dazzling visitors also need shelter—places to hide from predators or to take refuge during windy or rainy weather. Hummingbirds nest in shrubs and trees as well, building tiny nests from the smallest twigs, spider webs, lichens, and other soft natural materials. Trees and dense shrubbery provide the kinds of shelter hummingbirds seek, where they can feel safe raising a brood of tiny nestlings out of sight of potential raiders.

Finally, hummingbirds need water, just as all living things do—but it can be a little harder for a tiny bird to drink from a conventional birdbath. A dripping device that gently agitates your birdbath basin, or a mister that delivers a cooling spray to tiny tongues, can be just the thing to provide the hydration hummingbirds require.

HUMMINGBIRDS BY REGION

North America has a wealth of hummingbirds, but not every hummingbird can be seen in every region.

East of the Mississippi River, just one hummingbird species returns each spring and raises its young: the ruby-throated hummingbird, a glittering green fairy with the gleaming red throat its name implies.

While rufous hummingbirds appear to be expanding their territory eastward, making appearances at feeders from New Hampshire to Florida, only the ruby-throat returns dependably to nest and raise its young each year.

If you live in the West, your possibilities increase significantly. As many as seventeen different hummingbird species are regular visitors to the western states—some as casual guests at feeders along the border with Mexico, and others with long histories of established residency in the western deserts, mountains, and coastal areas.

Some western hummingbirds have widespread territories, spending the summer months from West Texas all the way to British Columbia. Northwestern residents can expect to see rufous and black-chinned hummingbirds at their feeders, while backyards in California and along the Pacific coastline may attract Anna's and Allen's hummingbirds as well.

Calliope hummingbirds, the smallest birds in North America, also range fairly widely across the western states—but they restrict their nesting activity to areas above 4,000 feet in elevation. Denizens of the high Sierra Mountains, the Grand Tetons, and other Rocky Mountain ranges, these tiny birds may be only half an inch shorter than other hummingbirds, but even this small difference is easy to see when birds gather in competitive groups around your feeders.

Black-chinned hummingbird

One of the most common western hummingbirds, the black-chinned can be difficult to identify until it flies out into the sun. The male's throat (also known as the gorget) appears black in the shade. Many hummingbirds seem to have this black chin when they're blocked from the sun. In bright light, the black-chinned's throat

Black-chinned hummingbird

turns a brilliant purple, while the area just under the bill remains black. Females are green-backed, with a grayish head and a dull gray breast and throat.

- **Habitat:** Wide ranging throughout the western states wherever there are tall trees and tubular flowers.
- **Food:** Flower nectar and tiny insects, as well as nectar from feeders.
- **Nest:** A flexible cup 6–12 feet up, hidden by leaves. Incubation takes twelve to sixteen days.

Ruby-throated hummingbird

If you live east of the Great Plains, the most dependable (and usually the only) hummingbird at your feeders is this beautiful species. In the shade, it's easy to mistake this bird for a black-chinned, as they are nearly identical without sun. Once you see the jewel-like gorget light up in the sun, however, you'll know exactly what bird you have. The female ruby-throat tends to be a bright green with some golden highlights. She's dull gray to white in front.

Ruby-throated hummingbird

- **Habitat:** Wooded areas and backyards with trees.
- **Food:** Plant nectar, tiny insects, and sugar water from feeders.
- **Nest:** A tiny cup on top of a tree branch; incubation takes twelve to fourteen days.

Anna's hummingbird

Widespread from southern Arizona to the Oregon and Washington coast, this hummingbird is easy to pick out from the others at your feeders. Anna's hummingbird has a bright magenta gorget and crown. The bird lights up in the sun, from its throat all the way to the top of its head. Females have a red patch in the center of the throat and a white stripe over the eye. This combination makes a female Anna's unusually easy to spot.

Anna's hummingbird

- **Habitat:** Open woodlands and along the edges of forests, as well as in backyards with tubular flowers.
- **Food:** Plant nectar, tiny insects, the sugar water we supply in feeders, and occasional small caterpillars.
- **Nest:** A tiny cup on top of a branch; incubation takes twelve to fourteen days.

Broad-billed hummingbird

One of the most common hummers in the wondrous southeastern Arizona/southern New Mexico birding region, this one distinguishes itself with its blue-green plumage and bright red bill.

Broad-billed hummingbird

- **Habitat:** Mountainous regions, where they forage in subalpine meadows up to nearly 10,000 feet.
- **Food:** Plant nectar, tiny insects, sugar water from feeders.
- **Nest:** A tiny cup between 3 and 10 feet up in a tree or shrub.

Rufous hummingbird

This widespread, bright orange hummingbird can be seen during migration and breeding season throughout the western states. Some appear in the East as well, a sign that this little bird may be expanding its range. Females are brownish with a warm, peachy wash.

- **Habitat:** Open shrubland, forest clearings, and meadows at just about any elevation.
- **Food:** Plant nectar, gnats, flies, and sugar water in feeders.
- **Nest:** About 30 feet up in a tree, hidden by surrounding branches. Incubation takes fifteen to seventeen days.

Rufous hummingbird (female)

Broad-tailed hummingbird

A bird of higher elevations, broad-taileds have the ability to enter a state of torpor on chilly mountain nights, slowing their heart rate and metabolism until morning. They are fiercely competitive with other hummers for plant nectar and feeder perches.

Broad-tailed hummingbird (female)

- **Habitat:** Open woodlands and meadows above 5,000 feet.
- **Food:** Plant nectar, tiny insects, sugar water from feeders.
- **Nest:** A branch with plenty of cover to maintain warmth on cold nights, not more than 5 feet from the ground.

Calliope hummingbird

The smallest bird in the United States is also fierce, migrating more than 5,000 miles annually and chasing off much larger birds, including hawks, to protect its young.

Calliope hummingbird

- **Habitat:** Meadows and thickets at about 4,000 feet, as well as lower elevations along rivers and streams.
- **Food:** Plant nectar, tiny insects, sugar water in feeders, and tree sap released by drilling sapsuckers.
- **Nest:** A cup on a conifer branch, using a spot where a pinecone was once attached; incubation takes fifteen to sixteen days.

HUMMINGBIRDS BY REGION

Southeastern Arizona and South Texas:

- Plain-capped starthroat
- Lucifer hummingbird
- Violet-crowned hummingbird
- Berylline hummingbird
- Broad-billed hummingbird
- White-eared hummingbird
- Blue-throated mountain-gem
- Rivoli's hummingbird

South Texas and Gulf Coast:

- Buff-bellied hummingbird

Southwest Border and West Coast:

- Anna's hummingbird
- Costa's hummingbird

West Coast only:

- Allen's hummingbird

Widespread in West:

- Black-chinned hummingbird
- Calliope hummingbird
- Broad-tailed hummingbird
- Rufous hummingbird

East:

- Ruby-throated hummingbird

PLANNING YOUR GARDEN

The trick to attracting hummingbirds is to catch their attention as they patrol your area for food sources.

Hummingbirds can see red and orange flowers and leaves easily as they fly, even from considerable distances. These colors signal hummingbirds to take a closer look at a garden or to expect a nectar feeder, bringing them into your yard with great efficiency.

Equally important, many flowers have a symbiotic relationship with hummingbirds. These blooms are usually tubular or bell shaped, with a

Fuchsia

deep well in which they produce the nectar that attracts the tiny birds. When the birds arrive to drink the nectar, they also collect pollen, usually from the extended stamen that hangs from the center of the blossom.

These flowering plants usually produce rows or clusters of blossoms on one stalk, so the hummingbird dips into each bloom in turn to sip the flower's nectar. As the bird drinks, it deposits the pollen it gathered from other flowers, effectively pollinating an entire plant.

Flowers that hang downward may look droopy to you, but they're actually positioned in a way that makes it easy for a hovering hummingbird to access the nectar and collect the pollen.

With the combination of red or pink color, tubular or bell shape, downward-hanging blossoms, and protruding pistil and stamen, these flowers create a paradise for hummingbirds while ensuring their own ability to reproduce.

Select a variety of plants, based on when they bloom during the spring and summer. To keep hummingbirds in your yard throughout the season, plants that bloom at different times will provide a continuous supply of natural nectar. For example, bee balm is native to the northeastern region and blooms in midsummer. Good complements to late-blooming bee balm might include columbine (spring

Bee balm

blooming), trumpet vine (early summer), and cardinal flower (late summer). In the West, adding several varieties of penstemon will keep your garden full of hummingbird-feeding blooms throughout the growing season.

Native plants are always the best choices for a hardy garden, but some carefully selected exotic species will bring the hummingbirds to your door. Fuchsia produces clusters of bright red, pink, or magenta hanging flowers. They're a favorite for hanging baskets and can be purchased at most garden centers early in the season. Rose of Sharon, shrub verbena, weigela, and common foxglove are all noninvasive exotic plants that attract hummingbirds.

HUMMINGBIRD GARDEN CHECKLIST

❑ Perennial, tubular flowers that bloom at different times in spring and summer.

❑ Blooming bushes that provide shelter and resting perches.

❑ Deciduous (leafy) trees for nesting.

❑ A water source that can generate mist, like a small fountain.

❑ No pesticides! Small insects are part of the hummingbird's diet.

HUMMINGBIRD PLANTS BY REGION

Red, orange, and pink flowers have the most success in attracting hummingbirds, but be sure to choose those that offer nourishing nectar as well as color.

Your hummingbird garden should flourish on its own, without a great deal of time and care. Choose perennial flowers that thrive in your region and that are appropriate for your climate and soil. Ocotillo, for example, may pull in hummingbirds from far and wide—but it only thrives in the desert, so it will wither and die in your northeastern garden.

In addition to the flowers on the following pages, talk with your garden center about the hardiest hummingbird-friendly flowers for your area.

Birding Tip: Friendly Hello

The hummingbird migration often starts before your garden has a chance to produce flowers. Attract migrating hummers to your garden by tying red streamers to your feeders, even if your nectar feeders are already red. The movement will help hummingbirds spot your feeders from some distance away.

Plants for the East

Choosing flowers can be the most fun part of creating your hummingbird garden.

It's also the most important contribution you can make to the hummingbirds' life cycle. Over time, many native plants have virtually disappeared from roadsides, open fields, and the edges of waterways, as housing and commercial development replaced natural habitat. When you choose plants that once grew wild in your area, you restore a little bit of the food supply hummingbirds have evolved to expect. The birds will come instinctively to these blooms, knowing that they provide the energy and nutrition hummingbirds need to maintain the frenetic pace of their lives.

Think beyond flowers that grow individually and include flowering shrubs, vines, and trees in your plans. These offer the additional benefits of shelter and resting places, shielding birds from chilly nights and aggressive predators.

Be careful, though, when you visit your favorite garden center to choose your plants. Many flower species are labeled as attractive to hummingbirds, but they are not hardy enough to withstand the Northeast's cold winters, or they are meant for dry climates and will drown in the humidity typical of the Southeast.

Ask the horticulturalist on staff to direct you to plants that are native to your area—especially perennials, which will die back in the fall and return to full bloom on their own year after year.

Trumpet vine (*Campsis radicans*)

Native trumpet vine grows wild in the national parks and wildlife refuges of the southeastern states, and it's a favorite trellis climber for homes from Georgia to Maine. These stunning orange, red, or yellow flowers are magnets for hummingbirds and orioles. As a ground cover or climber, trumpet vine can become invasive—so plant it where it can climb a pole, arch, or trellis, and prune it regularly and repeatedly throughout the growing season.

Zones 5–9, full sun, blooms summer to early fall

Trumpet vine

Cardinal flower (*Lobelia cardinalis*)

Here's a flower with a complete dependency on hummingbirds for its livelihood: its tubular flowers make it virtually impossible for bees to enter and pollinate it. Cardinal flower is the perfect addition to the edge of a pond or water feature. It thrives in moist soil and needs to be kept wet to ensure showy blooming. Most important, hummingbirds love this flower and will make your garden a focal point of their feeding activity.

Cardinal flower

Zones 2–9, partial sun or light shade, blooms midsummer to fall

Eastern red columbine (*Aquilegia canadensis*)

With its downward-facing flowers and its red color, this columbine attracts hummingbirds fairly easily. Put in several plants together to make a bed of columbine, which will persuade the birds to linger while they sample each bloom. Columbine grows in just about every region of the country, in colors from white to purple. The variety shown here is also known as Canadian columbine and is hardy in Canada's southern provinces. Columbine completes its blooming season fairly early in the year, so be sure to plant later-blooming flowers nearby.

Eastern red columbine

Zones 3–8, partial shade, blooms late spring

Coral honeysuckle (*Lonicera sempervirens*)

This perennial vine has the added benefit of year-round greenery, making it an excellent choice for gardens from colder zones to the most temperate. This honeysuckle may bloom in coral, orange, or yellow shades, all of which will attract hummingbirds—but the redder tones will do so more quickly. As a ground cover, trellis climber, or vertically staked vine, this flower will bring many birds to your garden.

Coral honeysuckle

Zones 3–9, full sun or light shade, blooms mid-spring

Plants for the West

With so many potential hummingbird species to attract in the western states and provinces, choosing the right flowers for your garden can be as simple as strolling through a wildlife refuge or park to see what blooms the birds actively seek out.

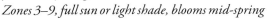

As in the eastern states, columbine is a favorite for hummingbirds at every altitude. The many varieties of penstemon, a plant with vertical rows of open, bell-shaped flowers, are excellent selections with proven results. Both of these plants offer varieties for virtually every climate the western region presents, whether your home is high in the Bighorn Mountains, on the edge of the Sonoran Desert, or in the midst of Nebraska's agricultural fields.

In the deserts, the red blooms of the ocotillo are magnets for black-chinned and broad-billed hummingbirds, which can be seen swarming these tall, spiny shrubs for hours on end. Fairy duster, a fluffy pink blossom that bursts into bloom with the first warm days, easily attracts the wealth of Arizona hummingbirds as they arrive from points south during spring migration.

Coral bells, with varieties as wide ranging as the climates across our continent, produce hundreds of tiny blooms from early to late summer. Hummingbirds love its frothy little blossoms, especially when many plants form a large cluster of blooms.

Check with your local garden center, cooperative extension, or Master Gardener program to determine which varieties of these plants are native to your area. Year after year, the right plants will give you seasons of beautiful blooms—and lots of fascinating hummingbirds.

Coral bells (*Heuchera*)

A native plant that thrives in a rock garden, along a path, or in a sun-dappled woods, coral bells bloom in shades of red and pink, sometimes with purple foliage. Place these plants close together to get a bed of coral bells, allowing several hummingbirds to feed at a time. After the first bloom, cut the stalks back to promote a second blooming later in the season.

Zones 4–9, sun to partial shade, blooms June to August

Coral bells

Penstemon (*Penstemon*)

These glorious funnel-shaped flowers attract birds daily, lingering to move up and down the stalks to drink from each flower. Dozens of varieties provide lots of choices for your garden (Parry's penstemon is shown here), based on your climate, elevation, and region. Many varieties are adapted to thrive with little water, making them appropriate for desert gardens.

Generally zones 4–9, full sun, blooms throughout the summer

Penstemon

Ocotillo (*Fouquieria splendens*)

The stalks of the ocotillo punctuate the landscape in the Sonoran and Chihuahuan Deserts from West Texas to southeast California. Once used as formidable fence material because of its tall, spiny branches, the ocotillo has another purpose: its red flowers provide food to desert hummingbirds. Black-chinned, broad-billed, and Anna's hummingbirds readily come to these blooms throughout the spring and summer.

Zones 8–10, full sun, blooms throughout the spring

Ocotillo

Fairy duster (*Calliandra eriophylla*)

A low-growing evergreen shrub with wispy puffballs for flowers, fairy duster is a favorite with butterflies and bees as well as hummingbirds. This is a perfect addition to a desert garden, as it tolerates drought and prefers sandy soil. In California, Baja fairy duster is the native variety—and its bright red puffs bring in the hummingbirds. The pink petals of the flower are actually its stamens, allowing it to pollinate liberally as birds and butterflies feed on its nectar.

Zones 8–10, full sun, blooms in early spring

Fairy duster

HUMMINGBIRD BEHAVIOR

Calliope hummingbirds appear to be fencing as they compete at a feeder

As human beings, we like to believe that animals share the same kind of family units and affection for one another as we do. We see male and female hummingbirds arrive at our feeders, and we think of them as mates, parents, brothers, and sisters. It's a natural assumption that birds, like people, feel some kind of relational connection to one another.

In the case of hummingbirds, however, nothing could be further from the truth. Hummingbirds see each other as competition for available food, and they become aggressive when another bird beats them to a perch or a flower. They search for food individually, scanning miles of territory to find new sources of nectar—and they will defend a flower bed or feeder as if it contains their last meal.

NESTING

How does something so small build a nest and raise young? Hummingbirds construct tiny nests in the crotch of a small, sturdy branch, attaching the soft cup to the twig with spider silk. The nest itself is the size of a walnut shell. It holds two or three tiny eggs, each not much larger than a pea. Baby hummingbirds are about a quarter of an inch long when they hatch. Most hummingbird species grow to about 3¾ inches tall.

Every hummingbird is a competitor to every other, so when a new bird invades an established territory, the bird that got there first is ready to defend its terrain. It's not unusual to see two birds bill-to-bill, looking as if they're about to engage in a swordfight. What results is a chase, and the stronger or more aggressive bird will return to the feeder. The other may choose another feeder in the area.

This territorial instinct is the main reason that hummingbirds will return to the same feeders and breeding spots season after season. Their ability to recall choice feeding spots even after migrating south, passing the winter in another country, and returning north speaks to the value of our nectar feeders to their survival.

Why do these birds eat constantly? They burn calories faster than any other animal. When in flight, a hummingbird's heart can beat up to 1,200 times per minute, and their wings flutter at up to 70 times per second. Those elegant moves break all kinds of records for bird behavior. Hummingbirds can fly as fast as 30 miles per hour, and their speed can increase to 45 miles per hour in a courtship dive.

Hummingbirds are the only animals that can hover in place for long periods. This ability to stay in one place while in the air allows the birds to sip nectar from flowers, for which there is usually no good perch available. Remarkably, hummingbirds can fly backward as well, a behavior not many birds can manage. You may even see a bird flying upside down, a feat copied only by the most skilled jet fighter pilots.

Given that the human heart rate when running is about 130 beats per minute, it's easy to understand why hummingbirds' appetites are never entirely sated.

Broad-billed hummingbird on nest

Eastern gray squirrel hanging from a branch to reach a seed bell

14: Uninvited Backyard Guests

Backyard birding can be joyous as colorful, musical little birds frequent your feeders and bring their young to your trees and shrubs.

As you create your bird paradise, however, it's important to realize that nature will take its course right in your backyard—and that course is not always benevolent.

PREDATORS

Bird feeders present easy hunting for hawks and owls, predators that soar over your neighborhood looking for small animals to catch and kill for dinner. These larger birds have every right to eat, just as your feeder birds do, but they may exercise that right in your backyard when your back is turned . . . or even when it's not.

Several hawk species rank high among birds that come to feeders, according to the citizen science program Project FeederWatch. Cooper's, sharp-shinned, and red-tailed hawks are among the most common birds of prey in the United States, and they will stake out feeding stations in large backyards to catch smaller birds for their meals.

If you live in an open area with surrounding fields, watch at dusk for owls—large birds gliding swiftly over meadows and pastures looking for rodents and small birds they can catch. Wooded areas also may attract owls, providing high perches from which they can watch for movements below that signal likely prey.

Most backyards do not attract hawks or owls, so the treacherous side of bird feeding may not visit your home. If hawks do avail themselves of your unintentional offerings, however, there's only one way to rid your yard of these hunters: stop feeding the birds altogether.

Red-tailed hawk

The good news is that your birds generally know when a hawk is nearby. When all the birds in your yard suddenly dash for cover behind leaves or thorns, it's time to look up to see what kind of hawk is circling overhead.

You may observe the occasional *Wild Kingdom* moment, but these are your chances to marvel at the agility and skill with which large birds of prey acquire their targets.

NUISANCE BIRDS

Who invited the pigeons?

You did, when you put out seed for the white-crowned sparrows, mourning doves, and juncos you hoped to attract.

Pigeons, starlings, house sparrows, and even crows can be facts of life for people who feed birds, particularly if you live in an urban or highly populated suburban area. All of these birds owe their livelihood to human development, and to their own ability to adapt. When natural food sources dwindled, these birds learned to eat what they could scavenge from humans. When trees fell to the path of progress, these birds began nesting in man-made nooks, on rooftops, and in whatever cozy cavities they could usurp from other birds.

A house sparrow plunders a purple coneflower for its seeds

Consequently, it's inevitable that house sparrows, starlings, the occasional crow, and rock pigeons will find their way to your feeders. Worse, they may move in for good, taking up residence in or near your yard to have ready access to all the good food you supply.

As these birds tend to arrive in flocks and tenaciously overstay their welcome, you may find yourself spending lots of money on seed to feed birds you don't want around.

What to do? If you don't want to stop feeding altogether, change the food you offer and the positions in which birds can eat it. Here are some strategies that work.

No Falling Seed

- Remove any ground-feeding options to discourage pigeons, crows, and starlings.
- Hang catchall plastic or net trays under your tube feeders to keep seed from falling to the ground. These trays sway when a large bird lands, so pigeons and crows won't try to perch on them.
- Starlings may still partake, but they will find less on the ground to satisfy their hunger.

Change Your Seed

- Most feeder birds like black oil sunflower seed, but house sparrows, starlings, and grackles have trouble cracking open black stripe sunflower seeds. Switch to black stripe instead of black oil to fend off these birds.
- Grackles and starlings also dislike safflower seed. Small birds like chickadees and titmice eat it up.
- Don't offer cracked corn, a favorite of house sparrows, crows, and starlings.
- White millet and canary seed attract house sparrows, grackles, starlings, and cowbirds. Avoid seed blends that contain them.

Rock pigeons can be aggressive feeder birds

Discourage Nesting

- House sparrows and starlings will take over nest boxes intended for other species, especially bluebirds. They also nest in unwanted places—in the letters of hanging signs, or in drain pipes or gutters.
- Both of these species were introduced to North America (see pages 53, 54 and 161), so federal law does not protect them.
- Keep an eye open for house sparrow and starling nesting activity and remove the nesting material as soon as possible, before the birds incubate their eggs. This will discourage the birds.

OUTDOOR CATS: A MENACE TO BIRDS

One of the most insidious intruders in your backyard masquerades as a beloved pet.

Indoor cats can sit for hours watching feeders—a sort of reality TV show for your kitty. Outdoor cats can't resist the instinct that presses them to attempt to catch ground-feeding and perch-sitting birds.

Outdoor domestic cats are the number-one killer of wild birds.
Shutterstock #1070747096

In fact, outdoor domestic cats have become the number-one direct threat to birds in the United States and Canada. The American Bird Conservancy (ABC) reports that in the United States alone, outdoor cats kill as many as 2.4 billion birds annually. How can this be true? Think about the number of outdoor cats in your own neighborhood, and then multiply that by millions of neighborhoods across the country. "Each outdoor cat plays a part," the ABC notes, even if the cats are well fed by their owners.

If you own a cat, chances are good that you've already taken steps to keep it away from your backyard birds. What can you do, however, when the neighbor's cat wanders into your backyard and starts stalking its feathery prey?

Start by checking the law in your community to see if there's already legislation regarding wandering cats. Your neighbor may not be aware that the law requires the cat to be leashed or kept indoors. If the law is in your favor, call your local municipal Animal Control office and let them deal with your neighbor.

If no law prevents the cat from spending its days outside, have a conversation with the cat's owner—perhaps while carrying the cat back to his or her home. Explain that you have created a bird garden in your yard for the purpose of attracting beautiful creatures, and that the roaming cat is taking too close an interest in the visitors at your feeders.

Your neighbor may be very resistant to keeping the cat indoors, particularly if the cat is accustomed to wandering at will. If this is the case, try a motion-activated lawn sprinkler, which will turn on and spray the cat when it enters your yard. The spray lasts only a few seconds, but a couple of good soakings should be enough to annoy the cat into avoiding your property. You can find this device in your favorite home improvement store's garden section.

You can help birds defend themselves from this menace by placing your feeders 10 to 12 feet from the nearest tree or shrub; this will bring birds close enough to cover to flee when necessary. Meanwhile, they will have a clear view of the surrounding yard so they can spot the cat approaching. Don't place the feeders too far from cover or the birds will not be able to escape into the trees if the cat pounces. Try shrubs like roses and hawthorns that offer thorns, an added level of protection. If a bird dives into a thorny bush when a cat approaches, it will only take one try before the cat learns not to reach into that bush again. Rose and hawthorn offer the added benefits of rose hips and berries in late summer, two treats for fruit-eating birds.

FOILING SQUIRRELS

It may take a few days or even weeks for birds to find your newly hung feeders, but squirrels will find them in a matter of hours.

Gray, black, or red, flying or land bound, squirrels are among the cleverest critters in the animal kingdom when it comes to finding new food sources. Highly motivated by seemingly inexhaustible appetites, these furry, broadtailed creatures work tirelessly to find ways to beat the birds to your feeders.

This feeder with a spinning bottom is one of the most popular squirrel-deterrent feeders in the United States

If you're feeding more seed and suet to squirrels than to your birds, you're not alone—virtually every backyard birder faces the squirrel dilemma.

Squirrels' remarkable flexibility, their ability to hang upside down by their back feet while feeding, and their amazing prowess in leaping from trees to feeders—and not getting hurt if they miss and hit the ground—all contribute to their success. All of these skills also prevent us from foiling them for long.

To compound the problem, squirrels can climb smooth objects like poles, balance on a wire or other slim avenue, and keep their footing on slick surfaces. If they were not such nuisances at our bird-feeding stations, we might be forced to admire and revere these talented animals.

That's why many manufacturers have invested large amounts of time and money in research and development, just to help backyard birders keep the squirrels out of their birds' food.

The result is a parade of products that can turn your squirrel problem into a source of endless amusement.

Feeders That Work

Spend an afternoon watching how your squirrels gain access to your feeders. Do they jump up from a spot below the feeder? Do they walk the edge of your neighbor's fence and hop over to a feeder nearby? Or do they climb up through a shrub that's close to the feeder? The more you know about the access path, the more likely it is that you can solve the problem, often without any outlay of funds.

Here are feeder options that will work if you are looking to foil your neighborhood squirrels. We've tried many of these solutions, and some of them do indeed do the job.

Trick Feeders

Trick feeders come in all shapes and sizes and in all price ranges. A popular option is a feeder with a spinning bottom that sends the squirrel flying when he applies his weight to the perch. Most birding specialty stores carry this feeder, which has a built-in rechargeable battery. No outdoor cord is required, but you

---

Birding Tip: Wood Is No Good

Don't use wooden bird feeders! Squirrels chew through these in a matter of hours, emptying them of their seed. Instead, choose feeders made of hard plastic or metal, durable materials that resist squirrels' industrious teeth.

Spring-loaded perches

will need to charge the battery every so often. Once the squirrels learn that they can't get to the food, they will back off.

Another option is a feeder with spring-loaded perches. This trick feeder (shown here) can hold the weight of small birds. When a squirrel puts its weight on the perch, however, it gives way and the squirrel slips to the ground. Squirrels learn quickly, so once they've determined the seed is out of reach, they will lose interest.

Weight-Activated Feeders

A weight-activated feeder holds nearly ten pounds of seeds, but its perch balances delicately as if it were part of an old-fashioned scale. When more than two small birds land on the perch, it rocks down and closes off the seed dispenser openings. Squirrels will try for days to find a way in, but the rugged construction and sensitive perch mechanism keep them from accessing any of the seed. Be sure to place this feeder a good distance from branches or other feeders so the squirrel can't keep its weight on another perch while trying to get past this one.

A second option is a little mesh feeder, a perfect addition to a small garden, which has a built-in spring that responds to weight. Two or three birds can use the perches and feast on the seed inside, but squirrels are too heavy. When they try to climb on, the mesh lowers and shuts off the feeder's holes. Squirrels can't even climb on top and reach down the feeder, as this will close the feeder holes.

A suet feeder with a squirrel cage lets woodpeckers in, but keeps squirrels out

Squirrel Cage

Here's a caged feeder that lets woodpeckers, nuthatches, sparrows, and other birds in but keeps squirrels out. The suet stays in the center of the cage, allowing birds to enter the cage, perch comfortably, and eat the suet in peace. The cage's mesh is too small to allow a squirrel to enter or to even reach in through the bars. (Be careful, however, to hang this feeder out of reach of the nearest tree or shrub. Cats climb into shrubs and wait for birds to land on feeders, and then catch or kill them. Cage feeders can help cats trap and hold small birds.)

Squirrel Feeders

It seems like a good idea on the surface: give the squirrels their own food and maybe they'll leave the birds' food alone.

If only it were that simple!

Squirrels will indeed rush readily to the feeder you offer them, whether it's full of peanuts in the shell or it holds an upright, bright yellow cob of corn.

The problem, however, is that squirrels have no sense of "mine" and "theirs." They will spend some time distracted from their job of finding a way to your bird feeders, gobbling down the nuts or corn cob. Once these food sources have been exhausted, however, they will be back at the bird feeders with renewed energy and vigor.

A feeder filled with whole peanuts will keep squirrels busy for days

So should we skip the squirrel feeders? One of the advantages of these devices is that they may be the only feeders in your yard that are not at the end of an obstacle course of challenges. If you're already using squirrel-proof feeders, your squirrels probably know they can't penetrate these—but it may not stop them from trying.

Distracting the squirrels with choice morsels of their own can buy you some squirrel-less time at your other feeders. Industrious squirrels will stop interfering with birds' feeding habits, at least for short bursts of time.

Placing a platform or dish feeder on the ground with squirrel treats in it—dried whole-kernel corn and nuts—also will keep squirrels busy. When food is plentiful without much expense of effort, squirrels will take the path of least resistance, leaving your seed feeders alone while they devour whatever is easiest to get.

Birding Tip: Don't Build a Pathway

Squirrels will find a highway to your feeders if you let them. Here are some situations to avoid:

- Keep trees trimmed back from feeders. Squirrels will run down the branches and leap onto the feeder.
- Look out for downspouts and wiring. Squirrels can scamper up a drainpipe or climb an electrical or cable wire to get to feeders close to your windows.
- Extend hanging hardware away from porch or deck railings so the squirrel can't jump from the railing to the feeder.

Alternatives That Work (or Don't)

Despite your best efforts and the most innovative squirrel-proof feeders on the market, your squirrels may still find a way into your sunflower seed–stocked hopper and tube feeders.

Baffles

All is not yet lost! Try some of the baffles that cut off a squirrel's access to the feeders before the animal gets close.

Some baffles work on the same weight-activated principles as squirrel-resistant feeders, but others create a tunnel or compartment that stops the squirrel in its tracks. None of these devices hurt the squirrels in any way, but they do frustrate the squirrels' efforts to reach your feeders' contents.

Your birding specialty store or home improvement store is well stocked with all kinds of baffles: tubular, flat, domed, and otherwise. There's a solution to fit any size feeder or space, and most are fairly inexpensive.

Choose baffles made from durable, teeth-resistant materials like steel, Plexiglas, or polycarbonate plastics. Squirrels will chew through anything they can to get to your seed, so look for materials that are impervious to this kind of punishment. The baffles you select should be easy to install and versatile enough to fit many different kinds of feeders; and—most important—they should not block your view of the birds visiting your feeders.

Small hanging baffle on a tube feeder

Squirrel-Blocking Solutions

Defeating the wily squirrel has become a hobby of its own, a high-spirited struggle between humans and nature. The wide-ranging list of solutions involves various kinds of nontoxic chemicals, odor agents, alternate seed combinations, and even the old-fashioned catch-and-release—all of which provide the fun of watching squirrel behavior as they experience one product or process after another.

Manufacturers now offer many products at outdoor recreation, farm and feed, and garden stores, with an even more inspired selection online (search "squirrel deterrents"). Most backyard birders try these products sequentially, seeing what works and using another solution to augment whatever success the first one offers.

How effective are all of these products? As in all fields of endeavor, some solutions may prove very effective in one region of the country or against a particular squirrel species, while others may have no discernible effect at all.

Chili peppers contain a natural chemical called capsaicin, which gives peppers their spicy heat. Squirrels appear to hate seed or suet coated with

Plain suet, like the cake in the feeder on the left, holds no interest for squirrels because it contains no seed. Squirrels also reject nyjer seed, seen here in the right-hand feeder.

capsaicin—at least until they get used to it. Treated seed and suet are generally a little more expensive than food that does not contain the hot chemical. Birds in South America eat so many chili peppers that some species are called "bird peppers." It stands to reason that the birds will not be put off by capsaicin-treated food, although these products receive mixed reviews from backyard birders.

Other possible deterrents include a cloth bag or sock filled with mothballs placed in the path to feeders; rags soaked with ammonia placed near feeders; coyote urine (available in bottles); organic squirrel repellents, available at garden centers; cayenne pepper mixed into conventional birdseed; or a high-frequency-emitting device that irritates squirrels (and other animals).

If you choose to engage in the eternal battle with squirrels, keep in mind that each deterrent you put in place may have an unintended impact on birds or other animals. Skip any kind of harsh chemicals, especially poisons, as they could be ingested by rabbits, voles, chipmunks, or other small furry creatures. Pesticides have a significant negative impact on birds—in fact, many bird species lingered for decades on the nation's endangered species lists because of toxic chemicals in pesticides. While these dangerous substances are now banned from use by law, newer chemicals may not have a long enough track record to determine their effects. Stick with natural, nontoxic deterrents to keep your backyard safe for wildlife.

LIVE CAPTURE

It seems like great sport to set and bait a trap, catch a squirrel, drive out into the country or woods some miles away, and release the squirrel there. Problem solved? Science says no. Removing squirrels from your area only alerts other squirrels that there are openings in your territory. New squirrels will drift in, overrunning your feeders in a matter of weeks—and squirrel breeding may increase as well until the gap is filled.

Spring Checklist

Feeders and Seed

☐ Take all of your feeders down and clean them thoroughly. Disinfect with a weak solution of one part household bleach to ten parts water.

☐ Get your hummingbird and oriole feeders out: early April for the southern states, early May in the North.

☐ Discard any remaining butcher suet as soon as daily temperatures rise above 40 degrees. Switch to packaged "all season" or "no melt" suet blends.

☐ Get out your mealworm feeder and add mealworms to attract bluebirds. Use live mealworms until the weather gets too hot for them.

Birdbaths and Ponds

☐ Remove water defrosters from your birdbaths. Clean and store them for next winter.

☐ Clean your birdbaths and refill them.

☐ Do a "wet run" of your water circulators (pumps) to make sure they're functioning properly. Check all electrical connections and repair or replace if necessary.

☐ Skim winter detritus off of the surface of your pond. Add barley or other algae inhibitor.

Nest Boxes

☐ Check all your nesting boxes for signs that birds roosted in them over the winter.

☐ If the boxes have been used, scrape out and clean them before birds begin nesting.

☐ Put out nesting material in suet cages or seed wreaths, or on its own.

Garden

☐ It's finally time to snip last year's blossoms from your perennials.

☐ Pick or prune off any remaining berries from last year's crop and discard.

☐ Rake any twigs or branches that fell over the winter into your brush pile.

☐ Rake up and discard the winter's seed shells and rejected seed under your feeders.

☐ Pull any new shoots under your feeders that may be sprouting from last year's birdseed. Watch for possible sunflower sprouts and transplant them to your perennial garden.

☐ Plan where you'd like to add annuals, new perennials, shrubs, or trees. Make a list to take to garden centers.

☐ Have fun planting!

Summer Checklist

Feeders and Seed

- ☐ As weather warms, change the nectar in your hummingbird feeders every three days.
- ☐ Change the orange halves on your oriole feeder every few days as well to keep oranges from generating mold.
- ☐ After heavy rains or in very humid weather, change the seed in your feeders to keep it from becoming moldy.
- ☐ Watch underneath your seed feeders for shell buildup. Rake seed and shells onto a shovel or dustpan and discard.
- ☐ Clean and disinfect feeders as needed.
- ☐ Watch your deck, railings, and squirrel baffles for bird droppings. Clean away this material as soon as possible.

Birdbaths and Ponds

- ☐ Change the water in your birdbaths daily throughout the summer.
- ☐ Maintain the level of algae deterrent in your pond.
- ☐ Add a mister to your bird bath to cool birds in the heat.

Nest Boxes

- ☐ Watch for nesting, feeding, and fledging activity.
- ☐ When birds have abandoned a nest after fledglings have flown, clean out the nest box. Remove the old nest and discard it.
- ☐ Keep an eye out for house sparrow nests in inconvenient places on your property. Remove and discard nests if you wish.
- ☐ Remember that no matter where they are located, it's illegal to disturb active nests of birds that are native to the United States.

Garden

- ☐ Leave dead flowers in place on seed-producing perennials (sunflower, coneflower, black-eyed Susan, and many others).
- ☐ Resist the urge to use pesticides—let the birds clear out your bugs.
- ☐ Monitor under your feeders for unwanted sprouts from germinating birdseed. Remove them as they appear.

Fall Checklist

Feeders and Seed

❑ In the northern states and provinces, leave hummingbird and oriole feeders out until mid-October for migrating stragglers.

❑ Bring out your high-capacity seed feeders. Fill them with sunflower and safflower seed to give birds extra energy during migration.

❑ Place your ground-level platform feeders and add millet for migrating or arriving juncos, winter sparrows, and siskins.

❑ When temperatures regularly rise only into the 40s, put out your butcher suet.

Birdbaths and Ponds

❑ Place your birdbath defroster in your birdbath when the first frost is predicted.

❑ Shut off water circulators when temperatures are predicted to drop below freezing.

Nest Boxes

❑ Clean out the last nests of the season.

❑ Scrape and wash out your nest boxes.

❑ Leave the boxes in place to provide shelter for roosting birds in winter.

Garden

❑ Leave dead blossoms in place on seed-producing perennials to feed birds throughout the migration and winter.

❑ Rake fall leaves. Compost or recycle most of this, but leave some under shrubs to provide shelter to overwintering birds.

❑ Prune dead branches and twigs from your shrubs. Add these to your brush pile.

❑ Leave as many berries in place as possible. Birds will return in winter to eat the fermented fruit.

Winter Checklist

Feeders and Seed

- ❏ Take in your hummingbird and oriole feeders. Clean these and store them until spring.
- ❏ Keep your seed feeders filled for overwintering birds.
- ❏ If you don't usually feed with nuts, add a peanut feeder in winter.
- ❏ Replenish suet often.
- ❏ Rub some suet on the bark of your largest trees for brown creepers, wood-peckers, and nuthatches.

Birdbaths and Ponds

- ❏ Check your birdbath defrosters regularly to be sure the ground fault inter-rupter (GFI) has not shut them off. Reset and find the issue if necessary.
- ❏ Maintain open water in your birdbaths as much as possible during the cold-est weather.

Nest Boxes

- ❏ Place some wood shavings in your clean nest boxes to provide warmth for roosting birds.
- ❏ Add a roosting box (hole in the bottom) if you wish. These boxes provide perches inside for birds and are usually larger to accommodate small flocks.

Garden

- ❏ Leave dead blossoms to allow birds to eat the seeds.
- ❏ Begin planning your spring garden goals. This is a great time of year to get catalogs, review websites, and make a list of the new plants, shrubs, and trees you will add when the weather warms.
- ❏ In warmer climates, planting may begin by late winter.

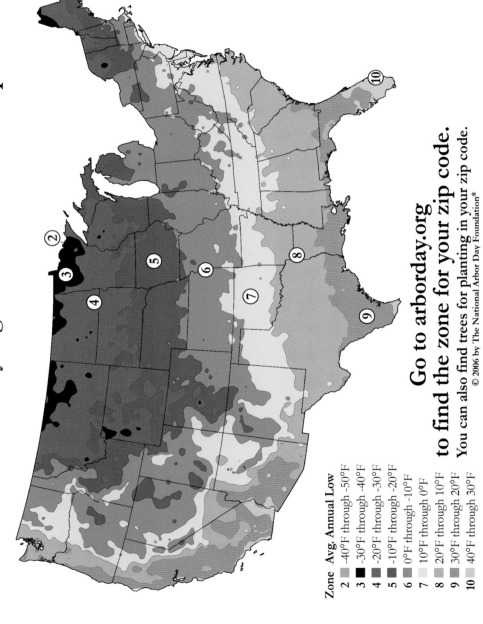

arborday.org Hardiness Zones Map

Go to arborday.org
to find the zone for your zip code.
You can also find trees for planting in your zip code.

© 2006 by The National Arbor Day Foundation®

Zone	Avg. Annual Low
2	-40°F through -50°F
3	-30°F through -40°F
4	-20°F through -30°F
5	-10°F through -20°F
6	0°F through -10°F
7	10°F through 0°F
8	20°F through 10°F
9	30°F through 20°F
10	40°F through 30°F

Arborday.org Hardiness Zones
Alaska and Hawaii

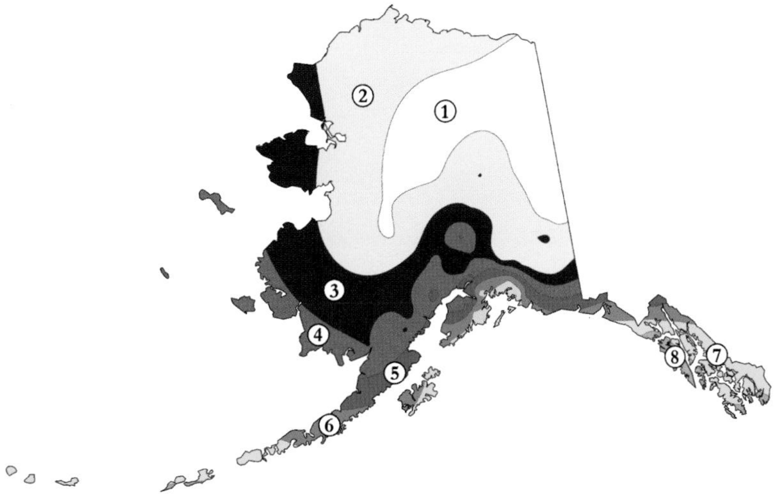

Zone Avg. Annual Low

1 Below -50°F
2 -40°F through -50°F
3 -30°F through -40°F
4 -20°F through -30°F
5 -10°F through -20°F
6 0°F through -10°F
7 10°F through 0°F
8 20°F through 10°F
9 30°F through 20°F
10 40°F through 30°F
11 Above 40°F

Go to arborday.org
to find the zone for your zip code.
You can also find trees for planting in your zip code.

© 2006 by The National Arbor Day Foundation®

Blackbird

Brewer's, 201, 202

Red-winged, 140, 141, 151, 153

Yellow-headed, 201, 202

Bluebird

Eastern, 21, 114, 181, 183

Mountain, 46, 98, 138, 184

Western, xviii, 65, 138, 185

Bobwhite   Bunting

Northern, 114, 181, 182

Indigo, x, 177, 183

Lark, 98, 103, 106, 135, 201, 203

Bunting

Lazuli, 185, 187, 189

Painted, 205, 216

Bushtit

13, 98, 102, 187

Cardinal

Northern, xiii, 26, 66, 139, 144, 172, 173

Catbird

Gray, 120, 130, 151, 157

Chachalaca

Plain, 205, 212

Chickadee

Black-capped, 34, 52, 63, 148, 169, 188

Boreal, 206

Chickadee

Carolina, 169, 170

Chestnut-backed,
52, 169, 188

Collared-dove

Eurasian, 164

Cowbird

Brown-headed, 54, 157,
160

Creeper

Brown, 31, 127, 154, 247

Crossbill

Red, 205, 208

White-winged, 205, 208

Crow

American, 65, 67, 116,
120, 142, 157, 234, 235

Dove

Inca, 212

Mourning, 13, 64, 93, 95, 102, 157, 158, 164, 195, 197

White-winged, 118, 195, 197

Finch

Cassin's, 119, 185, 186

House, xvi, 14, 22, 23, 24, 26, 28, 41, 60, 128, 141, 144, 150, 162, 163, 169, 185, 186

Purple, 150, 169

Flicker

Northern, 13, 33, 51, 52, 60, 63, 155, 168, 179

Flycatcher

Vermillion, 201, 203

Goldfinch

American, xvii, 137, 141, 148, 185

Lesser, 15, 24, 36, 98, 102, 185, 186

Grackle

Boat-tailed, 95, 215

Common, 32, 177, 178

Great-tailed, 195, 197

Grosbeak

Black-headed, 193

Evening, 207

Rose-breasted, 174

Hawk

Cooper's, 233

Red-tailed, 141, 233

Hummingbird

Anna's, 29, 221, 224, 230

Black-chinned, 220, 221, 224, 229, 230

Broad-billed, 29, 222, 224, 229, 230, 231

Hummingbird

Broad-tailed, viii, 99, 223, 224

Calliope, 99, 220, 223, 224, 230

Lucifer, 224

Hummingbird

Rivoli's, ix, 218, 224

Ruby-throated, 29, 94, 219, 221, 224

Rufous, 219, 220, 222, 224

Jay

Blue, 111, 126, 134, 142, 172, 174, 183

Green, 205, 211, 212

Mexican, 20, 189, 213

Jay

Steller's, 52, 98, 135, 189, 191, 193

Junco, Dark-eyed

Eastern race, 13, 15, 32, 33, 64, 93, 96, 97, 102, 106, 110, 124, 157, 160, 234, 246

Oregon race, 160

Kingbird

Eastern, 13, 37, 127, 130, 165, 181, 183, 189

Kinglet

Ruby-crowned, 64, 134, 165, 167

Magpie

Black-billed, 189, 190

Martin

Purple, 48, 51, 52, 137, 173, 176

Meadowlark

Eastern, 134, 137, 166, 201

Western, 134, 137, 145, 166, 201

Mockingbird

Northern, xiv, 97, 99, 112, 113, 114, 116, 117, 118, 120, 121, 124, 125, 130, 144, 145, 151, 152, 176

Nutcracker

Clark's, 115, 192

Nuthatch

Brown-headed, 217

Red-breasted, 48, 52, 135, 156

White-breasted, 48, 137, 153, 156

Oriole

Baltimore, xvii, 19, 133, 172, 173, 175

Bullock's, 20, 137, 194

Oriole

Orchard, 173, 175

Scott's, 8, 20, 214

Parakeet

Monk, 205, 216

Nanday, 205, 217

Phoebe

Eastern, 49, 120, 182

Say's, 189, 190

Pigeon

Band-tailed, 198

Rock, 162, 164, 198, 234, 235

Pyrrhuloxia

213

Quail

California, 195, 196   Gambel's, 195, 196

Redpoll

Common, 20, 115, 207

Robin

American, 19, 20, 21, 38,
49, 61, 62, 63, 66, 67, 100,
111, 112, 113, 114, 115, 116,
117, 118, 119, 120, 121, 122,
124, 125, 127, 142, 151, 152,
157, 175

Sapsucker

Yellow-bellied, 16, 63, 181

Scrub-jay

California, 20, 52, 191   Florida, 215

Scrub-jay

Woodhouse's, 20, 134, 189, 191

Siskin

Pine, 13, 25, 26, 150, 185, 246

Sparrow

American tree, 166

Chipping, 147, 149, 195, 209

Sparrow

Field, 171

Fox, 159, 177

Golden-crowned, 198

Sparrow

Harris's, 199

House, xvi, 14, 15, 16, 23, 32, 34, 47, 49, 50, 53, 54, 57, 60, 61, 63, 66, 126, 129, 142, 147, 149, 161, 162, 172, 177, 181, 234, 235, 245

Sparrow

Lark, 106, 195

Song, 64, 135, 149, 157

Sparrow

White-crowned, 32, 157, 158, 177, 195, 234

White-throated, 32, 64, 145, 159, 177

Starling

European, 53, 120, 147, 161, 163, 177, 234–235

Thrasher

Brown, 176

Curve-billed, 118, 194

Thrush

Varied, 52, 98, 115, 192

Titmouse

Black-crested, 204, 205, 209

Juniper, 52, 189

Tufted, 14, 46, 52, 169, 171, 209

Towhee

Eastern, 178

Spotted, 199

Turkey

Wild, 33, 95, 113, 138, 161, 177

Warbler

Pine, 172

Yellow, 144, 145, 157

Waxwing

Cedar, 111, 112, 115, 146, 165

Woodpecker

Acorn, 65, 200

Arizona, 205, 210

Downy, 30, 51, 153, 154, 155

Woodpecker

Gila, 205, 210

Golden-fronted, 211

Hairy, 12, 31, 51, 155, 200

Woodpecker

Ladder-backed, 200, 201

Pileated, ii, 179, 180

Red-bellied, 31, 48, 139, 179

Woodpecker

Wren

Red-headed, 130, 179

Bewick's, 51, 169, 188

Cactus, 118, 127, 136, 209

Wren

Yellowthroat

Carolina, 50, 51, 52, 54, 169, 170

House, 50, 52, 60, 61, 127, 167

Common, 144

APPENDIX D:
QUICK AND EASY PLANT REFERENCE GUIDE

Aster

White heath, 107

Bayberry
Southern wax myrtle,
113, 114

Beautyberry
American, 113, 114

Bee balm

75, 90, 91, 102, 104, 105,
225

Bellflower

Bluebell, 103

Black-eyed Susan

73, 75, 84, 90, 92, 104,
106, 245

Blanket

Indian, 97, 103

Blazing star

75, 80, 81, 91, 97, 98, 102,
105

Boneset

Common, 75, 106

Cactus

Prickly pear, 118

Cardinal Flower

228

Chokecherry

Western, 73, 111, 116

Cholla

Cane, 117, 118, 209

Columbine

Eastern Red, 228

Wild, 90, 91, 92, 94, 101, 102, 104, 225

Coneflower

Prairie, 100

Purple, 91, 105, 234

Yellow, 105

Coral Bells

229

Coreopsis

Plains, 104

Cotoneaster

122

Creeper

Virginia, 124

Crossvine

95

Dogwood

Pagoda, 120

Red osier, 120

Elderberry

Common, 121

Red, 116

Everlasting

Pearly, 101

Fireweed

Narrow-leaf, 99

Firewheel

97

Foxglove

110, 226

Globemallow

Desert, 103

Goldenrod

Canada, xv, 75, 79, 80, 90, 91, 93

Hawthorn

Highbush blueberry

40, 84, 115, 119, 151, 237   113

Holly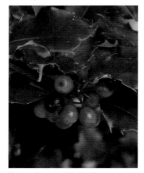

Honeysuckle

American, 88, 112   Yaupon, xiv, 113, 114   Coral, 228

Impatiens

Joe-Pye weed

Juniper

110   Spotted, xvi, 75, 78, 81, 91, 93   Rocky Mountain, 118

Lilac ....
78, 80, 81, 123

Lily ....
Glacier, 99

Lobelia ....
Great blue, 107

Lupine ....
Wild perennial, 106

Magnolia ....
Southern, 95

Milkweed ....
Butterfly, 104

Milkweed ....
Common, xvi, 84, 107

Swamp, 79, 92

Mistletoe ....
Mesquite, 119

Nettle

California hedge, 100

Ocotillo

102, 226, 229, 230

Onion

Nodding, 99

Oswego-Tea

104

Paintbrush

Giant red Indian, 98

Penstemon

James, 102, 229

Petunia

81, 109

Phlox

Wild Blue, 96

Poppy

Mexican golden, 102

Rhododendron

Evergreen, 95

Rose

Common wild, 112

Woods', 116

Serviceberry

Shadblow, 112

Snapdragon

110

Sneezeweed

Common, 75, 108

Spurge

Allegheny, 125

Stonecrop

124

Strawberry

Wild, 100

Sumac

Smooth, 120

Sunflower

Oxeye, 106

Tickseed

Lobed, 96

Trumpet Vine

227

Vervain

Blue, 74, 93

Viburnum

American cranberry,
73, 84, 88, 113, 117

Weigela

122, 226

Wisteria

Japanese, 122

Yarrow

Common, 96, 104, 106

Index

chickadees
    bird feeders, 23, 32, 33, 34, 147
    birdhouses and nesting, 48, 50, 51, 53, 63
    black-capped, 52, 148, 169
    boreal, 206
    Carolina, 169, 170
    chestnut-backed, 52, 169, 188
    and flowers, trees, and shrubs, 90, 91, 92, 106, 107, 110, 120, 121
    preferred diet, 13, 14, 15, 16, 235
chipmunks, 243
chokeberry, western, 73, 111, 116
cholla, cane, 117, 118, 209
cleaning
    birdbaths and ponds, 41, 42, 44, 45, 244
    bird feeders, 27, 34, 35, 244, 245, 247
    nest boxes, 53, 55, 56, 244, 245, 246
columbine,
    eastern red, 228, 229
    golden, 101
    wild, 90, 91, 92, 94, 102, 104, 225
coneflower
    purple, 91, 105, 234
    yellow, 105
coral bells, 229
coreopsis,
    lobed tickseed, 75, 96, 102
    plains, 104, 105
Cornell Laboratory of Ornithology, 2, 3, 11, 59, 145
cotoneaster, 122
CountryMax, 21
cowbirds, brown-headed, 54, 157, 160, 235
    nesting in other birds' nests, 54, 157
coyote urine, 243
creeper, brown, 31, 127, 154, 247
creeper, Virginia, 124

crossbill,
    red, 115, 205, 208
    white-winged, 205, 208
crow, American, 65, 67, 120, 142, 157

D

daisy, 90, 91, 98, 102, 105, 108
deer, 93, 110, 114, 125
dickcissel, 20
dogwood, 73, 90, 113, 115, 119, 120,
    pagoda, 120
    red osier, 120
dove
    bird feeders, 13, 15, 25, 32, 33, 234
    Eurasian collared, 164
    inca, 212
    mourning, 64, 118, 157, 158, 195
    nestlings, 64
    preferred diet, 93, 95, 102, 118, 124, 157
    white-winged, 118, 195, 197

E

Elderberry, 119
    common, 121
    red, 116

F

fairy duster, 102, 229, 230
Federal Migratory Bird Treaty Act of 1918, 54

preferred diet, 93, 96, 97, 102, 106, 110, 124
yellow-eyed, 102

K

kestrel, American, 48, 51, 52, 53
kingbirds
  birdbaths, 37
  eastern, 13, 37, 127, 130, 165, 181, 183, 189
kinglet, ruby-crowned, 64, 134, 165, 167
Knoblauch, Paul, 40

L

lilac, 78, 80, 81, 123
lily, glacier, 99
loosestrife, purple, 109
lupine, wild perennial, 106

M

magnolia, southern, 95
magpie, black-billed, 189, 190
maps by zones, 248–249
martins, purple, 48, 51, 52, 137, 173, 176
  birdhouses and nesting, 48, 51, 52, 137
meadowlark, 134, 137, 201
  eastern, 166
  western, 145, 166

mealworms, 20–21, 31–32,183, 244
migration patterns, 133–135
Migratory Bird Treaty Act, 54, 157
mistletoe, 94, 119, 191
mistletoe, mesquite, 119
mockingbird, northern, xiv, 97, 99, 112, 113, 114, 116, 117, 118, 120, 121, 124, 125, 130, 144, 145, 151, 152, 176
myrtle, southern wax, 113, 114

N

Native Plant Society, 89
nectar and nectar feeders, 17, 18, 29–30, 225
  and hummingbirds, 17, 18, 29–30, 225
  making nectar, 17–18
  and orioles, 18
  and red food coloring and honey,18
nest boxes. *See* birdhouses and nesting
nesting. *See* birdhouses and nesting
nuthatches
  bird feeders, 13, 14, 16, 20, 30, 31, 113, 116, 137, 239, 247
  birdhouses and nesting, 48, 50, 51, 63
  brown-headed, 217
  identifying, 10, 127, 135, 153
  red-breasted, 156
  white-breasted, 156

About the Author and Photographer

RANDI AND NIC MINETOR crisscross the country regularly to research and shoot photos for their books on birds, hiking, history, and America's national parks.

Randi and Nic have worked together on more than thirty books to date, including their comprehensive Falcon Guides Birdfinding guides, *Birding New England* and *Birding Florida*, and their *Best Easy Birding Guides* to Acadia National Park and Cape Cod. Nic also provided all of the photography for eight guides from Quick Reference Publishing to the birds, trees, and wildflowers of New York City and New York State, as well as the trees and wildflowers of the mid-Atlantic states. The Minetors have collaborated on ten hiking guides throughout New York State, including two editions of the bestselling *Hiking Waterfalls in New York*, and Randi has written six nonfiction books in the Death in the Parks series, about people who visit national and major state parks and become victims of fatal accidents, hubris, or sheer bad luck.

When not on the road, Nic is the resident lighting designer for the Eastman Opera Theatre, theatrical productions at the National Technical Institute for the Deaf, and exhibitions at the University of Rochester's Memorial Art Gallery. Randi writes for publications in the theater technology and health care trades, as well as for *North American Birds* and *Birding* magazines.

The Minetors live in Rochester, New York, where they have participated in migratory and breeding bird research projects for the Nature Conservancy and the New York State Breeding Bird Atlas. Randi serves as president of the Rochester Birding Association.

Fresh spring feathers make white-throated sparrows easy to spot.